I, *Yantra*

I, *Yantra*

Exploring Self and Selflessness in Ancient Indian Robot Tales

SIGNE COHEN

SUNY
PRESS

Cover: Female Purusha Yantra (India, seventeenth century, artist unknown). Watercolor on paper. Philadelphia Museum of Art. Gift of Stella Kramrisch, 1978.

Published by State University of New York Press, Albany

Printed in the United States of America

For information, contact State University of New York Press, Albany, NY
www.sunypress.edu

Library of Congress Cataloging-in-Publication Data

Name: Cohen, Signe, author.
Title: I, yantra : exploring self and selflessness in ancient Indian robot tales / Signe Cohen.
Description: Albany, NY : State University of New York Press, [2024] | Includes bibliographical references.
Identifiers: LCCN 2023023656 | ISBN 9781438496610 (hardcover : alk. paper) | ISBN 9781438496634 (ebook) | ISBN 9781438496627 (pbk. : alk. paper)
Subjects: LCSH: Tales—India—History and criticism. | Robots—India—Folklore. | Robots in literature. | Robots—Religious aspects. | Technology and civilization. | Civilization, Ancient.
Classification: LCC GR305 .C56 2024 | DDC 398/.45—dc23/eng/20231120
LC record available at https://lccn.loc.gov/2023023656

10 9 8 7 6 5 4 3 2 1

For Dan, Josh, and Alisha, who bring my world to life.

It is the obvious which is so difficult to see most of the time. People say "It's as plain as the nose on your face." But how much of the nose on your face can you see, unless someone holds a mirror up to you?

—Isaac Asimov, *I, Robot*

Contents

List of Illustrations xi

Acknowledgments xiii

Introduction 1

Chapter 1 The History of Automata in the West 17

Chapter 2 Interlude: Yavanas and the Creation of Automata 57

Chapter 3 Robots in the Royal Garden 63

Chapter 4 Body of Flesh, Body of Wood, Body of Stone: Humans, Androids, and Gods in Hinduism 85

Chapter 5 Mechanical Gardens and a Craving for Flying Machines: Androids in Jainism 113

Chapter 6 I, *Yantra*: Androids in Buddhism 129

Chapter 7 The Buddha, the Emperor, and the Killer Robot 151

Chapter 8 Interpreting Indian Robot Tales 173

Appendix Chapter 31 of Bhoja's *Samarāṅgaṇasūtradhāra* 193

Illustrations

Figure I.1	*Śrī yantra*	12
Figure 1.1	Al-Jazarī's robot band	26
Figure 1.2	Al-Jazarī's automated elephant clock	27
Figure 1.3	Kempelen's automated chess player	43
Figure 1.4	Repliee Q2	53
Figure 5.1	Siddhacakra	117
Figure 7.1	Emperor Aśoka	152

Acknowledgments

This book has been a labor of love many years in the making. I am grateful to the friends, colleagues, mentors, and students who have nourished my obsession with ancient Indian robots over the years, including all the students in my Robots and Religion course. A special shout-out to Adrienne Mayor for her kind encouragement, and to Kristen Jellison and Mara Sidney for their friendship and support.

Introduction

What Is a Robot?

This is a book about robot tales from ancient India, stories about mechanically constructed androids embedded in archaic Hindu and Buddhist texts composed in Sanskrit and Pāli. The fact that there are stories about automata in ancient Asian texts may come as a surprise to many readers. When we think of robots and androids, we usually think of an imagined future, rather than the past: *Star Wars, Star Trek, Bladerunner, Battlestar Galactica,* or the works of Isaac Asimov. But tales of artificially constructed humans can be found in old texts from many parts of the world; ancient Egyptians, Greeks, and Romans wrote about statues that moved and spoke, humans forged out of metal, and mechanical birds. Ancient texts from India, Tibet, China, and Mongolia describe mechanical men and women so lifelike that people mistake them for humans, artificially constructed geese and elephants, and programmed killer robots. Medieval western European texts tell of deadly androids guarding tombs, talking brass heads, and mechanical leopards, while medieval Muslim engineers not only fantasized about moving mechanical men but also gave detailed instructions for how to make them, using intricate forms of clockwork. Actual automata were made in early modern Europe, including mechanical musicians playing lovely little melodies and a lifelike little eighteenth-century automaton boy writing over and over, "I think, therefore I am," playfully challenging Descartes with a stroke of the pen held in his chubby little robotic hand.[1]

This book examines the depiction of mechanical beings in ancient Sanskrit and Pāli literature from India, although I will also refer to Chinese, Tibetan, Mongolian, and Tocharian translations and variants of Indian texts. To date, there has been no comprehensive and systematic study of these ancient robot tales, perhaps because they are preserved as fragments and brief narrative interludes in texts dealing with a variety of other topics, rather than as a cohesive collection of stories. The fullest treatment of Indian android tales to date is V. Raghavan's study *Yantras or Mechanical Contrivances in Ancient India,* especially his greatly expanded second edition from 1956.[2] While Raghavan's work is rich in textual attestations relating to ancient Indian automata, it does not contain a great deal of analysis and is fairly inaccessible to the general reader due to the large number of untranslated Sanskrit passages. My own article "Romancing the Robot and Other Tales of Mechanical Beings in Indian Literature"[3] draws on more comparative material but does not cover all the extant Indian textual references fully. Daud Ali's work on robots and royal gardens in medieval India is insightful in its analysis but does not attempt to cover the full scope of Indian literature on automata.[4] The present work is an attempt to fill the gaps in the existing scholarship and present a comprehensive study of premodern tales of automata from South Asia.

Narrative episodes featuring robots and androids are embedded in ancient South Asian texts from many different genres, such as fairy tales, didactic literature, *Jātaka* tales recounting the past lives of the Buddha, and works on art and architecture. I argue that these robot episodes nevertheless constitute a distinct, albeit fractured, subgenre of ancient South Asian narrative literature, that these texts encode specific religious beliefs about body, soul, and embodiment, and that they construct a cultural and religious discourse of what it means to be human. Robot tales interrogate the very nature of humanity, the borders between the natural and the artificial, and the limits of human ingenuity. If we can imagine a moving, talking machine constructed in the likeness of a human being, then what makes someone truly human, as opposed to a robot? Our flesh, our DNA? Our language, our consciousness, our self-awareness? Our ability to feel empathy for others, or our capacity to remember and draw on our own past? Our soul?

Narratives about robots, androids, and artificially constructed human beings occupy a central space in contemporary science fiction. Situated in the borderlands between the world of the imagination and the realm of technological possibility, these mechanical beings of literature, television, and film embody fundamental cultural anxieties about what it means to be human. Although the preoccupation with mechanical humans may seem particularly relevant at a moment in time when androids superficially indistinguishable from humans are on the verge of becoming scientific reality, an attentiveness to the long and complex history of imagined mechanical beings will help highlight some of the profoundly religious themes intertwined with the tales of our mechanical doubles, the robots.

Can we call premodern texts about automata science fiction? Yes and no. Most contemporary science fiction focuses on future scientific inventions, hypothetical technology that we can imagine based on our current scientific knowledge.[5] Like modern science fiction, ancient robot tales are often fantasies about advanced technologies, and in that sense there is definitely a science fiction aspect to these stories. But these premodern stories are embedded in literary contexts of their own; they are episodes incorporated into religious or philosophical texts, folktales, didactic literature, or even architectural treatises. I argue that each robot story can only be interpreted in its original context. An ancient Buddhist tale about killer androids may have a great deal in common with a modern science fiction novel on the surface, but it must still be read as a Buddhist text illustrating central Buddhist teachings.

Robots, Androids, Automata, and Yantras

What exactly do we mean when we talk about *robots* or *androids*? Various terms are used in English to describe mechanically constructed moving objects that are made to resemble living people or animals. The term *android,* from the Greek *andro-eides* (like a man) is used to describe a machine that has the appearance of a human being.[6] *Automaton,* also from Greek (moving by itself), is used to designate mechanically moving machines, especially those that imitate things from real life, such as humans or animals. This word is first attested in the seventeenth century. The term *robot* is a much more recent one. *Robot* was coined by the Czech writer Josef Čapek (the brother of the more famous Karel Čapek) in 1917, in his short story "Opilec" (The Drunkard). The term *robot* comes from the Czech *robota,* which means "forced labor," "servitude," or "strenuous work."[7] The word *robot* was made famous through Karel Čapek's play *R.U.R.* (Rossum's Universal Robots) from 1920. In this play, a *robot* is an artificial humanoid machine that is used for labor, although Čapek's robots long to become human. In this book, I will use the term *robot* to refer to both humanoid and animallike artificially constructed moving objects. I will use the term *android* to refer to a robot that is made to resemble a human being, as opposed to a robot that imitates an animal. The term *cyborg* (cybernetic organism), which refers to a human-machine hybrid,[8] will not be used in most parts of this book, simply because the concept is not attested in ancient India.[9]

This book explores premodern robot tales from India, composed in the ancient languages of Sanskrit and Pāli. Although these tales are almost completely unknown today, some of them traveled widely in antiquity. Robot stories from India were known in Tibet, China, Mongolia, Central Asia, and Southeast Asia. The following chapters will explore some of the most striking robot stories from India but will also delve into translations of lost Indian tales preserved in languages such as Tibetan, Chinese, Mongolian, and Tocharian. I have attempted to provide fairly literal translations of the original texts, with explanatory notes where needed.

As already mentioned, the term *robot* is a fairly recent one, while *android* and *automaton* are quite a bit older. But what words did people use to designate mechanically constructed men, women, and animals in ancient India? The key term that recurs in these old robot tales is the Sanskrit *yantra.* A *yantra* can be a mechanical person, animal, or ingenious self-moving machine, but the same word can also be used for something as prosaic as an automated watering system, an oil press, or a garden swing. In order to understand the context and deeper meaning of the ancient Indian robot stories in this book, we will first need to unpack the many shades of meaning of the significant term *yantra.*

The noun *yantra,* which is masculine in gender, is derived from a verb *yam,* which means to control or to harness. The *-tra* suffix is used in Sanskrit to designate tools or instruments, so a *yantra* is an "instrument of control," something that is used to control one's environment. Any sort of device that allows the users to exert control over their environment can be called a *yantra,* whether that device is an astronomical instrument, a chemical apparatus, a water fountain, a catapult—or a humanoid robot. The noun *yantra* can form compounds with other nouns, as seen in the Sanskrit *yantra-putraka* (a *yantra* boy; a male android),[10] *yantra-putrikā* (a *yantra* girl; a female android),[11] *yantra-hastin* (a *yantra* elephant; a mechanical elephant),[12] *yantra-mayūraka* (a *yantra* peacock; a mechanical peacock),[13] *dvārapāla-yantra* (doorkeeper *yantra,* an android guarding an entrance),[14] *yantra-haṃsa* (a *yantra* goose; a mechanical goose),[15] and so on. A similar word, *yanta,* is used in Pāli, the language of the oldest Buddhist texts. In this book, I will occasionally use terms like *robot, android,* and *automaton* to refer to some of the *yantras* described in Indian literature. While these terms may seem somewhat anachronistic when applied to ancient Sanskrit texts, I am choosing to use them in order to bring these fascinating artificially constructed beings from ancient Indian literature into conversation with their mechanical counterparts from other parts of the world and other time periods. In doing so, my goal is to highlight that many of the questions raised in ancient Indian tales are still immensely relevant to modern readers, and that these ancient tales of wooden men and women contain as many truths for our age as contemporary robot stories do. Stories of artificial human beings help us articulate what it means to be human, and both modern robots and ancient *yantras* help us think about how we define humanity.

But while *yantra* can certainly be translated as "robot" or "machine" in many contexts, the Sanskrit term also resonates with a deeper religious meaning that is absent from both "machine" and terms like *automaton, robot,* and *android.* It is highly significant that while the words we use in English to designate a mechanically constructed object that imitates a living being (*robot, android, automaton*) are associated with the machines' practical functionality or appearance (*robot* = "work," a machine used for labor; *android* = "like a man," *automaton* = "moving by itself"), *yantra* is an important religious term in Sanskrit. In addition to designating machines and automata of various kinds, a *yantra* can also be a mystical diagram that maps both the cosmos and a person's inner psyche.

At first sight, this second meaning of *yantra* seems quite unrelated to the first. The geometric diagram called a *yantra,* consisting of interlocking circles, squares, hexagrams, lines, and stylized lotus flowers is used in meditation and to call upon deities in rituals. Surely, these religious diagrams have little to do with mechanical elephants or doorkeepers.

One of the main arguments I am making in this book is that these two meanings of the term *yantra*—religious diagram and robot—are indeed deeply connected to each other. Both the robot and the diagram are ultimately perceived in ancient India as devices that represent the ultimate control over the elements of the world. I want to demonstrate that while the ancient Indian robot tales can be highly entertaining, exciting, and occasionally very funny, they are ultimately *religious* stories, articulating spiritual truths.

Yantras in Ancient India

Hinduism, perhaps the world's oldest religion, has no historical founder, and its origins are difficult to trace. Its sacred texts were transmitted orally from teacher to student for millennia without being committed to writing, which makes dating Hindu texts particularly challenging. Many scholars date the oldest Hindu text, *Ṛgveda,* a Sanskrit collection of poems to various deities who represent natural phenomena such as the sun, the storm, and the dawn, to around 1200 BCE on linguistic grounds. The term *yantra* occurs in the *Ṛgveda* itself, and although the word does not yet mean "machine" or "robot" or "sacred diagram," this ancient text still foreshadows later meanings of the term.

In the *Ṛgveda, yantra* can be used in the sense of "bond" or "restraint," as in the passage in *Ṛgveda* 10.149.1 that describes the sun god Savitṛ:

> Savitar brought the earth to rest with his fastening straps [*yantraiḥ*];
> in the place with no prop Savitar made heaven fast.[16]

Here, *yantras* are invisible bonds that hold the earth and sky in their place, a meaning closely related to the word's derivation from the verb *yam*, "to control." This image of *yantras* as bonds that control the order of the universe foreshadows the later meaning of *yantra* as religious diagrams of cosmic energies.

The term *yantra* is first used in the meaning "machine" or "mechanical device" in Sanskrit from around the third century BCE onward. The Hindu epic *Mahābhārata* (ca. 3rd c. BCE–3rd c. CE) is a vast poem that tells the story of a great battle between two rival branches of the same family. One passage of the text describes a *matsya-yantra* (fish machine), a revolving mechanical wheel containing an artificial fish, which the hero Arjuna has to shoot with an arrow, looking only at the reflection of the fish in the water, in order to win the hand of the princess Draupadī.[17] It is not clear precisely how the wheel and the fish are constructed, but something along the lines of a water-powered wheel seems likely based on the context. The *Harivaṃśa,* which forms an appendix to the *Mahābhārata,* mentions a machine that throws stones, *aśma-yantra* (stone machine), likely a catapult of sorts.[18] Embedded within the *Mahābhārata* epic is the *Bhagavadgītā,* perhaps the most well-known Hindu text today. The *Bhagavadgītā* consists of a dialogue between the warrior Arjuna and his divine charioteer Kṛṣṇa on the eve of a great battle and covers topics such as duty, karma, and the paths to salvation. Toward the end of the text, Kṛṣṇa brings up *yantras* in a startling metaphor:

> O Arjuna, the Lord dwells
> in the heart of all living beings,
> and he makes them move by his magic power (*māyā*),
> as if they are mounted on a *yantra.*[19]

This verse recalls the depiction of the *matsya-yantra* elsewhere in the *Mahābhārata,* but here it is not merely fish that are moved by a rotating *yantra; all* living beings are made to move in a similar manner, but the power that enlivens these creatures is the power of a divine being. This notion that the world itself is a machine, set in motion and brought to life, along with the beings that inhabit it, through the power of a deity foreshadows King Bhoja's vision of the cosmic *yantra* set in motion by Śiva in the *Samarāṅgaṇasūtradhāra,* a text we will analyze later in this book.

The other great Hindu Sanskrit epic, the *Rāmāyaṇa* (ca. 200 BCE–200 CE), tells the tale of the god Viṣṇu's incarnation as a human prince, Rāma, and his heroic rescue of his wife Sītā, who has been kidnapped by a ten-headed demon. This text mentions *yantras* that can throw arrows and stones.[20] The royal city of Ayodhyā, where Rāma lives, is described in the *Rāmāyaṇa* as *sarvayantrāyudhavatī*, "furnished with all sorts of mechanical weapons."[21] The demons' city of Laṅkā, likewise, has many *yantras*, including a special room devoted to them.[22] While it is not always possible to tell from the context precisely what these *yantras* are, the Sanskrit epics make clear that well-constructed machines and mechanical devices are characteristics of high urban civilizations.

Kauṭilya's *Arthaśāstra*, the famous Indian text on statecraft (1st–2nd c. CE),[23] mentions *yantras* that can be used to get rid of enemies and unwanted people. Chapter 12 recommends making a false wall or stone fall down on someone by releasing a mechanical device,[24] while section 2.5 muses on the necessity of having the door to one's treasury connected to a staircase attached to a *yantra* concealed by the statue of a deity.[25] The text also lists *yantras* among the equipment one might store in a fort's trench, along with stones, spades, axes, arrows, knives, and so on, presumably in order to be ready to fight off one's enemies.[26] Section 2.18 lists mechanical devices used in battle, both stationary and moving ones, presumably catapults or something similar.[27] The *Arthaśāstra* recommends employing *yantras*, along with assassins and dark magic, to cause panic among one's enemies.[28] While most of the *yantras* mentioned in this text seem to be weapons or trapdoors, the text also mentions a mechanical device used to raise water from a well.[29]

Viśākhadatta's play *Mudrārākṣasa* (Rākṣasa's Signet Ring, 7th–9th c. CE)[30] draws inspiration from the *Arthaśāstra* and even features its author, Kauṭilya, as one of its characters (under his alternate name Cāṇakya). In this play, a mechanical arch (*yantra-toraṇa*) is rigged to come crashing down and kill a person passing underneath. It seems entirely in character that the calculating Kauṭilya/Cāṇakya uses this deadly mechanism to further his own political ends.

The *Kāmasūtra*, Vātsyāyana's third-century treatise on the art of love, is particularly well known today for its descriptions of various sexual positions. The *Kāmasūtra* is far more than a mere sex manual, however, and also covers topics like courtship, finding a partner, and philosophical reflections on the nature of love and its role in a well-balanced life. In the section on courtship, the *Kāmasūtra* gives a list of sixty-four essential arts a good lover must master. Included in this list is a mysterious skill called *yantra-mātṛkās* (literally, "mechanical mothers").[31] Intriguingly, the commentary *Jayamaṅgalā* divides *yantras* into two kinds: *sajīva* and *nirjīva,* literally, "with life and without life." It is not entirely clear what is meant here, but it is possible that the commentator is referring to automated/nonautomated mechanical devices of some kind.

The seventh-century CE version of Budhasvāmin's *Bṛhatkathāślokasaṁgraha* contains an elaborate narrative involving a flying mechanical chariot, also referred to as a *yantra.* In this story, a master architect named Pukvasa travels to Saurāṣṭra to work on a project for the king. In Saurāṣṭra, he meets a young architect by the name of Viśvila, who is so fantastically gifted that his work is equal to that of Viśvakarman (All-Maker), the architect of the gods. Viśvila marries Pukvasa's daughter Ratnāvalī after demonstrating that he can even create artificial grains of rice that are indistinguishable in appearance from real rice. Viśvila ends up being a superb provider for his in-laws; he makes both *yantras* and household items out of wood and sells them. The king wants to send Pukvasa to Banaras for a new building project, but Viśvila offers to go instead. Everyone agrees, and Viśvila starts his job in the remote location. But back at home, Ratnāvalī becomes pregnant. Her parents are appalled that she could become pregnant during her husband's long absence and suspect that she has been unfaithful, but the king eventually discovers the truth: her husband Viśvila has built himself a mechanical rooster, *yantra-kukkuṭa,* and every night after work he flies home to his wife in it. But when the king learns of this secret, he insists that Viśvila must reveal his knowledge of how to build flying machines. The king puts pressure on Pukvasa, who again puts pressure on his son-in-law. But Viśvila only pretends to reveal the secret of his flying machine. Instead, he gives his father-in-law and the king false information, wakes up his wife in the middle of the night, and tells her that she now has to choose between her husband and her father. She chooses Viśvila, and the two of them fly off together in the night on the mechanical rooster, keeping the true secret of the technology of flying machines to themselves.[32]

The term *yantra* is also frequently used in alchemical Sanskrit texts for the various apparatuses used in distillation and treatment of metals in the attempts to produce gold and attain immortality. The classical Hindu alchemical text *Rasārṇava* (The Ocean of Nectar/Mercury, 11th c. CE) describes the consecration of these *yantras* with holy *mantras*, or sacred utterances.[33] Yaśodhara Bhaṭṭa's thirteenth-century CE alchemical text *Rasaprakāśa Sudhākara* (Effulgence of Mercury, Wellspring of Nectar) lists forty different *yantras* used in the alchemical process.[34] Ambikādatta Śāstri Vāgbhaṭṭa's thirteenth-century CE text *Rasaratnasamuccaya* describes the extraction of mercury from cinnabar (mercury sulfide) and the amalgamation of mercury and copper by means of an *ūrdhvapātana-yantra* (apparatus of upward sublimination).[35] This *yantra* and its operation are described in great detail, and the apparatus appears to have been in common use for extracting mercury from the cinnabar ore that occurs naturally in India. Significantly, the alchemical apparatus is often compared to the body of a *yogin* and of the god Śiva himself.[36] As White has pointed out, the structure of the alchemical *yantras*, consisting of an upper and a lower vessel fused together, also serves as a model for both the universe (heaven and earth) and the human body (upper and lower body).[37] The idea of the *yantra* as a model for the universe itself recalls the other meaning of *yantra* as a sacred diagram.

While all the *yantras* we have discussed so far are simple devices of various kinds, inventions to make life a little easier, the term is used from around the third century CE onward to describe mechanically constructed animals and people. The third-century CE folktale collection *Pañcatantra* describes, as we shall see, a mechanically constructed flying bird even more lifelike than Viśvila's rooster-shaped flying machine. The seventh-century CE biography *Harṣacarita* mentions a mechanical elephant,[38] as does the eleventh-century CE folktale collection *Kathāsaritsāgara*,[39] which also describes mechanical geese programmed to steal and an entire city populated by androids. The seventh-century CE prose writer Daṇḍin writes about an engineer by the name of Māndhātā, who can make fantastical machines, and his son Lalitālaya, who is an even greater engineer than his father. According to Daṇḍin, Lalitālaya created mechanical men (*yantra-putraka*) that dueled each other, as well as an artificial cloud that could bring actual rain, and a mechanical catapult throwing stones at elephants' heads.[40]

Daṇḍin himself was certainly familiar with automata, and he lists six different types of *yantras* in his *Avantisundarī*: stationary (*sthita*) automata, moving (*cara*) automata, water-powered (*dhārā*) machines, *dvīpa*, fire-powered (*jvara*) machines, and mixed (*vyāmiśra*) types.[41] The inclusion of a category of yantras called *dvīpa*, which literally means "island" is somewhat confusing, but Raghavan is likely correct when he emends this word to *dvipa*, which means elephant.[42] The elephant may here be a representative for mechanical animals in general. Several of Daṇḍin's categories foreshadow those in Bhoja's *Samarāṅganasūtradhāra*, as we will see in chapter 3. King Bhoja's eleventh-century architectural treatise *Samarāṅgaṇasūtradhāra* devotes a whole chapter to automata of different kinds, while a thirteen-century textbook on the art of dance, *Nṛttaratnavalī* by Jāyasenāpati, describes a dance hall filled with female automata (*yantranārī*) dancing and singing.[43]

Many of the Sanskrit and Pāli stories involving mechanical beings have a similar plot structure, which makes it possible to view the "robot tale" as a story genre in ancient Indian literature. The robot stories relate how a mechanical being is constructed by an artisan (S.: *yantrācārya* or *yantrakāra*, a "machine-maker," *yantakāra* in Pāli). The robot stories then describe the verisimilitude of the robot, demonstrated in a scene where the characters in the story are deceived by the robot, imagining that it actually is a human being or an animal. Then follows the disclosure that the robot is merely a machine, much to the astonishment of the observers.

In the following chapters, we will analyze these intriguing tales of *yantras* in more detail. I argue that even though these automata are certainly *yantras* in the sense of "mechanical devices" or "machines," many of them are also *yantras* in a religious sense as well.

Yantras as Sacred Diagrams

Before we analyze the tales of mechanical humans and animals in ancient Indian literature, we need to take a brief detour and explore the other—and as we will see, related—meaning of the term *yantra*. In a religious sense, a *yantra* is a sacred geometric diagram, made up of interlocking circles, squares, hexagrams, lines, and stylized lotus flowers, used in meditation, religious rituals, and magic, and their various components have rich symbolic meanings.[44] Similar diagrams are often referred to as *maṇḍalas* (literally, circle, sphere, region, domain) or *cakras* (wheels).

Although the terms *yantra, maṇḍala,* and *cakra* are often used synonymously, some scholars have attempted to distinguish between them. Tucci, for example, defines *yantras* as purely linear designs, as opposed to more intricate *maṇḍalas*.[45] Zimmer likewise stresses the linear nature of the *yantras*.[46] Eliade also suggests that *yantras* are the simplest forms of *maṇḍalas*, and that they are specifically used in Hinduism.[47] Brunner, on the other hand, in her study of *maṇḍalas* and *yantras* in Siddhānta, suggests that *yantras* differ from *maṇḍalas* in that they are only used for *kāmya* rituals (to fulfill personal desires), are small and portable, have linear designs, and always contain *bīja* syllables.[48] She therefore translates *yantras* as "coercive diagrams."[49] *Yantras*, as Rastelli has also observed, are frequently used as amulets to protect their wearers.[50] Bühnemann similarly draws a distinction between *yantra, maṇḍala,* and *cakra.* She defines *maṇḍalas* in Tantrism as "a structured space that is enclosed and delimited by a circumferential line, and into which a deity or deities are invited by means of mantras."[51] Above all, the *maṇḍala* is the ritual space where the devotees see the deities, regardless of the shape of that demarcated space. While *maṇḍalas* are often larger and drawn in one place, *yantras* tend to be smaller, mobile, and without colorization (fig. I.1).[52]

Figure I.1. The well-known *yantra* called *Śrī yantra* (The *yantra* of the goddess Śrī). *Source*: Wikimedia Commons, CC BY-SA 3.0.

While there are hundreds of different *yantras* and *maṇḍalas* in Hinduism, Jainism, and Buddhism, most of these diagrams contain similar structural elements. The main diagram is often a square, which represents the earth.[53] Interlocking triangles represent the masculine and feminine aspects of the world as well as some of the elements that make up the physical cosmos; upward-pointing triangles represent masculinity and the element of fire,[54] while downward-pointing triangles represent the feminine and water.[55] Circles represent the element of *ākāśa,* or ether.[56] Often, there is a small dot (*bindu*) in the very center of the *yantra*. This dot represents a point of absolute beginning, the divine force that creates the world. This is the center and the locus of power of the entire *yantra*.[57] Bühnemann describes the *bindu* in the middle of the *yantra* as "the principle from which all form and creation radiates.[58]

While it is unclear how and when such diagrams were first constructed, it has been suggested that Hindu *yantras* originate in ancient Vedic sacrifice, and that the sacred space of the *yantras* are a continuation of the Vedic sacrificial site, a place where humans can connect with the divine.[59]

What is the purpose of these diagrams? These geometric *yantras* or *maṇḍalas* can be used for communication with a deity, for curing illnesses,[60] for luck in love,[61] for conquering one's enemies,[62] or for obtaining wealth.[63] They are used in magical rites,[64] and well as in the worship of deities,[65] in astrology, and in Āyurvedic medicine.[66] *Yantras* and *maṇḍalas* play a vital role in Tantric initiation rituals, where the diagram becomes the place where the deities become visible to initiate for the first time and thereby confirm the initiate's new identity.[67] The architecture of many Hindu temples are even based on *yantras;*[68] in fact, Hindu temples can themselves be seen as three-dimensional *yantras*.[69] The Hindu Vāstuśāstras, or handbooks of architecture, suggest that temple construction starts with a grid, *vāstumaṇḍala,* which is itself regarded as the body of a cosmic being, underscoring the deep connection between the temple, the cosmos, the *yantra*/ *maṇḍala,* and the human being.[70]

But above all, *yantras* and *maṇḍalas* are diagrams of both the cosmos itself and all its powers and the inner psyche of human beings. By meditating on a *yantra,* a person gains insight into both her own inner world and the universe, as well as the divine energies that infuse them both. Tucci refers to *yantras* or *maṇḍalas* as "psycho-cosmogrammata,"[71] and this gloss captures the essential fact that a *yantra* is simultaneously a spiritual map of the cosmos itself and of the human psyche. The main purpose of a *yantra,* then, is the reintegration of consciousness through a process of meditation.[72] These *yantras* are ritually constructed spaces that become sites for religious transformation.

In Tantric Hinduism, there is sometimes further correlation between *yantras* and the human body; the various parts of the *yantra* are identified with the practitioner's body parts.[73] This identification is underscored by the lotus designs found in many *maṇḍalas* and *yantras;* while the lotus is a symbol of creation, purity, the feminine, and the water element,[74] it is also associated with the human heart.[75]

Yantras as Automata

When automata are referred to as *yantras* in Sanskrit literature, then, the implication is that they are not mere machines but rather *both* machines and cosmic diagrams/bodies/temples onto which divine forces are inscribed. Gaeffke suggests that *yantras* are used in Hindu rituals in order to "involve the whole cosmos in the ritual act."[76] "The *yantra* is the whole universe in its essential plan, in its process of emanation and of reabsorption," writes Tucci.[77] I will argue in this book that a *yantra,* in the sense of an android or automaton, serves a very similar function as a blueprint or diagram of a site for cosmic divine energies. Ragahvan, in his study of androids in Hindu and Buddhist literature, writes: "In the minds of the writers, who were essentially men of religious faith and spiritual yearning, the *yantra* or machine always suggested a highly apt analogy for the material universe or the mundane body activated by a God or presided over by a Soul."[78] An android in ancient India, then, is far from an imperfect human imitation of divine creation; it is, much like the *golem* in Judaism, a vehicle for understanding the deepest secrets of creation.

This book proposes that Hindu, Buddhist, and Jain *yantra* tales serve as vehicles for contemplating the nature of humanity and our role in a cosmos filled with divine and natural forces. As we will see, the boundaries between human, animal, machine, god, and cosmos are continuously redrawn in these narratives until these familiar categories assume new shapes and merge in unexpected ways.

Chapter 1 outlines the literary history of mechanical beings in Western literature, both for comparison purposes and to demonstrate later in the book where mutual borrowing between India and Europe may have occurred. The chapter then turns its attention to the theoretical frameworks that can be used to interpret tales of automata and proposes that while Freud's concept of the uncanny (*das Unheimliche*) is especially pertinent to early modern and modern Western android narratives, any corresponding notion is completely absent from ancient Indian android tales. Instead, the Indian narratives are better interpreted within the framework of classical Indian *rasa* theory.

Chapter 2 examines the recurring trope of the Yavana (Greek) robot-maker in the ancient Indian imagination. This chapter proposes that Indian texts may draw on a vague familiarity with the concept of ancient Greek automata, while redeploying Greek and Roman feats of engineering, real or literary, in the service of Indian ideologies.

Chapter 3 analyzes three eleventh-century Indian tales of automata associated with the royal court: a chapter on automata from King Bhoja's *Samarāṅgaṇasūtradhāra,* a story of a robot who praised the king from the same author's *Śṛṅgāramañjarīkathā,* and the tale of a friendship between a princess and the daughter of a demonic robot-maker from the story collection *Kathāsaritsāgara.* These three narratives all suggest that the cosmos itself is comparable to a machine or mechanical device, but not in the sense that the world is reduced to a simple mechanistic clockwork. Rather, the machine of the world becomes a mystical *yantra,* a site for the unfolding of cosmic divine forces.

Chapter 4 analyzes Hindu views of the body, including the notion that the human body can be compared to a machine. This chapter demonstrates that both the mechanical body of the automaton and the living bodies of humans or animals can be likened to Hindu *mūrtis,* or icons of the divine, and argues that the both the Hindu automaton and the human body can serve as vehicles for contemplation of the divine.

Chapter 5 explores Jain tales of automata in light of the views of sentience in the Jain tradition. What does it mean for our interpretation of Jain robot stories when the wood or metal from which an automaton is made is itself seen as sentient? This chapter further examines several Jain narratives involving flying *yantras*, and I argue that these flying machines allow the characters in the stories to see the world "from above" in a way that leads to a greater understanding of a very architecture of the cosmos, which is a significant part of the process of enlightenment in Jainism.

Chapter 6 turns to Buddhist tales of automata and analyzes the curious tale of a man who falls in love with a mechanical woman, only to discover both her unreality and his own. This chapter traces various retellings of this popular story of the painter and the mechanical girl from India, Tibet, and China and analyzes the robot's role as a metaphor for a soulless human being in Buddhism.

The seventh chapter analyzes the bizarre narrative of the legendary Indian emperor Aśoka and his encounter with a killer robot from Rome in the thirteenth-century Burmese Pāli text *Lokapaññatti*. I argue that the homicidal robots in this tale are part of a larger narrative about kingship, power, relics, and *stūpas*, and that their different approaches to the use of dangerous technology signal the difference between an enlightened Indian ruler and a European tyrant.

Chapter 8 discusses the classification of ancient Indian robot tales. Are they science fiction, fantasy, or religious myth? This concluding chapter contains a short summary of modern Indian science fiction literature and film and demonstrates that major themes from the ancient Indian robot tales discussed in the book are still present in contemporary Indian science fiction. The chapter concludes that tales of artificial humans invite us to interrogate our assumptions of both selfhood and humanity.

Chapter 1

The History of Automata in the West

Before delving into the intriguing but vastly understudied ancient Indian android literature, I will first give a brief overview of the history of androids in Western literature for comparison purposes. For a more detailed study of European androids—real and imaginary—in general, the reader is referred to John Cohen's brief *Human Robots in Myth and Science*, Gaby Wood's lyrical *Edison's Eve: A Magical History of the Quest for Mechanical Life*, Minsoo Kang's more detailed study *Sublime Dreams of Living Machines: The Automaton in the European Imagination*, and Adrienne Mayor's fascinating and lively *Gods and Robots: Myths, Machines, and Ancient Dreams of Technology*, which focuses on ancient Greek literature but is also rich in comparative data.[1]

There is a remarkable number of automata, machines, and androids of various kinds described in ancient literature, from Egypt, Greece, Rome, and elsewhere. Does this mean that such advanced technologies actually existed in the ancient world? This is not a simple question. In many cases, the answer is likely to be "no"; the earliest android tales likely represent flights of the authors' imagination, early tech fantasies. As we know from modern science fiction, humans like to imagine technology beyond our current capacity to create, and we like to speculate about what would happen if that technology were available. But it is also true that science fiction sometimes presages inventions to come, decades or even centuries into the future. Humans told tales of flying machines long before the first mechanical flight was possible—but perhaps it was this *idea* that humans were capable of mechanical flight that led inventors to grapple with the issue of how exactly such a machine could be constructed.[2] Similarly, it is likely that the earliest android tales represent fantasies of creation rather than technology actually available at the time. In general, I find it reasonable to assume that ancient tales of automata and mechanical beings are literary fantasies or myths if the narratives serve a greater religious or literary purpose and any technology involved is described in the vaguest possible terms, if at all. On the other hand, there are premodern texts that describe the construction of automata in such mechanical detail that they clearly seem to represent technology known to the authors (and occasionally also attested in other sources). There is, for example, a Chinese third-century tale that describes flying chariots, but these chariots are simply said to be powered by "wind" and not described in any detail.[3] This particular narrative, therefore, bears all the telltale signs of being a fantasy. When Hero of Alexandria writes of a wind-powered organ, on the other hand, he describes his invention in great and convincing mechanical detail, in a book devoted to inventions powered by steam or water pressure; in this case, the invention is likely to depict actually existing technology.[4]

"Before it became a high-performance machine, an automaton was primarily a *techno-mythological idea,*" writes Beaune.[5] Although functioning androids may be very recent as a technological possibility, the *idea* of mechanically made human beings is very ancient indeed. In the following summary, I will describe both fantasy technology and actual technological inventions, although it is sometimes difficult to know where exactly to draw the line between the two categories. In the following pages, I will give an overview of automata and androids in Egyptian, Greek, Roman, and medieval Muslim, Jewish, and Christian texts, as well as some early modern European sources. This overview serves two purposes in a book devoted to ancient Indian android stories: to show mutual influences, and to allow for thematic comparisons between Indian and Western android tales in the later parts of this book.

Androids in Western Antiquity

Turning first to ancient Egypt, we find that statues of deities represent the first imagined (and possibly also actual) automata.

Thoth, the Egyptian ibis-headed god of wisdom, is said to have fashioned statues that could reply to questions by either nodding their heads or moving their arms.[6] It is intriguing to note that the creation of this technological wonder is ascribed to a god, rather than a human creator, which suggests that the creation of something that appears sentient was understood as the act of a divine being.

But there are also other, more realistic reports of mechanically operated statues from ancient Egypt. The statue of the god Ammon was reported to be able to select the new king by reaching out to seize one of the members of the royal family and speak to him. John Cohen speculates that statues such as these may have been mechanically operated.[7] It is likely that some such mechanically operated statues actually did exist in ancient Egypt. There are preserved Egyptian statues with "speech mechanisms" hidden inside; there is a head of Thoth in the Louvre and a bust of Ra Harmakhis in the Cairo Museum, both containing a speaking trumpet hidden in the hollows leading down from the mouth.[8] Cohen suggests that some of the moving statues were jointed dolls that could be manipulated by priests pulling on strings, or alternatively that they were operated by steam or fire.[9] The movements of the statues may have been particularly impressive to the public due to the ancient Egyptian belief that statues possess *ka*, or "spirit."[10] The priests were thought to be able to make the spirit enter into the statue and give them speech and the power to move.[11] The fact that mechanisms have been found inside some of these statues suggest that some priests may have resorted to some degree of fraud in order to convince the people of their power to bring the statues to life.

But even though there may have been some fraud involved in the animation of these statues, it is significant that the *idea* of a statue with the ability to speak and move is not alien to Egyptian religious thought overall. Importantly, most of the "moving statues" from ancient Egypt are images of deities, whose *ka* was believed to inhabit and animate their images. Conceptually, it makes sense in the ancient Egyptian context for a statue filled with a divine soul to be able to move or even answer questions.

Ancient Egypt is also home to what may be the world's first *golem* tale. An artificially created human being is described in the ancient Egyptian Vandier papyrus (ca. 7th–6th c. BCE). In this narrative, a magician by the name of Merire travels in to the underworld to find new life for the dying pharaoh Sisobek. In the underworld, Merire encounters Osiris, the god of the dead, and asks him for another seventy-five years of life for the dying king. But while Merire is seeking extended life for Sisobek in the realm of the dead, the pharaoh himself is taking advantage of Merire's absence to marry the magician's wife and murder his son. When the goddess Hathor informs Merire of the pharaoh's evil deeds, Merire decides to seek revenge against the ruler who betrayed him. In his anger, Merire forms a man out of mud, and this magical mud man haunts the pharaoh's dreams and commands him to burn all his magicians to death. The manuscript is fragmentary, and it is not clear exactly how the story ends. Brunner-Traut has argued, based on the extant text, that this ancient tale may have inspired later Jewish *golem* legends, tales of an artificial person made from mud.[12] While *golems* in later Jewish literature are animated through the sacred name of God, the Egyptian mud man comes to life through the ritual of opening the mouth, which is associated with temple statues; the mud man is therefore, by implication, the structural equivalent of a temple statue brought to life.[13] Brunner-Traut draws comparisons between the mud man and the ancient Egyptian *ushabti*, votive statues that were buried with the dead in ancient Egypt in order to carry out their wishes in the afterlife.[14] Did the idea of androids originate in the idea of statues of deities coming to life and speaking through the power of the gods? An intriguing article by Denis Vidal proposes that the modern interaction between humans and anthropomorphized robots mimics ancient ritual interactions between humans and (images of) gods.[15]

Ancient Greece is also home to several android narratives. Many ancient Greek tales refer to mechanically constructed moving beings, "made, not born," as Mayor writes.[16] The Greek god of craftsmen and blacksmiths, Hephaestus, for example, has handmaidens made of gold that resemble "living young damsels, filled with minds and wisdom"[17] as well as moving tripods with golden wheels,[18] and bellows that work by themselves.[19] Berryman, however, refuses to believe that these moving handmaids and tripods were conceived as automata in the ancient world:

> [It] is surely an anachronism to suppose that the poet is imagining a clever mechanic building a machine. Hephaestus is only said to have the tools of an ordinary blacksmith: hammer and anvil, tongs and bellows. His tripods have wheels, but no other evidence of moving parts or starting devices. Nothing is said about internal mechanisms in the handmaidens or bellows; the technology of the day offers little to inspire the idea of building devices that work by themselves. The story could be interpreted as hyperbolically embellishing the power of a smith.[20]

The association of the androids with the god of blacksmiths is surely significant and points to the stories extolling the great power of art to make statues seem lifelike. We may recall the tale of Pygmalion, who creates a statue of ivory that is so lovely that he falls in love with his own creation.[21] While Pygmalion's statue is eventually brought to life by Aphrodite, the story is clearly more about the greatness of art (and the power of the gods) than about any actually existing ancient technology.

Similarly, Talos, the legendary bronze giant patrolling the island of Crete, is forged by the divine blacksmith Hephaestus, or alternatively by the god Zeus himself. According to Hesiod's *Work and Days*, Talos is part of an entire race of bronze creatures, formed by Zeus from the ash tree: "And Zeus the father made a race of bronze / Sprung from the ash tree, worse than the silver race, / but strange and full of power."[22] But Talos is actually a cyborg of sorts; he has both metal and biological components. Ichor, the divine blood of the gods, runs through his bronze body, sealed in by a bronze nail at his ankle.[23] Significantly, humans themselves are said to be forged out of metal in Hesiod's *Work and Days*, so descriptions of metal men like Talos are likely to be echoes of this primordial act of creation.[24] Mayor observes that in many ancient robot tales, the mechanical humans are made from the same materials that humans use to make crafts. As we will see, this also holds true in ancient India, where automata are usually said to be made out of wood, rather than metal.

There are also other stories from ancient Greece of statues of stone that are able to come to life, such as the stone virgins singing at the temple in Delphi.[25] Many ancient authors, including Philostratus, Strabo, Pausanias, and Juvenal, are familiar with singing statues from Egypt; they refer to a statue of the Ethiopian king Memnon at Thebes as capable of producing a speechlike sound when the rays of the sun touched its mouth.[26] The sound was believed to be Memnon's song to his mother, the goddess of dawn.[27] As we have seen above, some simple technology involving speech trumpets may have existed in ancient Egypt, and these inventions may have been familiar to Greek authors as well.

But Greek authors are also familiar with tales of statues moving by mechanical means. Plato tells of a statue of Aphrodite made by Daedalus that could move when quicksilver was poured into it.[28] It is not clear how Plato thought that quicksilver could have powered a moving machine, but it is interesting to note that mercury/quicksilver is also believed to be able to power automata in ancient India, as we will see in later chapters. The fabled inventor Daedalus is also credited with having made a moving statue that guarded the labyrinth.[29]

Other mentions of mechanically constructed animals or humans may belong to the realm of science or fantasy—it is quite difficult to tell. The descriptions of the famous automaton in the grand procession of Ptolemy II Philadelphus in Hellenistic Egypt in 279/278 BCE, for example, contains some fairly realistic details. The procession included a twelve-foot-tall statue of Nysa, Dionysus's nursemaid, which made the audience gasp as it rose up in its chariot, poured out milk, and then sat back down. The automaton was presumably operated by ropes tied to its various parts.[30] Perhaps more difficult to explain is the mechanical snail mentioned by the Greek historian Polybius (200–118 BCE) in his *Histories*, a snail moving by itself and leaving a trail of slime.[31]

Philo of Byzantium, also known as Philo Mechanicus (ca. 280–220 BCE), is credited with making a mechanical singing bird and a servant pouring wine.[32] Since he was an accomplished engineer, these inventions are perfectly plausible. His famous text *Pneumatics* is only preserved in a brief Latin fragment as well as in Arabic translations, and his ingenious devices were well known to the medieval Arabic engineers,[33] and may have inspired several later inventions.

More likely to be a pure fantasy is the story of Nabis, the Spartan dictator (r. 207–192 BCE), who is said to have kept an automaton created in the image of his wife, Apega, with deadly spikes concealed under its clothes. If any wealthy Spartan refused to give Nabis money, he would let his automaton embrace the man until the victim either paid up or died.[34] The notion of the ruthless female robot assassin foreshadows modern female killer robots like Eve in the 1991 film *Eve of Destruction* and T-x (The Terminatrix) in the 2003 film *Terminator 3: Rise of the Machines*.

Hero of Alexandria (10–70 CE), in his treatises on pneumatics, describes moving automata, including mechanical birds that fly[35] and birds that whistle when water flows through them.[36] Other parts of his work deal with the construction of automated animals that appear to drink water with a loud noise,[37] a statue of Hercules shooting an arrow at a dragon figure if an apple is removed from a tree next to the dragon,[38] and an automaton playing a trumpet by means of compressed air.[39] Hero's writings are clearly the work of an engineer who has worked with steam- and water-powered engines and do not appear to be fantasy. It is not clear which of his inventions were actually constructed and which ones were merely plans or ideas, but they are all described in realistic terms, using available technology.[40]

According to the historian Appian of Alexandria (95–165 CE), Mark Antony had a mechanism inserted into a wax model of Caesar to make it appear as if Caesar was rising from his bier, stab wounds and all, during his funeral procession.[41] Since no such spectacle is mentioned in the earliest accounts of Caesar's funeral, it is likely that this dramatic scene is the invention of Appian.

The second-century CE Greek geographer Pausanias describes an eagle made of brass placed at an altar by the race course in Elis. Touching an attached mechanism would make the eagle rise.[42] The second-century Roman author Aulus Gellius reports in his *Noctes Atticae* (Attic Nights) that Plato's friend Archytas once made a flying wooden dove or pigeon,[43] although the nature of the mechanism is not known.

The Romans were familiar with many of the Greek texts about hydraulics and water-powered automata. But in the Christian Clementine *Recognitiones*, a fourth-century Latin translation of a lost Greek (2nd–3rd c.) original, we leave the field of engineering behind and enter the realm of magic and mysticism. According to this text, the infamous sorcerer Simon Magus claimed to be able to create androids; he was able to "render statues animated, so that those who see them suppose that they are men."[44] Simon Magus famously created a boy out of air, which he claimed was far superior to the work of God, since God merely created man from earth. To render statues animated is a plausible feat of ancient engineering, but the notion of a magician creating a boy out of air is presented as an act of magic, rather than science. It is intriguing to note that Simon's creation of the boy is here presented as a direct challenge to God himself; Simon is not merely imitating the divine creator but claiming to outdo him. Simon Magus is a character familiar from the Acts of the Apostles in the New Testament. Here, he is a sorcerer from Samaria, gathering many followers: "Now for some time a man named Simon had practiced sorcery in the city and amazed all the people of Samaria. He boasted that he was someone great, and all the people, both high and low, gave him their attention and exclaimed, 'This man is rightly called the Great Power of God.' They followed him because he had amazed them for a long time with his sorcery" (Acts 8: 9–11). Simon soon realizes, however, that his powers are insignificant compared to that of the apostles, and he offers to pay them to teach him what they know. The apostle Peter then informs him that divine gifts cannot be bought for money. Simon Magus is often regarded as the prototype of the Dark Wizard literary archetype so often found in medieval and early modern literature. In the Clementine *Recognitiones*, he foreshadows later robot-makers who are "playing God," such as Albert Magnus or the literary character Victor Frankenstein.

The hermetic text *To Asclepius* (2nd–4th c. CE), which shows a strong Egyptian influence, also hints that there is something dangerous about making artificial humans. This text states that men made statues but were unable to create souls for them. They therefore invoked the souls of demons and angels, made them enter the statues, and used the statues to do good and evil:

> What we have said about man is already marvelous, but most marvelous of all is that he has been able to discover the nature of the gods and to reproduce it. Our first ancestors invented the art of making gods. They mingle a virtue, drawn from material nature, to the substance of the statues, and since they could not actually create souls, after having evoked the soul of demons and angels, they introduced these into their

> idols by holy and divine rites, so that the idols had the power of doing good and evil.[45]

The author of this Egyptian-Greek text was likely familiar with the ancient Egyptian ideas of bringing statues of the gods to life, but the idea of binding the souls of angels and demons to the statues seems to be a later Christian/Gnostic reinterpretation.

Androids in the Middle Ages

Ancient ideas about speaking statues and mechanically constructed animals and humans were further elaborated in the Middle Ages. The medieval Muslim engineers were familiar with ancient Greek texts on automata, and they built on the knowledge gained from these texts to develop elaborate working automata of their own. Hero's *Mechanics* was translated into Arabic in the ninth century,[46] and while automata were not a staple of medieval Muslim fiction, they were featured in actual engineering in the Arab-speaking world in the Middle Ages. In 827 CE, the caliph al-Ma'mun even had an artificial tree with mechanically singing birds at his palace, constructed according to the instructions by Hero.[47]

A well-known work on automata *Kitāb al-ḥiyal* (The Book of Ingenious Devices) was composed around 830–850 CE by three brothers, the sons of Mūsā ibn Shākir.[48] This work, which was commissioned by the Caliph of Baghdad, was influenced by the works of Philo and Hero[49] but also contained a number of clever original inventions. The Mūsā brothers, who were able mathematicians as well as engineers, describe the construction of automated fountains, including the world's first wind-powered fountain, a water-powered organ, an automated flute player, and automated water dispensers. Intriguingly, the concluding sentence of the *Kitāb al-ḥiyal* is: "The instrument [their musical automaton] is finished with the power and strength of Allah."[50] The Mūsā brothers further refer to their ingenious self-refilling mechanical oil lamp as *Sirāj Allah*, "the lamp of God," which strongly suggests that they saw their inventions as perfectly compatible with—and perhaps even inspired by—their religious faith.[51]

Human and animal automata are also described in *Kitāb al-asrār fi natā'ij al-afkār* (The Book of Secrets about the Results of

Thoughts), a treatise on mechanics attributed to the eleventh-century mathematician Abū 'Abd Allāh from Andalusia, also known as Ibn Mu'ādh. Although the only surviving manuscript, dated to 1266, contains drawings of water clocks and some of the other machines described, there are no illustrations of the human or animal automata in this text, likely due to the religious prohibition in Islam against depicting humans or animals in art.[52]

An even more influential work of Muslim engineering was al-Jazarī's (1136–ca. 1206) treatise *Kitāb fi ma'rifat al- ḥiyal al-handasiyya* (Book of the Knowledge of Ingenious Mechanical Devices), written in 1206. Al-Jazarī was the chief engineer at the Artuklu Palace in Eastern Anatolia (present-day Turkey), in the service of the Artuqid rulers.[53] He is clearly indebted to the work of the Mūsā brothers but also developed many new inventions of his own. Among the ingenious mechanical devices described in great detail in his illustrated treatise are a water clock with a scribe moving a rod,[54] a figure of two men pouring wine for each other and drinking it,[55] an automated elephant clock, and an automated figure offering a drink to the king.[56] A musical automaton features a whole band of water-powered musicians designed to float around on a lake and entertain the guests at royal drinking parties (figs. 1.1 and 1.2).

The mechanical skills of the Muslim engineers must have struck their Christian contemporaries as little short of supernatu-

Figure 1.1. Al-Jazarī's robot band. *Source*: Public domain.

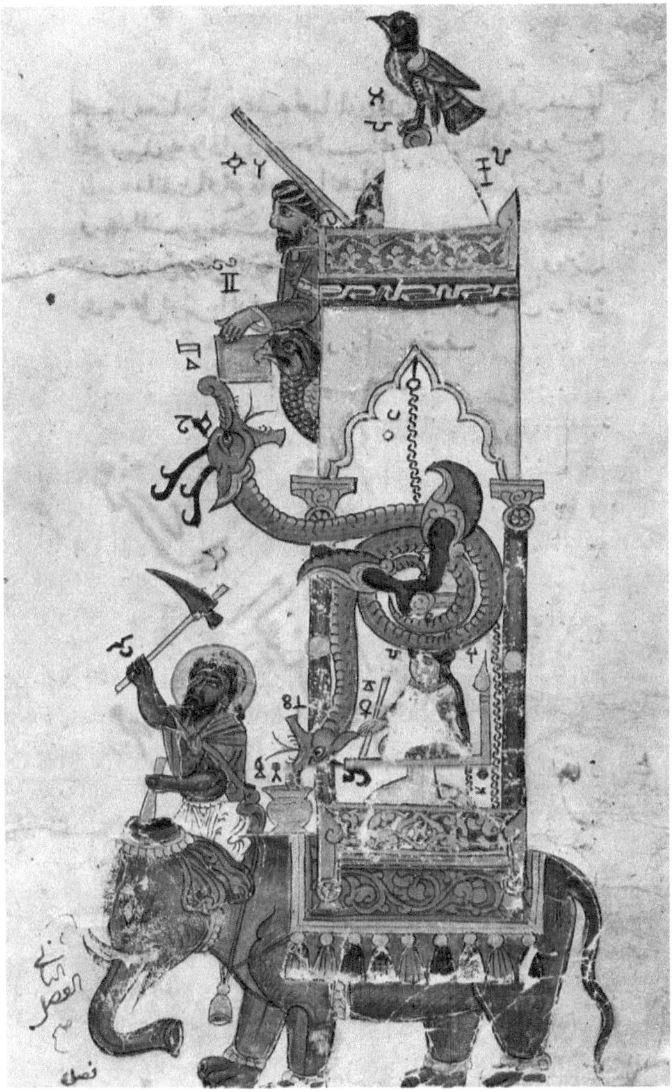

Figure 1.2. Al-Jazarī's automated elephant clock. *Source*: Public domain.

ral. A sense of wonder and awe infuses the French text *Aymeri de Narbonne* (ca. 1205–1220), attributed to Bertrand de Bar-sur-Aube, which describes Charlemagne's vassal Aymeri's encounter with a mechanical tree at the palace of a caliph, a tree formed by sorcerers out of metal and filled with artificial birds.[57] The fact that the creation of this wonderful tree was ascribed to sorcerers, rather than engineers, indicates that advanced engineering was not well known or understood in France at the time.

Western European (Christian) fiction from the Middle Ages and early modern era abounds in depictions of automata, supernatural or not. Why, then, is there no trace of automata in Muslim fiction from this time period, when the Muslim engineers were so clearly capable of creating such inventions? The automata we encounter in Muslim literature belong to a world of mechanical ingenuity, spinning wheels and automatic water clocks, rather than a realm of fantastic literature or myth. The robots move and perform tasks, and the audience is amused and delighted with how cleverly they have been made, but there is never any question of confusing humanlike robots with actual humans. Perhaps the distance between the almighty Creator and humans is simply felt to be too great in Islam to suggest any kind of parallel between God's creation of humans and the human creation of androids. In Islam, God creates living humans, while humans create mere machines, such as clocks and robots. The creation of automata is not considered an act of blasphemy, as so often in medieval Christian texts, perhaps because there is no way the construction of a machine, no matter how clever, could possibly be compared to divine creation. Although descriptions of automata abound in premodern Muslim texts, a recent study showed that modern-day Muslims may be somewhat hesitant to use humanoid robots in tasks such as teaching children the Qur'ān. While advanced humanoid robots have been shown to be particularly helpful in teaching children with autism, many Muslims express discomfort with the idea of a humanoid machine, rather than an actual human, imparting religious instruction to children.[58] One possible reason for this shift in attitudes toward robots over time may be that robot-making has now become so advanced that the androids resemble actual humans more than the medieval automata did.

Greek technical treatises on automata were far more influential among Greek-literate Muslim engineers than among Christians in the Middle Ages. Many of the Greek texts were not translated into Latin until the fifteenth century, and reading Greek in the original had fallen out of fashion in Western Europe.[59] Many medieval Latin texts describe automata as strange foreign artifacts, ascribed to the

Muslims or other outsiders, but these texts do not associate the automata with the ancient Greeks. It is recorded, for example, that the caliph Hārūn al-Rashīd sent Charlemagne (742?–814) a water clock with moving figures.[60] From what we know of eighth-century Muslim engineering, the technology to create such a clock was certainly available in Baghdad at the time.

But the Muslims were not the only ones reading ancient Greek texts in the early Middle Ages; Greek was also the cultural and religious language of the Byzantine Empire. The idea of Charlemagne being astonished by foreign automata is echoed in the twelfth-century French text *Le Voyage de Charlemagne,* which describes Charlemagne's journey to Constantinople, where he sees copper automata at the court of the Byzantine king Hugo.[61] Did such technology actually exist at the Byzantine court, where ancient Greek texts were still read in the original? The tenth-century Byzantine courtly ceremonial text that is usually referred to by its Latin name *De Ceremoniis* describes three different kinds of automata: a tree with singing birds, roaring lions, and moving beasts.[62] There is no mention of the materials the automata are made from, nor is there any detailed description of the mechanisms. Brett suggests that such automata must really have existed at the Byzantine court, however, since a traveler, Liutprand of Cremona, who visited Byzantium in the tenth century, also describes the exact same mechanisms.[63] Since the Byzantine Empire already had a highly developed technology for advanced water clocks (*klepsydra*),[64] with technology borrowed from the ancient Greek engineers, it is not unlikely that they could also have developed impressive automata.

What then of automata in Western Europe in the Middle Ages? While several are mentioned in literature, these are imaginary automata often associated with fantasies of dark magic rather than accurately described machines. It is likely that these automata are literary inventions rather than reflections of actually available technology.

An intriguing conceptual forerunner to the modern virtual assistant is the brazen oracular head that features in several premodern legends. While the notion of oracular heads may go back to the Greek legends of Orpheus,[65] the Norse myths of Mímir's head,[66] or Arabic legends of the oracular powers of severed human heads,[67] the notion of a mechanical device in the shape of a human head designed to answer questions is first attested in *Gesta Regum Anglorum* (*Chronicle of the Kings of England*) by William of Malmesbury, around 1125. Here, the author mentions the rumor that Gerbert of Aurillac, who later became Pope Sylvester II (ca. 946–1003), had made a speaking oracular head that could answer yes-and-no questions truthfully.[68] While there is no evidence that Pope Sylvester, who was interested in mechanical inventions, ever tried to construct an actual mechanical head, his legendary speaking brazen head became a popular trope in early modern literature. According to the Gautier de Metz's *L'image du monde,* the Roman poet Vergil had also created an artificial oracular head.[69] Brazen heads were subsequently ascribed to learned men like Robert Grosseteste, Albert Magnus, and Roger Bacon as well.[70] The notion of a talking brass head was satirized in Cervantes's *Don Quixote* (1605) and is also mentioned by Daniel Defoe,[71] Lord Byron,[72] and Nathaniel Hawthorne.[73] Why all the mechanical heads? Borlik interprets the brazen head as metonymy for the hubris of Renaissance intellectuals and artists.[74] What all these legendary and literary "mechanical heads" have in common is the uncanny ability of the mechanical artifact to answer questions about things normally beyond human ken. Kang reads the brazen head as a symbol of the "danger and glory of arcane knowledge,"[75] and LaGrandeur similarly associated the legendary brass heads with "recondite knowledge and cultural threat."[76] The legends about the much-too-knowledgeable brass heads attest to a profound unease with technology. It is surely significant that the makers of these eerie oracular heads were men like Albert Magnus, Roger Bacon, and Gerbert of Aurillac, who were all deeply interested in experimental science, perhaps to the discomfort of their contemporaries.

Although the Roman poet Vergil was not associated with the making of mechanical figures in antiquity, he acquired a reputation for such acts from the twelfth century onward.[77] According to John of Salisbury's *Policraticus* (ca. 1159), Vergil created a bronze fly that could really fly.[78] Alexander Neckum, in his *De naturis rerum* (ca. 1190), describes both a golden leech constructed by Vergil and a bronze knight placed on the palace roof, pointing to any rebellious province.[79] The twelfth-century *Le Roman d'Eneas,* which retells the story of Vergil's *Aeneid,* describes the tomb of an Amazon, Camille, which in this version of the tale contains an archer automaton.[80] The association between Vergil, tombs, and automata is also found elsewhere; the thirteenth-century text *L'image du monde* describes copper men guarding Vergil's own tomb.[81] Tombs are frequently associated with automata, as in the tomb of the (not quite dead) Blancheflor in the twelfth-century text *Le Conte de Flore et Blancheflor,* which contains mechanical representations of Blancheflor and her admirer Flore kissing.[82] As Linda Strauss has observed, automata are often associated with liminal spaces, such as tombs, temples, theaters, magicians' stages, and so forth, in European literature because the automata themselves exist at the boundaries between two worlds.[83] But why was Vergil (and his tomb) in particular associated with automata? It is possible that the insertion of Vergil into these tales of automata simply represents a lingering cultural memory of the origin of automata in Greek and Roman antiquity, with Vergil functioning as an emblem of the classical age in general. As we will see when we turn to android tales from India, the association of ancient Rome with human automata may have traveled beyond Europe; the medieval Pāli text *Lokapaññatti* features killer androids guarding the tomb of an Indian emperor, but the technology is specifically said to originate in Rome.

Automata are also mentioned in another twelfth-century French text, *Le Roman de Troie* by Benoît de Sainte-Maure. Here, the Trojan hero Hector is taken to an alabaster (tomblike) chamber containing four automata made of gold: a maiden holding up a mirror, a female dancer, a boy sitting on a throne, and a boy carrying a censer.[84] In the thirteenth-century French Arthurian text *Lancelot du lac,* the knight Lancelot encounters copper knights and a copper maiden, and discovers that they were powered by devils.[85] Lancelot would not be the last literary European figure to suspect that the devil must have had a hand in the construction of mechanical humans.

Famously, Albert (Albertus) Magnus, Bishop of Ratisbone (ca. 1200–1280), is said to have made himself a mechanical doorkeeper, or possibly a human speaking head.[86] His automaton was eventually smashed to pieces by Albert's student, the great theologian Thomas Aquinas, who declared it the work of the devil.[87]

William Godwin (the father of Mary Shelley, the author of *Frankenstein*) retells the story in his *Lives of the Necromancers*:

> It is related of Albertus, that he made an entire man of brass, putting together its limbs under various constellations, and occupying no less than thirty years in its formation. This man would answer all sorts of questions, and was even employed by its maker as a domestic. But what is more extraordinary, this machine is said to have become at length so garrulous, that Thomas Aquinas, being a pupil of Albertus, and finding himself perpetually disturbed in his abstrusest speculations by its uncontrollable loquacity, in a rage caught up a hammer, and beat it to pieces. According to other accounts the man of Albertus Magnus was composed, not of metal, but of flesh and bones like other men; but this being judged afterwards to be impossible, and the virtue of images, rings, and planetary sigils being in great vogue, it was conceived that this figure was formed of brass, and indebted for its virtue to certain conjunctions and aspects of the planets.[88]

According to some retellings of the legend, the automaton was a male, but according to others, it was a beautiful female,[89] which may also have bothered the chaste friar Thomas Aquinas. In his 1373 text *Rosaio della vita,* Matteo Corsini writes that Albert Magnus made a talking metal statue, but Corsini emphasizes that Albert Magnus merely consulted the courses of the planets in making this statue, and that no necromancy was involved.[90] Corsini writes that another friar destroyed the statue when he heard it speak because he mistakenly believed it to be an evil idol. The fifteenth-century bishop Alonzo Tostado repeats the same legend in his commentary on the book of Numbers, insisting that the friar in question was Thomas Aquinas, Albert Magnus's disciple.[91] Joachim Sighart (1824–1867) elaborates on Thomas's encounter with and rejection of a seductive female robot,[92] while G. L. Craike writes of a male automaton made of brass, destroyed by Thomas Aquinas because it talked too much and disturbed his studies.[93] Whether or not there was necromancy involved in the creation of the android, this tale was not enough to tarnish Albert Magnus's reputation for posterity however; he was canonized by the Catholic Church in 1931. The legend of Albert Magnus's android, in all its iterations, made its mark on the European imagination; evil robots and seductive female androids have been populating European literature ever since.

The thirteenth-century French Grail poem *Sone de Nansai* describes a Grail castle surrounded by ten mechanical leopards sitting on its walls, uttering sounds when the wind blows. These mechanical leopards, the text assures us, are powered *par engien*, by engine.[94] It is possible that these robotic leopards were inspired by travelers' tales of the mechanical lions from the Byzantine Empire, as described above.

What most of the aforementioned medieval android tales have in common is a striking lack of detail. It seems likely that these stories may have been inspired by the knowledge that actual mechanical clockworks and automata might exist, perhaps through some familiarity with Hero's works or through a vague impression that Muslim engineers possessed advanced technology, but with all details filled in by the authors' imaginations.

A few actual automata, as opposed to imagined ones in these literary texts, were also created in Europe the thirteenth century, however. Villard de Honnecourt made several drawings and charts of clockwork automata, including a mechanical angel and a mechanical eagle.[95] At the chateau at Hesdin in Artois, France, there were several android automata, built at the command of Robert II, Count of Artois (1250–1302), including mechanical monkeys and mechanical birds.[96] Johannes (Jean) Müller (aka Regiomontanus) (1436–1476) is said to have created an iron fly and a mechanical eagle for the Emperor Maximilian,[97] while Hans Bullmann of Nuremberg (d. 1535) is said to have created automata of both men and women, capable of moving and playing musical instruments.[98] The Italian clockmaker Gianello Torriano of Cremona (ca. 1515–1585) constructed various automata, including flying wooden birds and moving miniature soldiers. His only surviving work, however, is a lute player automaton now in a museum in Vienna.[99]

The fifteenth-century Italian engineer Giovanni Fontana even poked fun of the notion that an advanced automaton must be the work of the devil by designing an automaton in the shape of a fire-breathing she-devil, flapping her batlike wings.[100] He also designed fire-shooting rockets in the shapes of rabbits and birds, clearly intended to startle a public not used to flying fire-farting rabbits.[101]

Although some early tales of androids convey some discomfort with the notion that people can create something to rival God's creation of humans, the Church eventually began to use the new technology in its own way by incorporating mechanically moving figures into cathedral clocks. The Strasbourg Cathedral, for example, put a mechanical rooster on its clock around 1350. At noon, it flapped its wings, opened its beak, and crowed. The mechanical rooster can still be seen in the Strasbourg Museum.[102] The Strasbourg Cathedral also had an astronomical clock where a central Christ figure is encircled by the twelve apostles.[103] The figures included in the cathedral clocks were clearly meant to be devotional in nature, and as such were never subject to the same type of religious critiques as other automata. The famous clock tower in Berne, where a wooden jack strikes the hours, was likely constructed shortly before 1500 CE.[104]

In the Middle Ages, Jewish legends about *golems*, humanlike beings shaped out of clay, also begin to flourish. The *golems* of Jewish legends are artificially made humans, although their origins are more mystical than mechanical. The word *golem* occurs once in the Hebrew Bible, in Psalm 139: 16, where it refers to an "unformed substance": "Your eyes saw my unformed substance . . ." Here, the term *golem* seems to refer to Adam's material substance before the creator infused him with a soul, a sense that still lingers in later *golem* legends, where *golems* are said to lack a soul.

The first mention of a *golem* in the sense of an artificially created being occurs in the Babylonian Talmud (3rd–6th c. CE). According to one brief story, the learned rabbi Bar Nahmani (Rava) creates an artificial man and sends him to Rabbi Zera. When Rabbi Zera discovers that the man can't speak, he commands him to return to dust.[105]

The *golem*'s lack of speech is a trope that is found in many later legends, and it is sometimes interpreted as a mark that a *golem* does not possess a soul, in spite of its humanlike appearance. Idel argues that the *golem*'s lack of speech and return to dust are meant to demonstrate the perfection of the divine being; even the most impressive forms of human creation cannot possibly rival the works of the divine creator.[106] While the idea of creating artificial humans could potentially have been theologically problematic in Judaism due to the prohibition in the second commandment against creating "graven images," the legendary *golem* is not associated with blasphemy or idolatry, perhaps because of its ephemeral nature and its creation in the name of God. It is significant that the *golem* in this first brief tale is created by a learned rabbi who also has the ability to return his creation to dust. While the Talmud story does not give any information about how the rabbi created the *golem*, the commentator Rashi suggests that Rava used the mystical text *Sefer Yetzirah* to create the *golem*.[107] Since the *Sefer Yetzirah* was composed many centuries after the Talmud, this must be interpreted as the medieval commentator's desire to claim ancient origins for the popular Kabbalistic text.

How did the authors of the Talmud come up with the idea that a rabbi could create an artificial man in the first place? Moshe Idel speculates that the Talmudic story of the creation of an artificial man from dust may have been inspired by pagan tales of animated statues.[108] While this is certainly possible, we should also note that the tale of Rava's creation of the first *golem* is also an echo of the story of the creation of Adam from the book of Genesis; like Adam, the *golem* is formed from clay/dust and will return to dust at the end of its life.

Another possible source of inspiration for the *golem* story is the aforementioned Egyptian tale of the mud man from the Vandier papyrus. But it is also possible to trace the origins of the *golem* to the enigmatic *teraphim* mentioned in the Bible. These mysterious ritual objects, whose precise appearance and nature are not well understood, appear to have had some rudimentary human shape. They seem connected to divination and foretelling the future; divination by *teraphim* is mentioned in Ezekiel 21: 21: "For the king of Babylon stood at the parting of the way, at the head of the two ways, to use divination: he made his arrows bright, he consulted with images [*teraphim*], he looked in the liver." The *teraphim* are similarly associated with divination in Zechariah 10: 2, and the author of this text is clearly opposed to their use: "For the idols [*teraphim*] have spoken vanity, and the diviners have seen a lie, and have told false dreams." While the *teraphim* are presented in a negative light in these passages, they seem to be something positive or neutral when they are mentioned in 1 Samuel 19: 16 as a decoy hidden in David's bed in his place, allowing him to escape.

What exactly were the *teraphim*? Van der Toorn suggests, based on philological and comparative evidence, that they may have been oracular figurines representing deified ancestors, a view that is generally accepted today.[109] When Rachel steals the *teraphim* from her father in Genesis 31: 17–35, she may have done so in order to prevent him from discovering through these oracles where Jacob had gone,[110] a suggestion already made by commentators like Rashbam, Ibn Ezra, Kimhi, and Nahmanides.[111] Hamori proposes, however, that Rachel herself may have wanted to use the *teraphim* for divinatory purposes and that she was hiding them for this reason.[112] The *teraphim* were outlawed by Josiah (2 Kings 23: 24), perhaps because they were regarded as suspiciously similar to idols. The *teraphim* appear to have been human-shaped objects believed to have oracular power, and therefore at least conceptually forerunners of the idea that humans can create artificial devices and consult them for divinatory purposes. While the *teraphims* were clearly not *golems,* they may have been conceptual forerunners to the idea that humans can create virtual human-shaped assistants.

The term *golem* is used in third-century *Pirke Avot* to designate a foolish or uncultivated person, someone who is socially and educationally yet unformed.[113] While this usage likely goes back to the biblical idea of *golem* as an "unformed substance," it presages the image of the foolish and socially inept *golem* found in later Jewish legends. Intriguingly, some later classical Hebrew texts also refer to an unmarried woman as a *golem,* since she is as yet socially unformed and incomplete.[114]

The fifth- to seventh-century midrash *Leviticus Rabbah* specifically describes Adam, as he is created by God, as a *golem.* The creation of Adam here becomes a paradigm for some of the later *golem* literature: in the first hour, Adam ascends in the mind of God, in the second hour, God discusses the creation with the angels, in the third hour, God collects dust, in the fourth hour, He kneads the dust, in the fifth hour, He forms Adam's limbs, in the sixth hour, He makes him a *golem,* and in the seventh, He breathes a soul into him.[115] Adam is similarly described as a *golem* right before God breathes life into him in the fourth- to sixth-century *Genesis Rabbah.*[116] It seems, then, that a *golem* is here defined as something like a human body prior to the entry of the soul.

A medieval manuscript describes how Enosh, the son of Seth, creates an artificial man out of dust and breathes the spirit of life into it in order to show people the greatness of God. But then Satan intervenes, the statue comes alive, and people start worshipping it as a magical being. Idel interprets this story as a warning to Jews against practicing idolatry, but also as evidence that the Jews were familiar with pagan practices.[117]

Legends about creation of *golems* were soon associated with great learned Jewish men. The Spanish Jewish mystic Solomon ibn Gabirol (1021–1058) is said to have created a mute female *golem*, who worked as a servant girl. When the king of Spain accused him of sorcery, however, he dismantled the *golem*.[118] Intriguingly, this particular *golem* is not made from dust, but rather from wood: "And then he returned her to her original [state], to the pieces and hinges of wood, out of which she was built up."[119] Idel speculates that this legend may simply reflect that Gabirol was, in fact, a man of great technical ability.[120]

Eleazar of Worms (1160–1230) describes how to make a *golem* in his commentary on the Kabbalistic text *Sefer Yetzirah* (The Book of Creation). While the creation of *golems* is not mentioned explicitly in the text itself, the creation of *golems* nevertheless comes up frequently in the rabbinical scholarship on the text. In Eleazar's commentary, the *golem* is created by means of the letters of the Hebrew alphabet.[121] A person making a *golem* must use virgin soil from a place that has never been plowed, add water and make a body, and then begin going through all the possible permutations of the letters of the alphabet.[122] The person making the *golem* combines the twenty-two letters of the Hebrew alphabet into pairs of two, making 221 total combinations.[123] But Rabbi Eleazar adds that the *golem* cannot speak, since only God can create speech.[124] It is telling, perhaps, that the creation of the *golem* is tied to the text of the *Sefer Yetzirah,* an early medieval esoteric text that describes the creation of the universe through the letters of the *aleph bet*. The *golem* is a linguistic creation of life, mimicking the esoteric idea of the linguistic creation of the universe itself. The World is made from the Word, as is the *golem*. In another text, *Sefer ha-Shem*, Rabbi Eleazar refers to the permutations of the letters from the first half of the alphabet to create and those from the letters from the last half of the alphabet to destroy again that which was created.[125] The limbs of the *golem* are created by means of combinations of each letter in the alphabet with each of the four letters in the divine tetragrammaton, the four-letter name of God, YHWH.[126]

The thirteenth-century text *Sefer ha-Gematri'ot* describes the creation of an artificial man by means of the word *emet* (truth), which was also inscribed on Adam's forehead by God. When the letter *aleph* is erased so that only the word *met* (dead) remains, the artificial man will return to dust.[127]

The Polish rabbi Elijah Ba'al Shem of Chelm (1514–1583) is said to have created a *golem* by means of the letters in the sacred four-letter name of God, the *Shem ha-Meforash*.[128] When the letters were erased from the *golem*, he returned to dust.[129] A 1630 manuscript retells the story and adds that the *golem* was brought to life when the word *emet* (truth) was written on it, and destroyed by erasing the first letter, so that *emet* was changed to *met* (dead), as in the *Sefer ha-Gematri'ot*.[130]

Rabbi Loew/Leyb of Prague (1520–1609)[131] is rumored to have made a *golem* out of clay to protect the Jewish population of Prague when they were threatened with persecution following false accusations that they were using the blood of murdered Christian children in the Passover matzah. The *golem*'s tasks were to protect the ghetto at night and frighten away any attackers. During the day, the *golem* worked as a servant but was allowed to rest on the Sabbath.[132] The tale of Rabbi Loew's *golem* was first published in the seventeenth-century text *Nifla'ot Maharal* (The Maharal's Miracles), and it became the basis for numerous *golem* narratives, including Chaim Black's *The Golem: Mystical Tales from the Ghetto of Prague*; Gustav Meyrinck's very influential 1914 novel *Der Golem*; Paul Wegener's disturbingly anti-Semitic 1920 film *Der Golem: wie er in die Welt kam*; H. Leyvick's 1921 dramatic poem *Der Goylem*, initially performed in Hebrew in Moscow and later in Yiddish in New York;[133] and Isaac Bashevis Singer's 1969 novel *The Golem*. The tales of Rabbi Loew and his *golem* often feature a terrible threat to the small Jewish community in the Prague ghetto at the hands of the Christians. The *golem* stories can easily be read as tales of deliverance from anti-Semitic threats, dangers that must have resonated with the readers of nineteenth- and twentieth-century Europe who helped popularize the *golem* tales. The *golem* is here above all a divinely sanctioned protector, rising up to protect the Jewish community from extinction through genocide.

Importantly, the *golem* tales are not narratives of transgressive science but rather profoundly religious texts. *Golems* are always created by rabbis and their apprentices with the full consent of God himself. *Golems* are even discussed in legal (halakhic) Jewish literature; the nineteenth-century Hungarian Rabbi Yehudah Asud contemplated whether a *golem* could be part of a *minyan*, the quorum of men required for ritual prayer. He rejected this idea, since the *golem*, in his view, did not possess a soul due to its lack of speech.[134]

Androids in the Early Modern Era

The medieval European obsession with automata continued into the early modern era. Talos, the legendary bronze giant of Crete, makes an appearance in Spenser's *The Faerie Queene* (1590) as an "yron groome." McCullough has demonstrated that Talos is not merely an automaton in this text, however, but a mirror for the poet himself, vacillating between autonomy and political dependency,[135] which captures the idea that literary automata are often stand-ins for human beings who have been deprived of their free will.

René Descartes (1596–1650) introduced the idea that animals, while living beings, can be compared to complicated machines.[136] By logical extension, the same can then be said of humans, even though Descartes refrained from making that conclusion explicit, perhaps out of fear of how this radical idea would be received. The notion that a living organism functioned along the same lines and according to the same principles as a machine became very influential in the centuries that followed. Perhaps Descartes's insistence that the body is like a machine led to the intriguing (and highly unbelievable) legend that claims that Descartes himself created a robot named after his dead daughter Francine. According to legend, he took his "daughter" with him on a sea voyage to faraway Sweden, but the android was discovered by another traveler, who reported it to the captain. The captain, worried about sorcery, threw the robot overboard.[137] Descartes did indeed have an illegitimate daughter named Francine who died of illness when she was only five. There is no evidence that the philosopher ever tried to build an android replacement for his lost daughter, although he had drawn up some plans for automata, including a dancing man, a pigeon, and a mechanical spaniel.[138] Perhaps this legend of Descartes's robot daughter, which can be traced back to Bonaventure d'Argonne's *Mélanges d'histoire et de literature* (1700),[139] is nothing more than a fantasy inspired by the philosopher's idea that somehow, a living body and a machine were not all that different. In his intriguing essay "Descartes avec Milton: The Automata in the Garden," Scott Maisano argues that Cartesianism was later interpreted as a "retelling of paradise lost," his *cogito* a fall from the state of innocence where humans assumed that body and soul were one.[140] The legends of Descartes's android daughter can therefore be read as expressions of cultural anxiety over the idea that the human body could be understood as a machine.

But while Descartes did not, in all likelihood, construct an android, some of his contemporaries certainly did. A Spanish automaton from the sixteenth century in the form of a female zither player can be found in the Vienna Museum of Art History.[141] An android in the shape of a monk, nodding its head and rolling its eyes, is on display at the Deutsche Museum in Munich.[142] The French brothers Isaac (1590–1648) and Salomon de Caus (1576–1626) are credited with building a number of fountains with automated features, including a statue of Galatea drawn by dolphins and one of Neptune surrounded by moving tritons and horses.[143] Salomon de Caus was a hydraulic engineer who published a treatise about the construction of a steam-powered pump, and he is therefore sometimes falsely identified as the inventor of the steam engine. His younger brother Isaac was a landscaper who borrowed many of his brother's inventions for his own book, *New Invention to Lift Water Higher than Its Source.*

The eccentric Jesuit polymath Athanasius Kircher (1602–1608) is rumored to have worked on a mechanical head for Queen Christina of Sweden that was able to move its eyes, lips, and tongue and make sounds. The head was never completed, however.[144] While there is no surviving physical evidence of Kircher's mechanical head, diagrams of many of his other inventions have been preserved. He invented an improved magical lantern (a forerunner to modern film),[145] a magnetic clock,[146] a perpetual motion machine,[147] an automated water organ, and a speaking statue.

In the early modern era, automata were sometimes featured in religious works as metaphors for hypocrites and heretics and other inauthentic religious figures,[148] demonstrating an unease with these mechanical men and women. Ponti proposes that such anti-machine polemic is particularly prominent in Protestant literature because automata were associated with Catholicism, both literally and as stand-ins for religious icons.[149] The infamous Rood of Boxely, a crucifix in a Cistercian abbey in Kent featuring a seemingly "living" Christ with a moving head and eyes, was exposed as a fraud perpetrated with wires and became a prime Protestant example of Catholics using machines to fool the gullible.[150]

In the eighteenth century, more worldly automata became a popular obsession. The French inventor Jacques de Vaucanson (1709–1782) became famous for his mechanical duck, made in 1739, which would pretend to eat a grain, swallow it, and then excrete it afterward, to the amazement, delight, and occasional disgust of those who flocked to see it.[151] Vaucanson also made human figurines, such as a mechanical mandolin player, a fife and drum player, and a mechanical piano player who looked as if she were breathing.[152] It is said that in his youth, he created mechanically flying angels, which made the leader of the Jesuit order he was a member of order him to destroy his workshop. Vaucanson solved the problem by deciding to leave the Jesuits at that point.[153] Voltaire was so impressed by Vaucanson's figures that he described the inventor as "Prometheus' rival,"[154] suggesting that the inventor's work was as brilliant and as transgressive as that of the Greek mythological figure who ventured into forbidden realms and stole fire from the gods.

The Swiss inventor Henri Maillardet (1745–1830) created a mechanical boy who could draw four different sketches and write four poems.[155] The automaton is still housed at the Franklin Institute science museum in Philadelphia. But the most famous automaton makers of the early modern era were Pierre Jaquet-Droz (1721–1790) and his son Henri-Louis Jaquet-Droz (1753–1791) of Geneva. Their most well-known automaton is that of a female clavichord player who makes music, moves her limbs, appears to breathe, and looks back and forth at her music, her hands, and her audience.[156] Pierre and Henri-Louis Jaquet-Droz also made The Writer, a figure of a small boy writing a message at a writing desk,[157] and the Artist, a young boy who can make four different sketches, including portraits of King Louis XV and King George III.[158] Ironically, the little writing automaton writes, over and over: "I think, therefore I am," hinting to the astonished observer that perhaps there might be some sort of sentience imbuing the lifelike machine. At times, however, the wording is changed, and the little boy writes instead: "I do not think . . . do I therefore not exist?"[159] Although many of their automata were greeted with wonder and admiration, Pierre Jaquet-Droz was actually imprisoned (along with his writing automaton) during a visit to Spain and accused of heresy due to the uncanny lifelike quality of his machine.[160]

The idea that humans are, in one sense, machines was explored in eighteenth-century philosophical works as well. Julien Offray de La Mettrie's work *L'Homme machine* (The Machine Man) expands Descartes's idea that animal bodies can be seen as machines and suggests that humans are also machinelike in our functions, and that our biological components are similar to mechanical parts.[161] La Mettrie even argues that there is no need for a soul to explain the human body; all our abilities can be understood as biological functions.[162] His work was highly controversial at the time, copies of his work were ordered burned by the Church, and the author had to flee.[163] The French philosopher Étienne Bonnot de Condillac (1714–1780) was perhaps inspired by La Mettrie when he wrote his *Traité des Sensationes* (1754), where he argued that one could make a machine out of marble with a mind somewhat like a human, except that the machine's mind would initially be completely blank, a tabula rasa, which could then be filled with all sorts of thoughts.[164]

European inventors continued to experiment with automata, and in 1760, the German clockmaker Friedrich Knaus created an automaton he called the "Wondrous Mechanical Omniscriptor," a mechanical woman who could write texts on a sheet of paper.[165] A mechanical swan created by James Cox in 1777 was on display at the Great Exhibition of London in 1867, where Mark Twain saw it and was fascinated: "I watched a silver swan, which had a living grace about its movements and living intelligence in his eyes."[166]

The Hungarian inventor Wolfgang von Kempelen (1734–1804) constructed an "automatic chess player" in 1769 that became immensely popular in its time (fig. 1.3). The chess player is a wooden life-sized figure of a man sitting by a chess board. Dressed in a Turkish-style turban and exotic clothing, the figure was popularly known as "The Turk."[167] The Turk was able to play chess against any opponent and usually won, much to the amazement of people throughout Europe. This android appeared even more wondrous than Jaquet-Droz's automata, which had been programmed to write, draw, or play music; in its ability to outwit a human opponent at a complex game, The Turk seemed to demonstrate that a machine could actually *think*. Not only that: the machine was so good at playing chess that it beat both Napoleon Bonaparte and Benjamin Franklin! Perhaps this was why some observers found the machine to be uncanny and speculated that it was possessed by a demon; surely, no mere machine was able to play chess as well as a human being.[168] The automaton was later revealed, however, not to be a machine at all. Rather, a small man was hidden inside the box and controlled all the moves of the "mechanical chess player" through a series of levers.[169] Although there had been numerous speculations to that effect previously, the full "secret" of The Turk was not revealed until 1834, when a French magazine article published a full explanation of how a man could be hidden inside the machine.[170] But although Kempelen's machine was a hoax, his idea was remarkably prescient; today, chess programs can easily beat even the most accomplished human players.

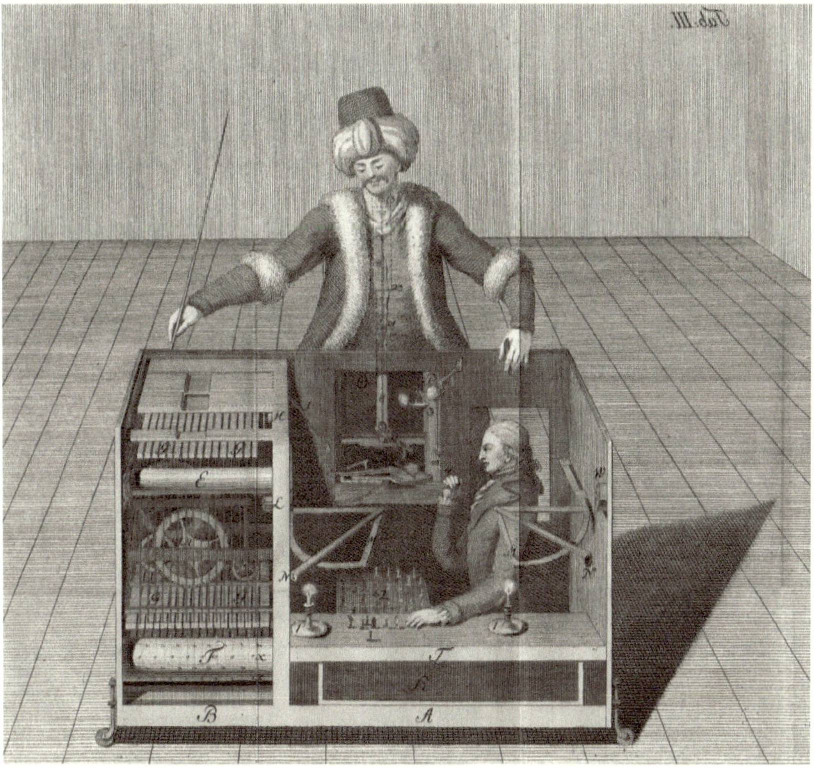

Figure 1.3. Kempelen's automated chess player. *Source*: Public domain.

Modern Western Android Tales—A Selection

One of the first modern android novels is the 1897 *L'Eve future* (The Future Eve) by Villiers de l'Isle-Adam.[171] As the title indicates, the novel is a meditation on the creation of woman, both in a very literal sense and as a metaphorical social creation. The novel depicts the agonies of the intelligent and sensitive Lord Ewald, who is captivated by the lovely Alicia Clary but tormented by the fact that she appears bourgeois and soulless to him. He seeks out the inventor Thomas Alva Edison, who creates an artificial woman called Hadaly at his request.[172] The android resembles Alicia in appearance but is ironically capable of expressing more genuine sympathy and spiritual depth than Alicia herself. The android thus becomes a more perfect version (in Ewald's mind) of Alicia. Ewald falls in love with the android and sets out on a sea journey with her, only to lose the coffin containing his artificial beloved when a terrible storm strikes. The novel's critique of man's desire to shape woman according to his own desires still resonates with many readers. The female android as a metaphor for a woman shaped by male desires and expectations is a theme that recurs in many later novels and films,[173] and one that we will also find in Indian robot tales.

Another female android that left her indelible mark on later science fiction is Olimpia from E. T. A. Hoffmann's 1816 short story "Der Sandmann" (The Sandman). In this narrative, a young man named Nathaniel is infatuated with the lovely Olimpia, who unbeknownst to him is actually an android. Nathaniel notices the stiffness of her movements and her lack of coherent speech, but he interprets these as charming feminine qualities. No matter what he says to her, Olimpia merely replies, "Ah, ah!," which Nathaniel in his delusion interprets as an expression of sympathy and understanding. The story, which ends with Nathaniel's madness and death, is analyzed at length in Freud's 1919 essay on the uncanny ("Das Unheimliche"). Freud defines the uncanny as "that species of the frightening that goes back to what was once well known and had long been familiar."[174] In this case, the sense of the uncanny arises from the profound alienation when that which should be familiar (the human form) is suddenly not (Olimpia's mechanical components). Freud quotes E. Jentsch, who cites as an example of the uncanny the "doubt as to whether an apparently animate object really is alive and, conversely, whether a lifeless object might not perhaps be animate."[175] Olimpia ushers in a new era of fictional androids, characterized above all by a strong sense of uncertainty about what is real and what is not.[176] She hovers at the borderline between human and machine, woman and nonwoman, and her very liminality is a source of dread and anxiety. It is also worth noting that Olimpia is initially introduced in the story as the "daughter" of the robot-maker Coppelius, echoing the somewhat incestuous father-daughter theme from the legends of Pygmalion and Galatea, or Descartes and his mechanical Francine. Sarah Higley has argued that many legends about men creating artificial women point to "an important link between male making and reproduction,"[177] a theme that we will also see in Indian android texts.

Another major milestone in the literature of artificially created beings appeared two years after "The Sandman": Mary Shelley's *Frankenstein*. Mary Shelley's 1818 novel *Frankenstein, Or the Modern Prometheus* drew on a rich literary history of fictional creators and creatures. Practically speaking, Shelley may have been inspired by a recent visit to Neuchatel, where the Jaquet-Droz automata were on display,[178] but she also drew on several literary premodern sources. Mary Shelley may have been familiar with ancient tales of automata and their makers from discussions within her family; her father William Godwin was later to write *Life of the Necromancers* (1834), which lists many legendary automata and their makers. In this work, which warns against "boundless ambition" leading humans astray and causing them to indulge in dark arts of various kinds, Godwin mentions the statue of Memnon at Thebes, the oracular head of Orpheus at Lesbos, and mechanical creatures ascribed to both Vergil and Albert Magnus. As *Frankenstein*'s subtitle indicates, Shelley's novel is inspired by Ovid's tale of Prometheus, the giant who creates humankind from clay "in godlike image" but is later punished by the gods for stealing the divine fire to give to humans. The medieval Jewish *golem* legends may have been a source of inspiration for *Frankenstein* as well.[179]

Significantly, *Frankenstein* resonates with religious themes throughout. Frankenstein's monster reads *Paradise Lost* and identifies with Adam after Eden, rejected by his creator. The plight of the alienated creature, rejected by its maker, as a metaphor for the human condition is a theme that recurs in many later science fiction novels and films. Rather than an object of wonder, the nameless being created by the inventor Victor Frankenstein is variously referred to in the text as a "creature," "monster," and "daemon" (although he is frequently referred to as "Frankenstein" following the immensely popular 1931 film starring Boris Karloff). Perhaps more than any other tale of artificially created humans, *Frankenstein* stresses the transgressive nature of the creation; Victor Frankenstein's experiment is a violation of both moral and natural laws, a dire warning against scientists "playing God."

The classic Frankenstein films added to the narrative of transgressive science. The first Frankenstein film, the brief 1910 *Frankenstein*, shows the monster being created chemically in a vat and eventually vanishing on his maker's wedding night, chased away by true love. The 1931 film, however, starring Boris Karloff as the brooding monster, makes the monster into something of a tragic hero, an innocent creature misunderstood by society. The film further introduced several now-classic horror movie tropes into the narrative, such as the hunchback assistant and the hunt for a human brain. This film was followed by the almost equally popular *Bride of Frankenstein* (1935) and *Son of Frankenstein* (1939). Eventually, a whole franchise developed, which included such films as *The Ghost of Frankenstein* (1942), *Frankenstein Meets the Wolf Man* (1943), *House of Frankenstein* (1944), among others, as well as the immensely popular comedy spoof *Abbott and Costello Meet Frankenstein* (1948).

Karel Čapek's 1920 play *R.U.R.* or *Rossumovi Univerzální Roboti* (Rossum's Universal Robots) popularized the term *robot* that had been introduced by the author's brother in a short story the previous year. The play features a robot factory that produces artificial humans, made from organic materials. They are forced into labor by humans but eventually form a rebellion. Rossum, the robot-maker, initially created these androids to show that there was no need for a god. Rossum's nephew exploits the robots as free labor, while the play's heroine, Helena, wishes to free the robots and insists that they must be paid for any work that they do. She ends up destroying the formula for making more robots. In the end, the robots kill almost all humans, but the robot version of Helena and her lover become the new Eve and Adam of a new race of robots.

The play *R.U.R.* is significant in the history of Western androids both for its introduction of the term *robot* and for its emphasis on the robot as a metaphor for the dehumanized worker, exploited by an industrial society.

The theme of the alienated worker is also prominent in the German director Fritz Lang's film *Metropolis* (1927), one of the most well-known android films. This silent impressionistic film is set in a dystopian future when society is divided into a wealthy upper class and an exploited labor class. The film's stunning images of the factory workers depict them as machinelike (even if they are fully human), as insignificant cogs in the larger machinery of the factory. Eventually, the factory owner's sheltered son, Feder, discovers that the factory workers are living under appalling conditions, and he descends into the depths of the factory to rescue them. An obvious Christ figure, Feder descends from the paradisiacal world above down into the depths of the suffering men. But the film's most charismatic figures are its two female main characters, both played by Brigitte Helm: the pure and loving human woman Maria and the evil robot Hel. Significantly, Hel is created out of transgressive desire; the mad inventor Rotwang creates her in the likeness of his friend's deceased wife, for whom he harbored a secret obsession. Both the android's name, evoking the Norse goddess of the underworld, and the pentagrams surrounding her creation in the film suggest that the creation of this artificial woman is a sinful act. To drive the point home, the film juxtaposes images of Hel with engravings showing the Whore of Babylon. Hel is eventually destroyed, burned as a witch on the town square, while laughing gleefully.

Isaac Asimov's short story collection *I, Robot* (1950) introduces the question of robot ethics with his Three Laws of Robotics that state that a robot 1) cannot injure a human being, 2) must obey a human being (except when this law would be in conflict with the first rule), and 3) protect itself, except when this would be in conflict with the first two rules. The Three Laws of Robotics have influenced later science fiction literature and films but have also contributed to the formation of the actual field of ethics related to artificial intelligence.

Fred M. Wilcox's 1956 film *Forbidden Planet* features the iconic Robby the Robot, a benevolent and often witty robot who assists a crew of explorers from earth arriving on the planet Altair IV. Robby became so popular with audiences that he was reused for many other films and television shows, such as *The Addams Family* and *Lost in Space*. Robby is, as so many fictional robots after him, unable to kill or harm a human being, a plot point likely influenced by Asimov's third law of robotics.

Ira Levin's novel *The Stepford Wives* (1972) describes the experiences of a young woman who moves to a suburban neighborhood with her husband and begins to suspect that the much-too-perfect housewives of suburbia have actually been replaced by robots. In the novel and in the very popular 1975 film, the robots become a symbol of the dehumanization of traditional housewives, robbed of individuality and humanity by men's and society's demands for perfection (perfect homes, perfect appearance, perfect marriages, etc.).

Michael Scott's 1973 film *Westworld* features android cowboys in a futuristic amusement park who begin to malfunction and attack the park's human guests. The film's main antagonist, the Gunslinger, played by Yul Brynner, is one of the most memorable run-amok robots in film. *Westworld* is an exploration of the darker side of android fantasies: What if humans lose control over the technology they create? What if robots were to turn on humans?

The android character Data in the television show *Star Trek: Next Generation* may possess superhuman intelligence, memory, and strength but is nevertheless so intrigued by humanity that he strives to become human. Data is said to be different from his human colleagues in that he lacks emotions, but the character is actually shown to be both sensitive and sympathetic to human suffering throughout the show.

Ridley Scott's film *Blade Runner* (1982) features androids ("replicants") that are almost indistinguishable from humans, presumably just different in their lack of ability to feel empathy. The titular blade runner, Deckard, is tasked with eliminating a group of rogue replicants deemed a danger to society. While pursuing the replicants, Deckard discovers that Rachael, with whom he has fallen in love, is also a replicant, although she does not initially recognize this herself. At the film's end, as Deckard prepares to run away with Rachael, the viewer begins to suspect that Deckard himself may also be a replicant, although this is never made entirely clear in the film. The lingering question about the humanity of the main character, Deckard, suggests that the film's theme is, as Telotte suggests, the "postmodern problem of determining just what constitutes reality itself,"[180] a question that is also central in Buddhist robot tales, as we will see.

The film's sequel, *Blade Runner 2049* (2017) features a main character, K, who knows that he himself is a replicant. Like Deckard, he is tasked with hunting down rogue replicants. While killing ("retiring") a replicant, he discovers a box containing the remains of a female replicant who died during a caesarean section, which suggests that replicants can actually give birth. The female replicant is identified (through DNA, which these replicants possess) as Rachael. K fantasizes about being Rachael's child and thus more human than other replicants in that he is born, rather than created. Eventually, it is revealed that K is not Rachael and Deckard's child but simply had the memories of that child implanted in him. K eventually dies, while Deckard (revealed in this film to be a replicant himself) is about to reconcile with his daughter. Like the original *Blade Runner* film, *Blade Runner 2049* destabilizes our commonsense notions of what it means to be human. Are we human because we possess human DNA, or is our humanity a psychological construct shaped by our memories and consciousness?[181]

James Cameron's 1984 film *The Terminator*, the first in a successful franchise, introduces the memorable cyborg antagonist, T-800, "The Terminator." The Terminator is an assassin who travels back in time from 2029 to 1984 to kill Sarah Connor, whose future son will lead a resistance movement against an army of machines. Significantly, the Terminator, while human in appearance, is completely devoid of human emotions, such as fear or pity. The idea of the robot as a ruthless killer is an old trope in android literature, going back at least as far as Talos, the bronze giant of Crete, and may be interpreted as a metaphorical exploration of the dehumanizing effect of war on its soldiers.

Although this is not the place to explore androids in modern Western literature, film, and television in greater detail, mention must also be made of Donna Haraway's seminal essay, "A Cyborg Manifesto: Science, Technology, and Socialist-Feminism in the Late Twentieth Century."[182] The cyborg represents, to Haraway, not just a fusion of human and machine but any identity that transgresses rigid boundaries, such as those between male and female, between human and animal, and between human and machine. The cyborg stands for the constructed postmodern self, no longer bound by the metanarratives of modernism. She embraces the freedom inherent in the cyborg and exclaims: "I would rather be a cyborg than a goddess." In Haraway's manifesto, the cyborg becomes a powerful symbol for women seeking to free themselves from rigid socially constructed categories. Haraway's cyborg feminism inspired Marge Piercy's science fiction novel *He, She, and It* (1991), which blends traditional *golem* legends with the idea of a cyborg as a creature able to overcome rigid categories of gender and human versus machine.

Themes and Tropes of Western Android Narratives

In this all too brief survey of Western androids, we can distinguish some recurring themes. Many Western android tales involve ideas of the robot-maker somehow "playing god" or challenging the authority and sanctity of a divine creator. John Cohen writes: "The overriding urge of a Prometheus or an Odin to create a man is but a way of challenging the supremacy of the gods."[183] While this may indeed be true of some Western robot-makers, it is not the only motive found in tales of artificially constructed beings. In the Jewish tradition, as we have seen, the creation of a *golem* is a profoundly religious act, meant to give the robot-maker a sense of the awesome power of the first moment of creation and a glimpse of the greatness of God. In Jewish tales, the creation of a *golem* does not challenge the divine creator; rather, the creation is always done in his name and with his consent. And in Islam, as we have seen, there is not even a question of comparing a machine, even one that is humanoid in form, to an actual human being made by a divine creator.

The gendered aspect of Western robot tales is striking. Why are most robot-makers male? It is possible to read robot tales as male fantasies of procreation without the aid of women. Robot-makers often refer to themselves as "fathers" and their creations as their "offspring," but this artificial creation is usually undertaken without any female input whatsoever; the robots have no "mothers." Tales of female robots created by men are often narratives of power;

men create female figures that do not possess a will or agency of their own. Read in this way, many android tales are symbolic explorations and critiques of gender inequity in patriarchal societies.

Other robot tales wrestle with questions of slavery or exploitation of workers. Machines can do the work that human workers used to do, but humans can also be treated like mere machines. Androids in fiction are often symbolic stand-ins for humans robbed of their humanity: slaves, exploited workers, women reduced to sex bots or Stepford wives.

Even if human beings are capable of creating humanlike machines, should they? Or is the creation of false humans an act of religious transgression, a form of blasphemy against a divine creator? While there may have been an aspect of religious piety in the Egyptian belief that statues of gods could come to life and speak, other premodern tales of artificially created beings present these forms of creation as more transgressive than pious. Many of the android tales in European literature are stories of hubris, human creators fantasizing about imitating the gods and bringing inanimate matter to life.[184] While the Hindu and Buddhist stories in this volume may share some superficial similarities with their European counterparts, they are also, as I hope to show, radically different in outlook and orientation, both because there is no insurmountable difference between gods and humans, and because there is no absolute distinction between spirit and matter. There can be no question of the creation of humanlike automata being transgressive or blasphemous in Hinduism or Buddhism, because these religious traditions view both humanity and personhood very differently than the Western traditions.

In this book's exploration of ancient Indian robot tales, we will see many of the same themes as in the Western android stories: critique of traditional gender roles and labor practices, human imitation of divine creation, piety and rebellion. At the heart of the Indian stories, as in the Western ones, there is a deep preoccupation with the question of what exactly it means to be human. But as we will see, some of the answers in the ancient Indian stories are very different from those provided by the Western tales. It is my hope that the ancient android narratives presented and analyzed here will spark further dialogue and debate about the essential philosophical, religious, and ethical questions these texts raise.

The Uncanny and the Wondrous: Freud and Abhinavagupta

Many Western robot tales depict human automata as something uncanny, something associated with anxiety and terror. The concept of the uncanny (*das Unheimliche* in German) was first applied to automata by the German psychiatrist Ernst Jentsch (1867–1919). In his 1906 essay "Zur Psychologie des Unheimlichen" (On the Psychology of the Uncanny), Jentsch argues that a sense of the uncanny arises from the uncertainty the observer feels when it is unclear whether something is animate or inanimate.[185] A doll is supposed to be an inanimate object, but it can easily become a thing of terror if it is thought to move on its own accord. Jentsch uses E. T. A. Hoffmann's 1816 short story "Der Sandmann" (The Sandman) as an example of the uncanny in literature: is Olimpia, the woman the protagonist falls in love with, a real woman or not? Hoffmann builds a slow sense of dread throughout his short story precisely by letting the reader feel that something about the much-too-perfect Olimpia is terribly off, even if his protagonist fails to see it. Sigmund Freud (1856–1938), building on Jentsch, also treats the uncanny at some length in his 1919 essay "Das Unheimliche" (The Uncanny).[186] Freud does not merely define the uncanny, as Jentsch does, as a form of dreadful uncertainty, but specifically associates the uncanny with both the fear of blindness and the fear of castration. Influential as Freud's reading of "The Sandman" has been, later interpretations of the notion of the uncanny tend to focus on the feeling of the uncanny that is triggered by an uncertainty about whether something is "real." This anxiety surrounding objects that inhabit the borderland between the animate and the inanimate is explored in great detail both in science fiction and horror literature, and especially in European and American android tales. Kang proposes that androids make us uneasy precisely if they pose a threat to our "reality schema," our ordered sense of the categories of existence.[187]

The Japanese roboticist Masahiro Mori introduced the concept of the "Uncanny Valley" in his influential essay "Bukimi no tani" (The Uncanny Valley or The Valley of Eeriness).[188] Although Mori's "Uncanny Valley" is often read as a response to Freud's notion of the uncanny, Kimura shows that Mori likely arrived at the notion of the "uncanny" (*bukimi*) independently of Freud.[189] Mori argues that humans are particularly unsettled by inanimate objects that resemble humans too closely. An automated vacuum cleaner is rarely perceived as uncanny because its form (small, round, clearly an appliance) is too far removed from the human form to cause any discomfort. The robot Repliee Q2 (fig. 1.4), developed at Osaka University in Japan, however, which is deceptively human in form and appears to blink and breathe and is capable of responding to questions, would definitely fall into the category of "the uncanny" for many observers.

There is no notion corresponding to the "uncanny" in ancient Indian literature. In classical Indian poetics, works of literature are classified according to *rasa*, or "mood," according to the emotional experience the work evokes.[190] The *rasa* theory, first introduced in Bharata's famous dramaturgical treatise *Nāṭyaśāstra* (ca. 1st c. CE)

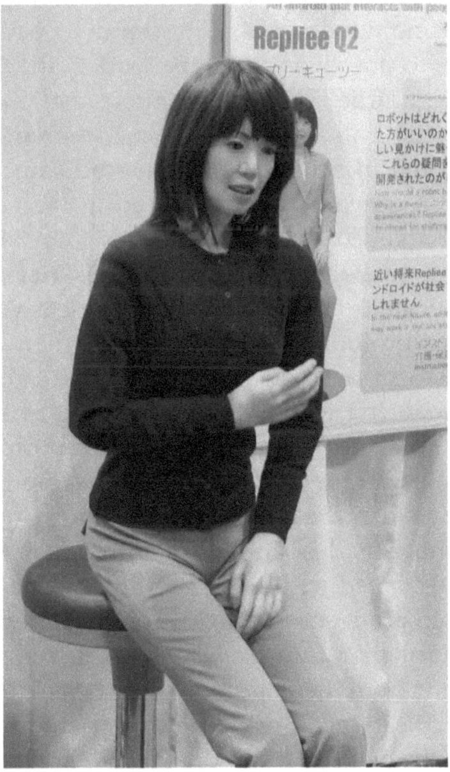

Figure 1.4. Repliee Q2. *Source*: Brad Beattie, Wikimedia Commons, CC BY-SA 3.0.

and elaborated by the tenth-century Kashmiri philosopher Abhinavagupta in his *Abhinavabhāratī*, distinguishes between eight basic moods in literature:[191]

śṛṅgāra (love)
hāsya (humor)
raudra (anger)
kāruṇya (compassion)
bībhatsa (disgust)
bhayānaka (fear, terror)
vīra (heroism)
adbhuta (wonder)

For Bharata, *rasa* is an emotion that can be communicated on the stage, and he locates that emotion in the performative event itself, rather than in the audience.[192] But this definition of *rasa* was later expanded in Ānandavardhana's ninth-century treatise *Dhvanyāloka* to be applicable to poetry and literary works other than drama as well. Another significant shift in the interpretation of *rasa* is represented by Bhaṭṭanāyaka's *Hṛdayadarpaṇa* from around 900 CE, a text only preserved in fragments but quoted extensively by later authors. For Bhaṭṭanāyaka, *rasa* is located in the reader/listener/audience rather than in the work itself or the characters in that work. According to Pollock, Bhaṭṭanāyaka's ideas about *rasa* as an experience located in the audience "are clearly of an order of magnitude more profound than anything earlier, and they were to utterly transform aesthetics."[193] While the *yantra* tales from ancient India analyzed in this book are not part of the classical *kāvya* literature to which theories of *rasa* are normally applied, I would nevertheless argue that these tales exemplify *adbhuta* and are meant to invoke a sense of wonder in their audience.

As Ali points out, descriptions of automata in Sanskrit literature are often associated with a "cluster of terms denoting wonder, marvel, surprise, strangeness, and curiosity,"[194] and he notes that the genre of story literature (*kathā*)—to which almost all of the robot tales in this book belong—seems to take a "special interest in wonderment."[195] In fact, the very term *adbhuta* is said by Indian grammarians to be derived from a prefix *at-* that means "wonder" or "surprise."

There is no Uncanny Valley in ancient Indian literature, but there is a "Valley of Wonder," a sense of amazement at that which is new and marvelous and clever. This is not to say that there cannot be a darker side to this wonder; as we will see in some of the Buddhist stories analyzed in this book, a robot can be a profoundly disturbing thing because it may make a person question such things as the reality of the soul. But this is a productive darkness, rather than a terrifying one; the encounter with the android has the potential to inspire enlightenment. Inspiring enlightenment is, in fact, the ultimate point of the *rasas* in Indian literature; as Abhinavagupta writes in his *Dhvanyālokalocana,* the *rasas* are "like a taste of the ultimate reality."[196] The *rasas* are not, therefore, mere passing emotions evoked in the audience by an expertly wrought work of literature, but rather they are a realization of one's own consciousness, spurred by these emotions that are not tied to one's own ego.[197] The resonance between the classical *rasa* theory and Indian science fiction is illustrated by the name of the once immensely popular, but now unfortunately deactivated website adbhut.com, which published original science fiction stories online and tried to introduce the science fiction genre to a wider Indian audience. The familiar term *adbhuta*—"wonder"—resonates with a literate Indian audience and invites them to see this new and relatively unknown genre of science fiction in the light of classical *rasa* theory as a vehicle for enlightenment.

Tales of mechanical beings may seem very familiar at first sight, but like all creatures of the human imagination, they do cultural work that is embedded in a particular historical, cultural, and religious context. While the ancient Indian *yantras,* like their modern Western counterparts, interrogate the boundaries of humanity, they also serve other kinds of cultural and religious functions. These *yantras* destabilize our commonsense notions of self and identity and decenter the human; they break down the boundaries between the human and the divine world, not as in the Western trope of "playing God" as an act of religious transgression but rather as a form of transformative spiritual insight.

Chapter 2

Interlude

Yavanas and the Creation of Automata

As we will see in many of the narratives analyzed in the chapters to follow, the creation of *yantras* is often associated with foreign artisans identified as Yavanas. Who exactly were the Yavanas in ancient India, and why was the construction of elaborate *yantras* so often attributed to them?

The term "Yavana" is derived from the Greek term "Ionian," via Old Persian "Yauna" and Prakrit "Yona." The Persian word was first used in the Behistun inscription of Darius I from 519 BCE, where the Yaunas (Greeks in this context) are listed among the people subjugated by Darius.[1] While the related term "Yavana" is initially used in Sanskrit to designate Greeks, Yavana is later used for any foreigners from the Mediterranean or West Asia, and eventually any foreigner at all, including Arabs and Europeans.[2] The Yavanas were sometimes also associated with the Kambojas and the Śaka (Scythians), or with tribal people such as the Kirātas and Śabaras.[3] While the Yavanas are regarded as Mlecchas (foreigners, non–Sanskrit speakers) in Sanskrit texts, they are often perceived as quite knowledgeable, which led to a problem of classification for Hindu authors, who generally regarded all Mlecchas as *śūdras*. Some texts therefore suggest that the Mlecchas are degraded *kṣatriyas*, who have lost their original status due to neglect of sacred rites.[4]

In the Tamil Sangam literature of South India, the Yavanas are often casually mentioned in association with trade and craftsmanship.[5] Zvelebil concludes that the Yavanas in Tamil texts may have been Greeks, Syrians, Jews, Southern Arabians, Eastern Africans, Romans, or Byzantines, which hardly narrows down the question of their ethnic background.[6]

The oldest reference to Yavanas in Tamil literature is from the second- to fifth-century CE poetry collection *Purananuru*, dating from around the first century BCE to the fifth century CE.[7] *Purananuru* 56.16–21 mentions Yavana merchants bringing cool, fragrant wine in beautiful ships.[8] The Yavanas are also depicted as merchants in the *Akanāṉūṟu*, another poetry anthology from roughly the same time period.[9] *Akanāṉūṟu* 149.7–11 describes the large and beautiful ships of the Yavanas bringing gold and leaving again with pepper.

In verses 59–61of the song *Mullaippāṭṭu*, which is part of the early *Pattuppāṭṭu* anthology (ca. 1st century BCE to 4th century CE), Yavanas are bodyguards in the royal military camp and described as having hard eyes and a terrible appearance, strong bodies, and concealing a horse whip (*mattikai*) in the folds of their clothing.[10] The Tamil term *mattikai* is likely a borrowing from the Greek *μάστιξ* (whip) and points to a Greek origin for these Yavana soldiers.[11]

Yavana artisans are also mentioned in the sixth-century epic poem *Maṇimēkalai*.[12] *Maṇimēkalai* 1.45 refers to an earthen lamp held in the hand of a well-crafted statue made by Yavanas.[13] *Maṇimēkalai* 19.108 confirms that Yavanas are known for their workmanship through a description of a lovely pavilion (*maṇṭapam*) made by artificers from Magadha, goldsmiths from Maratha, blacksmiths of Avanti, Yavana artisans, and Tamil craftsmen.

While most Indian texts depict Yavanas in a fairly positive light, the *Yugapurāṇa* predicts that Yavanas will conquer northern India, oppress the population, and kill women and children.[14] Although the text refers to these events in the future tense, the account of the Yavanas seems to be inspired by the memory of the Greek campaigns in India under Alexander the Great and later Indo-Greek rulers. Another negative account of a Yavana can be seen in the *Harivaṃśa*, which describes a warrior known as Kālayavana, "The Black Yavana,"[15] who is the offspring of a nymph (*apsaras*) and a sage (*ṛṣi*) but also a partial incarnation of Krodha (Wrath). This Yavana warrior attacks the city of Mathura with an army of Yavanas. Kṛṣṇa succeeds in luring Kālayavana into a cave where he kicks a sleeping sage, who promptly burns the Yavana to ashes.

Buddhist literature is also familiar with Yavanas (Yonas) and depicts them in a more positive light. Several of the third-century BCE edicts of Aśoka refer to Yonas,[16] and some of the edicts from outlying areas of his empire are trilingual, including text in Prakrit, Greek, and Aramaic. The Greek text is clearly an attempt at conveying Aśoka's message of *dhamma* (righteousness) to the Yonas. The identification of the Yonas with Greeks in the Aśokan edicts is confirmed by the fourteenth rock edict, which refers to a Yona king by the name of Amtiyoko, who has plausibly been identified with Antiochus II Theos.[17] The most well-known Yona in Buddhist literature is Milinda (Menander), one of the two main characters of the *Milindapañhā* (The Questions of Milinda), a Pāli Buddhist text dating to around the beginning of the common era. The text consists of a dialogue between the Buddhist monk Nāgasena and the Yavana king Milinda, who likely represents the third-century BCE Indo-Greek Bactrian king Menander I, and the conversation ends with the conversion of the wisdom-seeking Yavana king to Buddhism.[18]

A connection between Yavanas and *yantras* is made in several Indian texts. Why are Yavanas so often associated with the making of *yantras*? It is possible that the authors of the Indian *yantra* tales may have been familiar with literature about automata from ancient Greece or Rome, although the intricacy of some of the *yantras* created by Yavanas in the Indian imagination goes far beyond anything imagined by Hero of Alexandria or other ancient Greco-Roman engineers. It is also likely that the high level of craftsmanship among Greek or Roman artisans, as noted by the Tamil authors in a more prosaic way, fueled the Indian imagination and invited speculations about what other fantastical devices these foreigners were capable of producing.

Mechanical flying chariots constructed by Yavanas are mentioned in several Indian texts. The first such mechanical chariot is found in the fourth- to fifth-century CE Jain story *Vasudevahiṇḍī* (The Wanderings of Vasudeva) by Saṅghadāsa. The *Vasudevahiṇḍī* is ostensibly a retelling of the *Bṛhatkathā*, a lost Sanskrit literary work referenced by many later authors,[19] but the *Vasudevahiṇḍī* itself is composed in Old Mahārāṣṭrī. Here, we find a description of Indian traders who travel by sea to the country of the Javaṇa (Yavana), where one of them learns the art of making automata (*yantra*) from a Yavana master and ends up producing a fantastic flying chariot that allows passengers to travel through the air (see chapter 5 for more analysis of this narrative). The Yavanas in this story are clever artisans who live in a remote location. A variant of this story is found in Budhasvāmin's Hindu text *Bṛhatkathāślokasaṃgraha* (ca. 9th c. CE), which is a compendium of material taken from the lost *Bṛhatkathā*; here, the science of creating flying machines (*ākāśa-yantra*, literally, "ether machine") is said to be known only to Yavanas, who keep this technology secret.[20] We will return to the idea of secret foreign technology (in this case "Roman"), in chapter 7.

The seventh-century Sanskrit text *Harṣacarita* by Bāṇa, a biography of the king Harṣavardhana of Kanauj (606–647 CE), mentions a king Kākavarṇa who is carried away by a mechanical chariot (*yantra-yāna*) and vanishes. The chariot is said to have been constructed by a Yavana condemned to death.[21] The partially preserved Tamil version of the *Bṛhatkathā*, ascribed to Konguvel, also features Yavana carpenters.[22]

In the autobiographical portion at the beginning of *Avantisundarī*, Daṇḍin (7th c. CE) mentions a gifted architect called Māndhātā, who is capable of constructing flying chariots and is said to surpass "even the Yavanas" is his art.[23]

But Yavanas are not only capable of creating flying chariots in Indian literature; they can also create artificial humans. Yavanas are featured in Saṅghadāsa Kṣamāśramaṇa's eighth-century CE commentarial work *Bṛhatkalpabhāṣya*, where we learn that mechanical images (*janta-paḍimā*) of humans, capable of walking and opening and closing their eyes, are frequent among the Yavanas in their country.[24]

A Buddhist tale, retold in many different versions, features a painter from India who travels by unspecified means of transportation to the land of the Yavanas and encounters a mechanical woman there (see chapter 6). In this case, the *yantra* is so lifelike that the poor painter assumes that the mechanical woman is real and falls in love with her.

How can we account for the trope of the Yavana *yantra*-maker in Indian literature? It is difficult to know for certain, but it is possible that a vague familiarity with ancient Greek automata—real or literary—combined with firsthand encounters with skilled foreign artisans in India inspired the idea of the Yavana robot-maker.

But while Indian authors may have fantasized about marvelous automata created by the Greeks, there is at least one example of a Greek author spinning similar fantasies about India as a land of fantastic androids. The first-century CE author Flavius Philostratus, in his *Life and Times of Apollonius of Tyana*, describes bronze cup-bearers pouring wine for guests at a party Apollonius attends in India:[25] "Then Iarchas rose, and raising his voice invited the king to take refreshments, and on his gratefully accepting the invitation four Pythian tripods glided in of their own accord, like the moving tripods which Homer describes, and behind them came cup-bearers of dark bronze resembling the figures of Ganymede or of Pelops among the Greeks."[26] While this reference to Indian automata in an ancient Greek text has caused a flurry of speculation about ancient Indian robot-making technology, this passage seems inspired by the description of moving tripods in the *Iliad* and may simply be a flight of the author's imagination. Several ancient Greek authors were fascinated by India, but the information they provide about Indian culture is often extremely fanciful and includes descriptions of dog-headed men and ants the size of foxes. The description of the cup-bearing automata, which are known from ancient Greek texts, but not from Indian ones, may simply be yet another indication that India was a wonderful and exotic place in the ancient Greek imagination.

But in his 1943 edition of the *Āgamaśāstra* of Gauḍapada, the sixth-century Hindu philosopher, Bhattacharya drew attention to a legend mentioned in the sixteenth-century text *Gururatnamālā* by Sadāśivabrahmendra that connects Gauḍapada with a character called Apalūnya, which could possibly be an Indian version of the Greek name Apollonius. Bhattacharya further points out that the commentator Ātmabodhendra writes that Gauḍapada influenced both a certain Ayārcya and his followers, who included a yogin from the western border by the name of Apalūnya.[27] Could there be actual references to Iarchas and Apollonius in Sanskrit texts? And if so, could it be that the descriptions of Apollonius's adventures in India were more historically accurate than previously assumed? Swain's 1995 article "Apollonius in Wonderland" demonstrates conclusively that the Sanskrit references to Apalūnya and Ayārcya are likely very recent insertions into the Sanskrit texts. He is not accusing Bhattacharya himself of fraud but speculates that the names may have been inserted into the Sanskrit texts, which were first published in 1895, specifically to convince readers of a historicity of Apollonius's journey to India. Swain points out that the ancient Greek name Iarchas cannot possibly become Ayārcya in Sanskrit, especially since the Sanskrit spelling seems to reflect the modern English pronunciation of the name, rather than the ancient Greek one.[28] Even if there is no confirmation of Apollonius's journey to India in Sanskrit texts, it is nevertheless intriguing that the ancient Greeks and the ancient Indians both fantasized about each other as advanced robot-makers.

But the trope of the Yavana robot-maker in ancient Indian literature is more than just a vestige of cultural contact or a vague memory of the feats of ancient Greek engineers. While the Yavana robot-makers in Indian texts may be cultural others with access to mysterious foreign technology, they are primarily figures of the Indian imagination, creating mechanical men, women, and flying machines that—like other *yantras*—invite those who encounter them to a deeper understanding of a sacred cosmos.

Chapter 3

Robots in the Royal Garden

Yantras and the Puppet Theater

Why are the human automata described in ancient Indian texts usually made of wood, while those depicted in ancient Greek texts are made of metal? There may be several different reasons for this, but one that immediately comes to mind is a possible connection of *yantras* to the Indian puppet theater with its wooden dolls, moved by strings.[1] The puppet theater was immensely popular in ancient India, and it has even been suggested that India was the origin of puppet play.[2] Vātsyāyana, in his famous treatise on the art of love, the *Kāmasūtra,* recommends that young men cultivate an interest in puppet theater in order to gain women's affections.[3] The *Mahābhārata* epic compares human beings, manipulated by fate, to wooden puppets controlled by strings: "Man is without power when it comes to existence and non-existence, like a wooden puppet strung on a string (*sūtraprotā dārumayīva yoṣā*)."[4] It is surely significant that one of the words frequently used to designate an automaton in Sanskrit, *putrikā* (literally, "daughter"), is also one of the Sanskrit words for a puppet.[5] But puppets are more than just metaphors in the *Mahābhārata;* as the warrior Arjuna is heading into battle, the princess Uttarā and her friends ask him to bring back clothes for their puppets, signaling how important puppet play was to courtly life.[6] A puppet may even, like the automata of Hindu myth, be brought to life by a god. According to one tale, the goddess Pārvatī once made herself a puppet that was so beautiful and so lifelike that she thought it wise to hide it from her husband, the god Śiva, so he wouldn't fall in love with it. She hid the puppet in the mountains but visited it every day to play with it and dress it up in lovely clothes. But Śiva grew suspicious because of Pārvatī's long absences, so he decided to follow her and see what she was doing. And when he saw the puppet, he did indeed fall in love with it and decided to bring it to life.[7] Śiva's enchantment with the artificially created woman recalls the many robot tales where men fall in love with female automata.

But puppets are also associated with *yantras* in the sense of magical diagrams as well. In his study of Indian Gombeyata puppetry in Karnataka, Schuster describes pieces of paper or palmetto leaves with inscribed *yantras* placed inside seventeenth-century puppets in order to give them power.[8] These *yantras*, placed inside the hollow back of the head or the space under the arm guard, are symbolically animating the artificial beings of the puppets. Schuster further describes a Gaṇeśa puppet with a battery-operated motor in the hollow in the back of the head "where, in times past, a *yantra* might have been slipped." When the motor is turned on, a *maṇḍala* revolves around the deity's head. This battery-operated puppet evokes multiple *yantras* at once: the puppet is itself almost a *yantra* in the sense that the puppet resembles an artificially constructed human; it contains a mechanism (*yantra*) that produces a *maṇḍala* (*yantra*), a mechanism located at the site where an older *yantra* (line-drawn *maṇḍala*) might have been. As we will see in the following pages, one of the most significant texts on automata from premodern India, the *Samarāṅgaṇasūtradhāra*, even evokes a puppet master "holding the strings" in its title.

The *Samarāṅgaṇasūtradhāra* of King Bhoja

One of the most elaborate descriptions of automata in Hindu literature is, perhaps surprisingly, embedded in an eleventh-century treatise on architecture. The *Samarāṅgaṇasūtradhāra* (The Commander/Puppet Master of the Battlefield) is a monumental work on architecture, covering topics ranging from town planning, house and temple construction, to art and sculpture.[9] The work is commonly ascribed to Bhoja, the scholar-king of Malwā, a kingdom in west-central India.[10] Bhoja, the sixth ruler of the Paramāra dynasty, is mentioned in several medieval Sanskrit historical records, such as the *Udaipur-Praśasti* and the *Navasāhasāṅkacarita* as well as in various inscriptions.[11] He was likely born around 982–989 CE and ascended the throne of Malwā around 1010 CE.[12] Under his enthusiastic patronage of literature and the arts, Bhoja's capital city Dhārā became a center of intellectual life in India. A total of eighty-four Sanskrit texts are ascribed to King Bhoja himself, on topics ranging from politics, astronomy, and medicine to grammar, music, and philosophy. H. C. Ray has suggested that while these works were likely composed at Bhoja's court, many of the texts may have been composed by authors patronized by the king rather than by Bhoja himself.[13] Singh argues, however, that the style of many of the works ascribed to Bhoja suggest unity of authorship, and that the king himself may be the author of the majority of the texts ascribed to him.[14]

Bhoja's own life is steeped in legend. The fourteenth-century Sanskrit text *Prabandhacintāmaṇi* ascribed to Merutuṅga describes an attempt on the young prince Bhoja's life by his uncle Muñja, who wanted his own son to be king in Bhoja's place. Muñja sent armed troops led by the king of Vatsa to assassinate Bhoja in a forest temple. But when the assassins observed the beauty of the young prince and heard his eloquence, they instead agreed to bring back a letter from Bhoja to his uncle. Bhoja composed a lovely verse to his uncle, wrote it down on a fig leaf in his own blood, and sent it to his uncle along with an artificially constructed head. Muñja was so overwhelmed by the beauty of the poem that he repented his evil actions and restored Bhoja to his rightful place on the throne of Malwā.[15] It is not clear how the mechanical head enters into the story of the young prince, but we should note that the presence of a mechanical head may indicate some possible influence from medieval and early modern European tales of oracular heads (see chapter 1).[16] Another source of legends of King Bhoja is the fifteenth-century Telugu poem *Bhojarajīyam* by Ananta-Amatya, but this work does not mention either automata or an artificial head in connection with Bhoja.[17] Bhoja's life story is also retold in the sixteenth- to seventeenth-century Sanskrit text *Bhojaprabandha* by Ballāla of Benares.[18] In this text, the creation of the artificial head is ascribed to the king of Vatsa, who has become fond of the young Bhoja and does not wish to kill him as promised. Instead, he makes an artificial head and passes it off to Muñja as the decapitated head of Bhoja himself.[19]

Bhoja himself seems to have been a devout Hindu. During Bhoja's reign, Buddhism was in decline in most parts of India, while both Jainism and Hinduism flourished.[20] While the worship of the Hindu god Viṣṇu was popular, Śaivism was even more prominent.[21] Malwā itself was a center of Śaivism, and kings of the Paramāra dynasty, Bhoja included, commissioned the building of many temples to Śiva.[22] One of the works ascribed to Bhoja is the Śaiva text *Tattvaprakāśa*, and there are several prominent Śaiva elements in the *Samarāṅgaṇasūtradhāra* as well, beginning with its opening line. An entire chapter of the *Samarāṅgaṇasūtradhāra* is moreover devoted to the construction of *liṅgas*, the phallic representations of the god Śiva. It is not surprising, therefore, that the construction of automata is closely tied, as we shall see, to Śiva himself in the *Samarāṅgaṇasūtradhāra*.

Although the *Samarāṅgaṇasūtradhāra* deals with many of the same topics as other standard ancient Indian texts on architecture, it devotes an entire chapter to automata, something that is conspicuously absent from other architectural treatises. The thirty-first chapter of the text is titled *Yantra-vidhāna* (Establishing a *Yantra*). A full translation with notes of this rather complex technical chapter is given in the appendix.[23] In the following pages, I want to highlight some of the main themes of Bhoja's treatise on *yantras*.

The Puppet Master and the *Yantra* of the World

What is the meaning of this text's curious title, "The Commander of the Battlefield" or "The Puppet Master of the Battlefield"? A *sūtradhāra* (literally, "one who holds the strings") is the term for a stage manager in the classical Indian theater. It is likely that the stage manager got this title because he directs the movements of the actors on his stage just like someone holding the strings and controlling the movements of the puppets in the puppet theater. But *sūtradhāra* also means an "architect" in Sanskrit. The title of this text, then, reflects a multiplicity of interrelated meanings; *Samarāṅgaṇasūtradhāra* means "The Architect of the Battlefield," and it refers simultaneously to the king's strategic role in warfare and also to the crucial role played by mechanical inventions and their creators in maintaining the state. If the text is indeed the work of King Bhoja himself, the title may refer to the king's own role in the defense of his state; he is both the one who "pulls the threads" and controls the state, an architect in a literal sense, and a builder of automata and machines. The title of the text resonates in a particularly meaningful way with the contents of this chapter, which deals with automata of various kinds. A maker of automata is of course a puppet-maker of sorts, one who makes the inanimate come to life. In this chapter, there are multiple symbolic *sūtradhāras* involved: the engineer who constructs the automata, the king himself, the author of the text, and of course above all the cosmic *sūtradhāra*, the god Śiva himself, who controls the threefold *yantra* of the world. The title of the work is found in 31.86: "The harnessing of the elements, controlled and generated by *sūtradhāras*, gives great pleasure." Here, the *sūtradhāra*, which could be understood in this context as an architect, a puppet master, or a machine-maker, is defined as a person with the power to harness the elements. The elements are described in great detail in the text, perhaps to underscore the fact that the maker of *yantras* controls the elements of nature.

While the *Samarāṅgaṇasūtradhāra* is a general treatise on architecture, this particular chapter both broadens and narrows the scope of how architecture may be defined; the chapter begins with the greater architecture of the cosmos itself, described as a cosmic *yantra*, and proceeds to analyze the architecture of various mechanical *yantras*, down to the level of their constituent elements.[24] The theme of homology between the human body and the cosmos that can be seen in Hinduism as early as the *Ṛgveda* is here reinterpreted as a homology between the cosmic *yantra* of the world and the body of the *yantra* as automaton.

The author defines *yantra* in the third stanza of this chapter: "When the elements (*bhūta*) spontaneously move along their own path, that which restrains and controls (*yam*) them is known as a *yantra*." While the term *yantra* does indeed come from the verbal root *yam*, which means "to control," the author's claim that a yantra represents control over the elements is interesting, particularly in light of the extensive discussion of the five elements in the chapter.

The *Yantra* and the Elements

The verses in the *Samarāṅgaṇasūtradhāra* on the relationships of various types of machines and automata to the five elements serve to align Bhoja's ideas with classical Hindu natural science:

9. When the elements (*bhūta*) spontaneously move along their own path, that which restrains and controls them is known as a *yantra.*
10. When the elements move along according to their own inclination and whim, it (the machine) controls (*yam*) them, and therefore it is called a *yantra.*
11. There are four elements (*bīja*): earth, water, fire, and air. Because it is the basis of the others, ether is also mentioned.
12. Some say that mercury is a separate element, but they are not correct. Since mercury is naturally of the earth, it should be treated as such (as part of the earth element).
13. Because mercury is earthly, it should not be regarded as separate from the earth element. But if its ability to produce fire is taken into account . . .
14. . . . then it is not different from fire. But because of its scent, it is different from fire and strongly connected with earth.

From the era of the older Upaniṣads onward, Indian authors have recognized the same five elements as the ancient Greeks: earth, water, fire, air, and ether. Intriguingly, these elements are not just referred to in the *Samarāṅgaṇasūtradhāra* by the classical term *bhūta* (element) but also by the more uncommon term *bīja* (literally, "seed"). The term *bīja* carries connotations of organic life, origin, and growth and is often associated with the seeds of plants. By using this unusual term to refer to the five elements, the *Samarāṅgaṇasūtradhāra* hints that the constituent elements of the world can also be imbued with a potential for life and growth.

Further, *bīja* can also signify "semen," a meaning that is surely also significant when the term is associated with the erotic god Śiva in this chapter. But *bīja* also carries more esoteric meanings; significantly, *bīja* is used to refer to the mystical syllables inscribed in a *yantra* (religious diagram); a *bīja* or "seed syllable" is a mystical sound that is a part of a *mantra* or a seat for a deity and that carries cosmic power. In alchemy, *bīja* is a compound made of gold or silver that is used in the advanced stages of alchemical work.[25] The first stanza of this chapter of the *Samarāṅgaṇasūtradhāra* therefore resonates with multiple interconnected meanings: the universe is both machine and mystical diagram, both mechanical and organic, made up of *bījas* that are both sacred sounds, seeds of organic life, physical elements, and the life-giving seed of Śiva himself. Seen against this cosmic backdrop, then, the automata described in the rest of the chapter are, like the machinery of the universe itself, *yantras* in all meanings of the word. They are machines but also devices for meditation and religious contemplation, and sites of wonder.

The *Yantra* and the Four Goals of Life

What is the purpose of creating *yantras*? The mechanical devices described in this chapter are meant to amuse and entertain, but the chapter also claims that the creation of *yantras* have a deeper meaning. Stanza 2 asserts that the purpose of this chapter on *yantras* is to establish a "basis for *dharma, artha, kāma,* and *mokṣa,*" which are the four goals of human pursuits (*puruṣārthas*) in Hinduism.

Dharma is an individual's social and religious duty, *artha* is wealth and prosperity, *kāma* is erotic love and fulfillment, and *mokṣa* is spiritual liberation. Ideally, a person will achieve all these goals at various points in life. What are we to make of the author's claim that a chapter on the construction of mechanical devices can help someone attain all these goals?

The author explains in stanzas 16–20 that someone who knows *yantras* will be beloved by both kings and women, which will naturally bring both wealth and love. Presumably kings will want to pay for a *yantra*-maker's services, while women will be charmed by his skills. It is a little more difficult to understand the author's argument for why these *yantra*-making skills will also help a person obtain *dharma*. The author notes that the *yantra*-maker will get a "dwelling among coquettish women, a palace of the greatest wonder . . . a dwelling that is an abode of pleasure, a house of marvel, just like that of the gods, because of the beauty and activity seen there. These things satisfy, and that satisfaction was known by the ancient ones as *dharma* (religious duty)" (18–19). It is possible that the *dharma* in this case is tied to the idea of a householder's dutiful observances or religion, with the implication that it is easier to fulfill these duties if one has a house and a wife. But there may also be a subtext here related to *yantra* diagrams, which are, as we have noted previously, often associated with the magical acquisition of love and wealth. The author further remarks: "Because of his accumulation of wealth, his renunciation and liberation (*mokṣa*) are not difficult to obtain." The underlying idea seems to be that a person who lives according to *dharma* will naturally attract wealth, which will bring about love but also eventually a desire to renounce worldly possessions and seek spiritual liberation.

The *Yantras* of the *Samarāṅgaṇasūtradhāra*

The *yantras* mentioned in the *Samarāṅgaṇasūtradhāra* range from simple devices such as spinning wheels to elaborate automata powered by water or mercury. The author introduces a fourfold classification of *yantras* into automatic (*svayamvāhaka*), those with wind-up mechanisms (*sakṛtprerya*), those who have mechanisms hidden inside, and those who have the mechanism far away (stanzas 10–11), and notes that the automatic *yantras* are the superior ones. The author notes, somewhat cryptically, that "that which has become invisible is the most effective of all. They praise it because it causes wonder among men" (12), a possible reference to devices whose machinery is not visible to the observer. Stanza 72 likewise notes that "a mechanical girl, an elephant, a horse, or a monkey" will cause wonder among men. The notion of wonder (*adbhuta*) is particularly noteworthy here because of its connection with the *rasa* doctrine of Indian aesthetics, as we saw in chapter 1.

A human automaton is described in some detail in stanzas 102–105:

> It is made of wood, well-made like a pillar and covered in discarded hide; made in the form of a man or a young woman, it is very charming.
> When it has an iron arrow and threads in every hole, it creates the movement and stretching and contraction of the neck.
> It shakes hands, spits betel juice, bows respectfully, looks in the mirror, plays the lute, and so forth.
> If something like this is seen, it produces a sense of wonder, because strings are drawn and released and opened regularly (seemingly) because of its (the automaton's) own intellect (*buddhi*).

These verses are particularly helpful in envisioning what a human-like automaton would have looked like and how it would have functioned. The references to strings, threads, and holes suggest that the automaton may have been very similar to a puppet in construction, and that its limbs may have moved because someone pulled strings. But the fact that it creates the illusion of being sentient (moving because of its own *buddhi*) indicates that it was created to be as lifelike as possible. The *yantra*'s tricks are likely to have appealed to an audience, and one can speculate that a *pan*-spitting automaton would have been especially fun to watch.

One automaton that is particularly noteworthy is a water clock in the shape of a rider on an elephant, accompanied by a display of the movement of the planets (stanza 70). This is a perfect match for the elephant clock whose construction is described in the *Kitāb fi ma'rifat al- ḥiyal al-handasiyya* (Book of the Knowledge of Ingenious Mechanical Devices) by the Muslim engineer al-Jazarī, a work composed in 1206, some two hundred years after King Bhoja wrote the *Samarāṅgaṇasūtradhāra*. Did al-Jazarī model his clock on the device described by King Bhoja? There are some hints in this chapter of the *Samarāṅgaṇasūtradhāra* that its author may be familiar with medieval Muslim texts on automata; the mention of a mechanical singing bird and automated flute players suggest at least some passing acquaintance with the Mūsā brothers' ninth-century text *Kitāb al-ḥiyal* (see chapter 1). It is possible, therefore, that both Bhoja and al-Jazarī's descriptions of the elephant clock are inspired by an earlier lost Arabic text on engineering, perhaps a work of the Mūsā brothers that is no longer extant.

Another *yantra* described in some detail in the *Samarāṅgaṇasūtradhāra* is a mechanical singing bird: "It is a thumb in length, and a quarter thumb in height, with two cavities, thin and round, made straight, with a hole going through the middle, joined together and made of sturdy copper among wooden birds, one which is like that on the inside, struck by the force of passing air, produces a sweet sound while moving and becomes a wonder for those who listen" (stanzas 89–90). In this case, the mechanically singing bird seems to be powered by moving air and is very similar to the one described by Hero of Alexandria (see chapter 1).

A substantial section of the thirty-first chapter of the *Samarāṅgaṇasūtradhāra,* verses 109 to 221, are devoted to descriptions of the royal pleasure garden, filled with fountains, automata, automated bathhouses, and rotating swings. Although other forms of automata are also mentioned in the text, including automated servants (63), elephants (73–74), birds (73), mechanical girls (74, 101–102), automated horses and monkeys (74), automated flute players (75), a mechanical singing bird (89–90), a mercury-powered bird (95–96), a mechanical doorkeeper (106–107), and various cranes and trebuchets (108), the *Samarāṅgaṇasūtradhāra* privileges the automata found in the king's marvelous garden over other machines, which is perhaps not surprising in a text ascribed to a royal author. This description of the king's automated pleasure-garden owes a great deal more to the tenth-century Jain text *Yaśastilakacampū* by Somadeva Sūri, which will be discussed later in this book.

One feature of the king's pleasure-garden in the *Samarāṅgaṇasūtradhāra* that is particularly noteworthy is that it takes the form of a yantric diagram:

> One should make a square in the form of a *puṣpaka,* with four entrances, surrounded with walls, with a gate in the shape of a sword. Over that, one should build a strong oblong courtyard reservoir in the middle. One should make a *karṇikā* in the middle of that, embellished with

> lotus flowers. In each of the four corners of that, one should make a charming wooden girl, her eyes fixed on the lotus in the center, with ornaments and with elegant dress. (150–152)

In Bhoja's vision, the pleasure-garden filled with *yantras* (machines) itself becomes a *yantra* (religious diagram). Like Bhoja's garden, most *yantra* diagrams are enclosed squares with four entrances and a lotus flower at the center. A *puṣpaka* (flowery) is a flying chariot in Hindu myth (and therefore a form of mechanical *yantra*) but also a name for a type of multistoried (square) temple in Hindu architecture. By describing his garden as a *puṣpaka,* Bhoja evokes both fantastic *yantras* and sacred construction. The *karṇikā* in the middle of the garden is also a religiously significant element. A *karṇikā* is the pericarp (fruit coat) of a lotus flower but also the name for the central portion of a yantric diagram, where the most important deity is located. Stylized lotus flowers are parts of many *maṇḍalas* as symbols of purity, enlightenment, and transcendence. A *karṇikā* located in the middle of the garden therefore reinforces the idea that the garden itself is a sacred diagram. The four wooden girls surrounding the lotus in the center are charming garden decorations, but in the context of the iconography of a *maṇḍala,* these *yantras* are positioned where lesser deities would be in a religious diagram. The subliminal message of Bhoja's garden architecture therefore seems to be that mechanical devices are wondrous devices that serve a larger religious purpose. Above all, this chapter of the *Samarāṅgaṇasūtradhāra* embeds the automata the author describes in a deeply Hindu context; the automata are all part of a cosmic *yantra* ruled over by Śiva himself.

The Cosmic *Yantra* versus the Clockwork Universe

When the first stanza of the *Yantravidhāna* chapter of the *Samarāṅgaṇasūtradhāra* speaks of the god who sets in motion the machinery of the world, this idea may at first sight seem deceptively familiar to Western readers: "The conqueror of the God of Love [Śiva], who is praised as the one who has set in motion the wheels [*cakra*] of the orbs [*maṇḍala*] of the sun and moon, the one who regulates all beings and who always moves the fundamental element (*bīja*), the threefold machinery (*yantra*) of the world, with its invisible center—may he come to our aid." The idea that the universe is constructed like a machine or a clockwork, constructed by a divine clockmaker, is frequently encountered in Western literature. The idea of the clockwork universe can be traced back to *De Mundo* (*Περὶ Κόσμου*) by Pseudo-Aristotle (3rd c. BCE?), which compares the divine being to an engineer, pulling one string and triggering many effects.[26] Cicero (106–43 BCE) similarly compares the world to a machine or water clock.[27] In the thirteenth century, the astronomer John of Sacrobosco famously referred to the universe as a *machina mundi*, "the machine of the world," in his *Tractatus de sphaera*. The German astronomer Johannes Kepler (1571–1630) also described the universe as similar to a clock.[28] The notion of the universe as a clockwork or machine operating according to natural laws is often erroneously ascribed to the mathematician and scientist Isaac Newton (1643–1727). While Newton did not himself use the metaphor in his surviving writings, his rival mathematician Gottfried Wilhelm Leibniz (1646–1716) ascribes to Newton and his followers the view that the universe is a clockwork: "According to their doctrine, God Almighty wants to wind up his watch from time to time. . . . He has not, it seems, sufficient foresight to make it perpetual motion."[29] As the French author Bernard de Fontenelle (1657–1757) put it: "The universe is but a watch on a larger scale."[30]

When the *Samarāṅgaṇasūtradhāra* opens with a stanza referring to the "threefold machinery" (*yantra*) of the world and the "wheels of the orbs of the sun and the moon," it is at first glance tempting to see a similarity to the Western notion of a clockwork universe in the Sanskrit text. While the notion of the universe as a cosmic machine is certainly present in the *Samarāṅgaṇasūtradhāra*, it is important to note that a *yantra* in Indian literature is not quite the same thing as a Western "machine" or "clockwork," although *yantra* could have either meaning, depending on context. The opening of the *Samarāṅgaṇasūtradhāra* skillfully weaves together both meanings of the Sanskrit term *yantra*: machine and sacred diagram. While the Western idea of a "clockwork universe" to some extent reduces the visible universe to its mechanical operations and distances it from a divine being, the Sanskrit text presents of vision of a different sort of machinery, a *yantra* imbued with divine power. Bhoja's image of the universe places the divine being at the very center of the cosmic *yantra*. The god Śiva here functions as the Prime Mover; but he is not the god of European Deism, winding up a clockwork world and withdrawing from all human contact. Śiva may have set in motion the "wheels of the orbs of the sun and moon" in the beginning, but he is also the one who continues to move both the fundamental element (*bīja*) of the world and the cosmic *yantra* itself; he is the living center of Bhoja's *yantra*. The use of the three terms that can all signify a sacred diagram in the opening stanza of the chapter, *yantra, maṇḍala,* and *cakra,* signals to the audience that while the cosmos is a *yantra* in the sense of a "machine," it is also a sacred diagram, with Śiva at its center.

What Bhoja describes is not a European clockwork universe but a *yantra* as a mystical map of all reality, a map that is also reflected in the descriptions of the machines that follow later in the chapter. The Hindu worldview is not a mechanistic one; although the universe is compared to a machine, it is not *reduced* to a machine. Rather, the machines, in all their ingenuity, become sites for the unfolding of cosmic divine forces, just like the universe itself. Bhoja's vision of the cosmos is imbued with life as well as divine presence.

The very last stanza of the chapter (223), returns to the image of the world as a cosmic *yantra,* underscored yet again by the use of the significant term *maṇḍala*: "This entire circle [*maṇḍala*] of twelve kings, made up of the crest-jewels of the protectors of the earth, whose circle is the joining of arms and pillars, rotates voluntarily. He, the sole joy of the earth, the divine king, quickly composed this chapter on *yantras,* by means of the mechanical devices created by his intellect." In this final vision, the earth itself is protected by a *yantra/maṇḍala,* made up of the kings who watch over the earth, as they join each other to form a figurative protective circle. It is not clear who these twelve kings are, but they appear to function here as human/architectural elements—"arms and pillars"—that create a symbolic *yantra* of protection for the world. It is against this background that Bhoja presents his own composition of the chapter on *yantras*; these mechanical devices are created "by his intellect," for the good of the world.

Mercury Engines, Śiva's Seed, and the Alchemical Subtext of the *Samarāṅgaṇasūtradhāra*

While the list of the five elements in stanza 5 of the machine chapter of the *Samarāṅgaṇasūtradhāra* is the classical one found in Hindu texts from the Upaniṣads onward,[31] the discussion of the ambiguous status of mercury (stanza 12) deserves some attention. Why is it even necessary to discuss whether mercury is a separate element here, since the author so quickly dismisses the view as erroneous? Mercury-powered automata are described in some detail in stanzas 95–99, and these passages have inspired a number of highly speculative theories flourishing on the internet about ancient Indian technology, spaceships, ancient aliens, and so forth.[32]

Most popular writing on this subject has focused exclusively on whether such highly advanced technology could possibly have existed in India at the time of King Bhoja.[33] My interest is not in the possible existence of ancient "mercury vortex engines,"[34] however, but rather in the symbolic significance of mercury within the Hindu tradition, and more specifically in Hindu alchemy. I argue that the text's focus on mercury hints at an alchemical subtext to the *Samarāṅgaṇasūtradhāra*, a subtext that also resonates with Śiva-centered devotion.

Mercury, or quicksilver, is a silvery chemical element that is liquid at room temperature. Mercury occurs naturally in India as cinnabar, or mercuric sulfide, a dark red mineral that has to be refined in order to produce the pure element. The cinnabar is crushed and heated in a furnace, which separates the mercury from the sulfur. Mercury plays a vital role in Indian alchemy, as demonstrated by the multitude of alchemical works in Sanskrit with *rasa* (mercury) in the title: *Rasārṇava* (The Flood of Mercury), *Rasahṛdaya Tantra* (The Tantra of the Heart of Mercury), *Rasamañjari* (The Ornament of Mercury), *Rasapaddhati* (The Path of Mercury), and so on. Mercury is associated in alchemical texts and beyond with the transmutation of other metals into gold, with longevity and immortality, and with the seed of the god Śiva.

Mercury is called by many names in the synonym-rich language of Sanskrit, but it is worth noting that most of these names hint at the element's life-giving qualities. Above all, mercury is associated with *rasa*, a Sanskrit word that can be loosely translated as "fluid" or "sap" or "essence." Simply put, *rasa* is the lifeblood of all living things: the sap of a plant or a tree, the marrow inside the bones of an animal or a human being, the essence of any living thing. As David Gordon White has pointed out, the term *rasa* has been associated both with life and with immortality (nondeath) from Vedic times onward.[35] As we have seen, the emotions that are evoked by Sanskrit plays and poems are called *rasa* as well; they are the life sap that bring the words to life for the audience. *Rasa* can also mean "seed," both the seed of a plant and the sperm of a man, and especially the semen of the god Śiva. When mercury is referred to in Sanskrit as *rasa,* or *rasapati* (the chief of *rasas*), or *siddharasa* (perfected fluid), this is not merely hinting that pure mercury is a liquid, but more significantly that it is an essential life-giving fluid. When mercury is further referred to as *sūta* (that which is born or begotten) in the *Samarāṅgaṇasūtradhāra,* the element's life-giving force is again emphasized.

Although it is theoretically possible to read the passages on mercury-powered *yantras* in the *Samarāṅgaṇasūtradhāra* as references to actual technology, it is nevertheless important to keep in mind the enormous symbolic significance of mercury in Hinduism. Mercury-powered engines are mentioned in early literature elsewhere; Hero of Alexandria described self-opening temple doors powered by boiling water and pulleys in the first century BCE, but he also mentioned that there are others who use a system powered by heated mercury.[36] Although the details of the mercury-powered doors are left vague, Mayor points out that self-moving medieval and early modern toys were, in fact, on occasion designed with the help of mercury; the shifting weight of mercury flowing to the end of a tilted tube would shift the center of gravity so that the device appeared to move on its own accord.[37] But while the description of the mercury-powered bird in the *Samarāṅgaṇasūtradhāra* may indeed be inspired by Hero, this passage must also be read in the context of mercury as a symbolic substance in Hinduism, fusing ideas of lifeforce, seed, and alchemical immortality into one.

The alchemical subtext of the *Samarāṅgaṇasūtradhāra* is further hinted at by the use of the alchemically significant term *bīja* for the five elements. As mentioned above, *bīja* is used in alchemical texts for a gold- or silver-based compound that is used in higher-level alchemical work. The thirteenth-century alchemical treatise *Rasarat-*

nasamuccaya defines *bīja* as follows: "When [the original substance] takes on the same color [as the added substance] through the process of *nirvāhaṇa* and becomes soft and useful for different chemical processes, then it is called *bīja*."[38] The use of the term *bīja* for the constituent elements of the physical world therefore signals to an audience familiar with alchemical terminology that these elements are not just the physical building blocks of the cosmos but also substances that may play a part in an alchemical transformation that could lead to immortality.

The Robot Who Praised the King

Robots are also prominently featured in another text ascribed to King Bhoja, the lyrical storybook *Śṛṅgāramañjarīkathā*.[39] The text opens with King Bhoja himself sitting on a throne in his garden—a garden that recalls that of the *Samarāṅgaṇasūtradhāra*—and telling stories to his favorite courtesan, Śṛṅgāramañjarī. The courtesan's name means "Bouquet of Love," and her name is also found in the title of this *Śṛṅgāramañjarīkathā*, "A Tale for Śṛṅgāramañjarī." The narrator begins by describing Bhoja's city of Dhārā and all its wonders and then goes on to depict the royal garden and all its magnificent features, including the fantastic automata that populate the garden and bring delight to the king and his retinue:[40]

> Here is the city of Dhārā, the ornament of the world. By its splendor it puts the glory of the city of the gods to shame. . . . In this city, where there are many enchanting abodes, there is a mechanical fountain house that enchants the minds of the people. . . . The work of the Creator of old is put to shame by the production of its moving automata. . . . Mechanical ducks made of white jewels and seated in the middle of the open mechanical lotus flowers sometimes eat the streams of water, under the impression that they are lotus fibers. Sometimes the fountain house is filled with laughter when the grove of white waterlilies bloom, and sometimes it seems to dance when the jeweled mechanical musicians play the lutes in their hands. Sometimes it seems to sing when a

pair of mechanical bees, made from black precious stones, hum inside the buds of open lilies. Sometimes the thirsty *cakora* birds,[41] their beaks open and their minds anxious, try to sip the radiance of the crystal pillars because of the illusion of moonlight even in the daytime. Streams of water, two or three lotus stems thick, flow from the corners of the eyes of the winged crocodiles and from the mouth of the peahen with the downturned glance, and from the breasts of artificial jeweled women, from the end of the hair braid of the golden artificial woman just stepping out of her bath, from the nail tips of the jeweled courtesans, from the mouths of a family of monkeys climbing a mechanical tree. . . . The mechanical children of the tortoise can be seen now and then, and in other places, the mermaids (*matsyāṅganī*) are afraid to tread with their lotus feet because they watch the mechanical crocodiles with fear as they emerge. . . .

The fountain house creates wonder even in the mind of experts by the threefold symphony of song, dance, and instrumental music performed by mechanical musicians. Blooming lotus flowers are carved on the walls, and they laugh at the spectators whose minds are dazed by the wondrous mechanical contrivances. It is surrounded on all sides by rivers made for playing, their banks muddy with the musk of deer. The sand is powdered camphor, and the waters are fragrant with pure sandal wood. The lotus groves are formed from the rays of rubies mingled with those of emeralds.

We should note that the *yantras* of this garden create "wonder even in the mind of experts" and are no doubt also meant to invoke *adbhuta* in the text's audience as well. After some lovely descriptions of the royal garden, King Bhoja addresses one of the mechanical men in his garden:

"O, mechanical man, even though our assembly approves of it, the narration of one's own virtues still seems inappropriate. Therefore, you should describe the king now." His friends gazed at the mechanical man with wondering

> eyes as he began to speak: "In that city lives the great king of kings, the divine Bhoja, who is capable of carrying the burden of the world. His footstool gleams red due to the glittering rays of the rubies in the crowns of all the kings who bow before him. The vine of his fame is ever nourished by the sprinkling of water in the form of tears from the eyes of the women of the arrogant enemies his arms have crushed."

The idea of an artificially made being praising the king is echoed in a later Hindu text that also features King Bhoja, the eleventh- to twelfth-century story collection *Vikramacarita* (The Deeds of Vikrama), also known as the *Siṃhāsanadvātriṃśakā* (Thirty-Two Throne Stories).[42] In the *Vikramacarita,* King Bhoja discovers an ancient throne that belonged to the legendary King Vikrama, and before he can ascend the throne, each of the thirty-two female statues that surround and adorn the throne tells a story illustrating one of the virtues of Vikrama. In the end, the statues admit that Bhoja himself possesses all these virtues, and they allow him to sit on the throne. The statues themselves, who were once female attendants of Pārvatī, cursed to become statues after flirting with Śiva, are released from their curse through the telling of the tale and ascend to heaven. It is very possible that the *Vikramacarita* was inspired by the *Śṛṅgāramañjarīkathā,* and that the female statues (*puttalikās*) that praise the king are vaguely based on the mechanical man who praised the king in the *Śṛṅgāramañjarīkathā.*

The elaborate descriptions of the king's gardens in the *Śṛṅgāramañjarīkathā* are strongly evocative of the *Yantravidhāna* chapter of the *Samarāṅgaṇasūtradhāra,* and the same mood of wonder and amazement at the technical marvels of the garden infuse both texts. In his insightful analysis, Daud Ali argues that the *Śṛṅgāramañjarīkathā* must be understood in the larger context of the history of gardens and garden technology in ancient India, and he compares the marvels of Bhoja's mechanical garden to the traditional descriptions of jeweled trees and wishing trees in Buddhist literature.[43] Ali observes that while the water technology of the South Asian courts, both actual and literary, may have been influenced by the Sassanians of Iran, the description of the mechanical garden in the *Śṛṅgāramañjarīkathā* is nevertheless "almost entirely unprecedented" in Indian sources, with the sole exception of the *Yaśastilakacampū* (ca. 959 CE) by the Jain author Somadeva Sūri, which also describes a mechanical fountain house equipped with automata of various kinds.[44] Ali argues that the Indian pleasure-garden represents a courtly fantasy of plenitude and erotic play, and that the garden becomes a "place of human artifice" in a South Asian courtly context.[45]

Ali draws attention to the fact that the *Samarāṅgaṇasūtradhāra*, the *Śṛṅgāramañjarīkathā*, and the Jain text *Yaśastilakacampū*, which described a wondrous mechanical garden, were all composed in central/western India within a 150-year time span, from around 950 to 1100 CE and suggests that there may have existed "a wider interest in automata that was not simply literary but included, at least notionally, the possibility of real-world technologies."[46] He points out that a "fashion for automata" spread across the Abbasid-Byzantine Empire by at least the tenth century and argues that this is the reason for the "rather sudden appearance of human and animal automata in Sanskrit texts of the tenth and eleventh centuries."[47] Ali is no doubt correct in his claims that there are likely influences from both Islamic and Byzantine sources on these medieval Indian texts; we should nevertheless note that *yantras* had already been a significant part of the Indian literary imagination for many centuries at this point in time. It is likely, however, that the far greater specificity of detail in the literary descriptions of *yantras* in India in this time period may be explained as a result of familiarity with Islamic technology, whether through direct observation or through literary texts.

The Princess and the Demon's Daughter

Yantras, royalty, and wondrous also gardens coalesce in a story from the fairy tale collection *Kathāsaritsāgara*, which dates from approximately the same period as the *Samarāṅgaṇasūtradhāra*, and the *Śṛṅgāramañjarīkathā*, around the eleventh century CE. But in this case, the *yantras* are not the creations of a royal engineer but rather the inventions of a demon (*asura*) who is the master of illusions. This tale, from the twentieth chapter of the collection, begins with a mysterious young woman by the name of Somaprabhā who enchants the young princess Kaliṅgasenā with her magical skills and her wondrous basket of automata. Somaprabhā is the daughter of the *asura* Maya, the master builder among the demons. But Maya gave up his demonic nature, sought refuge in the god Śiva, and built a palace for the god Indra. The other demons were upset with him for siding with the gods, and he therefore built himself a magical underground palace in the Vindhyā mountains, where the demons could not find him. He dwells there with his two daughters, Svayamprabhā, who has taken a vow of chastity, and the younger daughter Somaprabhā, who is the friend to the human princess Kaliṅgasenā: "Somaprabhā opened the basket and showed her [Kaliṅgasenā] some wonderful wooden automata made by her magic. One of them flew through the air on her command when a pin in it was touched, got a garland of flowers, and returned quickly. Another one likewise brought water as desired, one danced, and one held a conversation. Somaprabhā entertained Kaliṅgasenā for a while with the wonderful devices, and then she put the magical basket away in a safe place." Not only do these *yantras* inspire wonder in the princess; Kaliṅgasenā is so enchanted by the *yantras* that she can no longer eat or sleep in her friend's absence. This worries her royal parents, but when they are introduced to Somaprabhā, who puts on a magical puppet show for them, they are also overcome with wonder:

> For fun, Kaliṅgasenā went to a Buddha shrine built by the king, and they brought the basket of magical toys. Somaprabhā took a magical *yakṣa*[48] and sent it off to fetch what they needed for worshipping the Buddha. The *yakṣa* travelled far through the sky and brought masses of pearls, lovely jewels, and golden lotus flowers. Somaprabhā worshipped with those and (magically) displayed all sorts of wonders, including the different Buddhas with their dwellings. When King Kaliṅgadatta heard this, he came with the queen and saw it for himself. He asked Somaprabhā about the magical display, and Somaprabhā said: "O king, these magical devices were created in different ways by my father long ago. Even as this great *yantra*, which is called the world, is made of five elements, so are all these *yantras*. I will describe

> them one by one: The *yantra* dominated by the earth element closes doors and that sort of thing. Not even Indra can open a door that has been closed by such a *yantra*! The water-*yantra* produces shapes that seem to be alive, and the *yantra* dominated by the fire element shoots out flames. The wind-*yantra* performs actions like going and coming, and the *yantra* made from ether utters a particular language. I got all these from my father, but the wheel *yantra*, which guards the water of immortality, is known to my father and no one else."

Later, Kaliṅgasenā visits her friend Somaprabhā at her magical dwelling in the Vindhyā mountains, and she meets her sister, the ascetic Svayamprabhā, who gives her a fruit that gives the princess freedom from old age and death. Then Kaliṅgasenā sees the wondrous garden of Maya: "The garden was filled with birds with bright and golden feathers and pillars that seemed to be made of bright jewels. It created the idea of walls where there was no division and of open space where there were walls. It looked like dry land where there was water, and it looked like water where there was dry land. It looked like another and marvelous world, created by the *asura* Maya's powers of illusion." It is likely that this *Kathasaritsagara* tale is inspired by the descriptions of gardens and automata in the *Śṛṅgāramañjarīkathā* and the *Samarāṅgaṇasūtradhāra*. While the former texts present the wondrous *yantras* as great feats of engineering, however, the *Kathāsaritsāgara* reinterprets the *yantras* as supernatural. Somaprabhā is no ordinary young woman; she can fly, and she is the daughter of the demon Maya. While there are several Western examples of automata believed to be the works of the devil (see chapter 1), the *yantras* in this tale are in no way perceived as inauspicious or tainted by evil even if they are the work of a demon (*asura*). In fact, the narrator of the tale hastens to tell us that Maya is in fact a convert to Śaivism; he "gave up his demonic nature and fled to Śiva." Maya is well known to a Hindu audience as the architect of the heroic Pāṇḍava brothers' magnificent assembly hall in the *Mahābhārata* epic, so introducing him as the creator of automated marvels in this tale is not very much of a stretch.

Somaprabhā, the demon's daughter, is quite orthodox in her philosophical outlook; her description of *yantras* dominated by various elements seems to owe a great deal to the *Samarāṅgaṇasūtradhāra*. Her elder sister, Svayamprabhā, is presented in the text as a devout Hindu ascetic, and the magical fruit and water that can delay aging seem to be a result of her sister's yogic skills rather than her father's demonic magic.

The *yantras* in this tale are childish toys, carried in a basket, perhaps hinting at the Indian automaton's origin in the puppet theater. Somaprabhā makes her *yantras* dance and speak and perform little stories for the king and queen, just like wooden puppets might, and the royal couple is delighted by the show, like the audience of a puppet show might be. And yet, this tale contains subtle hints of an alchemical subtext that signals that these *yantras* are nevertheless more than just toys. Somaprabhā's name, which means "radiance of the moon" or "radiance of Soma," evokes for the reader the sacred drink of Soma from ancient Vedic mythology, which can grant both immortality and wisdom. When Somaprabhā and her sister Svayamprabhā (self-radiant) introduce the princess to a garden that contains the waters of immortality and give her fruit that can grant eternal life, the implication seems to be that this immortality is somehow interconnected with the wondrous *yantras* and with the demon's supernatural knowledge. The *yantras* in the story do indeed provide their audience with a glimpse of something religious in the puppet show that takes the spectators away to the abodes of heavenly Buddhas. But it is also highly significant that immortality itself seems to be associated with the *yantras*; Somaprabhā tells her friend that there is one *yantra* that is known only to her father that guards the waters of immortality. Like King Bhoja, Somaprabhā hints that understanding the secret of *yantras* is knowing the secret of life itself. Even though the automata in this text are created by a demon, they are no infernal devices. Rather, they are, like the ones described by King Bhoja, vehicles for wonder.

The *yantras* described in the three eleventh-century texts discussed in this chapter, the *Samarāṅgaṇasūtradhāra*, the *Śṛṅgāramañjarīkathā*, and the *Kathāsaritsāgara*, all stand at the intersection of technology and religion, as sites for the contemplation of the interplay of the elements of the natural world with divine forces. While automata in early Western literature often inspire anxiety about technology and its troubled relationship to religion, both King Bhoja's machines and those of Somaprabhā become instruments of mystical devotion.

Chapter 4

Body of Flesh, Body of Wood, Body of Stone

Humans, Androids, and Gods in Hinduism

What Is a Human Being in Hinduism?

Before we delve into more tales of artificially constructed humans in Hinduism, it is first necessary to investigate what it means to be human in a Hindu context. How is a human being different from an animal, or a machine? Is a human being more than just a body? What is the relationship between the body and the mind? What, if anything, survives after the death of the physical body?

The earliest preserved texts of Hinduism are the four Vedas, the *Ṛgveda* (The Wisdom of the Verses), *Sāmaveda* (The Wisdom of the Songs), *Yajurveda* (The Wisdom of the Sacrificial Formulas), and *Atharvaveda* (The Wisdom of the Atharvan Priests). The oldest of these texts is the *Ṛgveda,* likely composed around 1200 BCE in Vedic Sanskrit. The Vedas do not always differentiate clearly between the human body and an immaterial self. The Vedic term *tanú* can, according to context, be translated as either "body," "self," or "person." Additionally, the Vedas describe a person's *prāṇá* (life-breath) and *mánas* (mind). All in all, in the oldest time period of Hinduism, we find a view of a human being as a body-mind-breath continuum rather than a sharply divided mortal body and immortal self, as in later Hindu texts. There are, however, hints in the Vedas that the mind can roam separately from the body.[1]

The famous *Puruṣasūkta* (Hymn to Man, *Ṛgveda* 10.90) presents the human body as the victim of a primordial ritual sacrifice but also as a model for the entire cosmos.[2] In this hymn, a cosmic giant simply called *puruṣa* (man) is sacrificed to the gods in the beginning, and the universe is then created from various parts of his body:

> 1. The brahmin was his mouth. The ruler was made his two arms. As to his thighs—that is what the freeman was. From his two feet the servant was born.
> 2. The moon was born from his mind. From his eye the sun was born. From his mouth Indra and Agni, from his breath Vāyu was born.
> 3. From his navel was the midspace. From his head the heavens developed. From his two feet the earth, and the directions from his ear. Thus they arranged the worlds.[3]

In these verses, the different castes, or social classes, formed from different parts of the body of the primordial man. The *brahmans* (*brahmins*) are the priests, who in later Hinduism are regarded as the highest caste. The *kṣatriyas* are the rulers, kings, and warriors, the second highest caste in classical Hindu society. The *vaiśyas* are the farmers and merchants, the third ranked caste, and the *śūdras* are the servants, or lowest of the four castes. The priests are associated with the mouth of the cosmic man because it is their duty to recite the sacred texts, the rulers and warriors are associated with strength and therefore the arms of *puruṣa*, the freemen or farmers are connected with fertility and therefore the area around the genitalia of the cosmic man, and the servants are associated with the feet and therefore the lowest part of *puruṣa*.

But the primordial human being is not only the model for the social classes but also for the physical world. In this hymn's vision of the world, all the parts of society and cosmos correspond to different parts of one great human body, which also here includes the mind. The idea that the entire universe is, so to speak, present in the human body, is a significant one, and one that resonates through several of the later Hindu texts presented in this volume.

The Upaniṣads, philosophical Hindu texts composed from the eighth century BCE onward, do in most cases distinguish clearly between the *ātman*, the immortal self of a human being, and the mortal body.[4] According to these texts, salvation and freedom from the cycle of death and rebirth can be attained by those who realize the profound truth that the *ātman* of a living being is identical to *brahman*, the divine force that permeates the entire universe. Here, the *ātman*, or eternal self, is the most essential part of any living being, while the mortal body becomes far less interesting. While the distinction between the eternal *ātman* and the mortal body holds true in most Upaniṣadic passages, we should also bear in mind that some of the older *Upaniṣads* actually use the term *self* (*ātman*) to refer to the body as well, a meaning that is lost in later Hinduism.[5] These passages have preserved an older, holistic view of a mind-body fusion that precedes the dualism present in the later Upaniṣads. For the most part, however, the *ātman* or self is an immaterial and eternal principle in the Upaniṣads, separate from the physical body. The *Taittirīya Upaniṣad* proposes that there are five different layers of the *ātman*: a self made of food, a self made of breath, a self made of mind, a self made of perception, and a self made of joy.[6] These five "sheaths" or layers, ranging from the physical to the entirely abstract, preserve the older idea of a person as a body-mind continuum. The *Kaṭha Upaniṣad*, on the other hand, declares that the body is like a chariot, and that the self is the one who rides in the chariot, with the intelligence as the charioteer.[7] Here, we see the self as entirely distinct from the body, a mere passenger in its temporary physical form. This notion of the self as the rider in the vehicle of the body can perhaps be seen as a precursor to the idea of an intelligent controller governing a soulless robot (see the *Kathāsaritsāgara* tale discussed later in this chapter). The Upaniṣads introduce the idea that the *ātman* will be reincarnated into a new body after death, which further demonstrates the absolute difference between body and self.[8]

The Hindu Āyurvedic medical tradition, first attested in the Sanskrit texts *Carakasaṃhitā* (ca. 100 CE) and *Suśrutasaṃhitā* (ca. 4th c. CE), generally holds that a human being consists of a body, psychic being (*sattva*), senses, mind, and *ātman*. The body is made up of the physical elements of wind, fire, water, and earth, as well as the substances of space, time, and extension.[9] Larson points out that Indian medical texts assume that a person gets their physical body from their parents, while their mental constituents are a karmic inheritance from the person's previous lives.[10] In order for a person to remain healthy, it is vital that the three bodily humors (*doṣa*)—phlegm (*kapha*), bile (*pitta*), and wind (*vāta*)—are properly balanced.[11] These humors regulate the physiological and psychological functions of a human being; if the three are perfectly balanced, a person will remain healthy and happy, while an imbalance will result in disease.[12] Diminished *vāta* or wind leads to weakness and digestive and respiratory issues; diminished *pitta* affects body temperature, emotional stability, and energy; while diminished *kapha* leads to thirst, lack of mobility, and lack of appetite.[13] The *Carakasaṃhitā* also evokes the homology between the human body and the universe, which was already hinted at in the *Ṛgveda*: "This human being is coincident with the world; whatever kinds of entity are to be found in the world those same are to be found in the human being and whatever are to be found in the human being are to be found in the world."[14]

Doniger has pointed out the gendered nature of much of the ancient Indian material on the body; legal texts treat women as fertile fields and men as the owners of the fields, for example.[15] It is worth noting that Indian texts, when discussing human conception, suggest that men contribute the hard parts of the baby (bone and sinew), while women contribute the soft parts (flesh and blood).[16] It is intriguing, then, that all makers of automata mentioned in ancient Indian texts are male, and that the automata and androids are invariably made from hard materials, such as wood, which may here function as a symbolic substitute for the bone the male contributes to the creation of a human being. The creation of an android, then, symbolically becomes a male-only form of procreation, a giving birth without the need for female involvement.

The well-known Hindu text *Bhagavadgītā* (ca. 200 BCE–200 CE) compares the body to worn-out clothes to be discarded:

> As a man throws away old clothes
> to put on new, different ones,
> so the self throws away old bodies
> and puts on new ones.[17]

Here, the self is not only separate from the body but also superior to it. Bodies get worn out and must be discarded, while the immaterial and unchanging self lives eternally.

But where exactly are the lines between the material and the immaterial parts of a human being drawn? The Sāṃkhya school of Hindu philosophy teaches that there are two eternal principles in the world: *puruṣa* (spirit) and *prakṛti* (matter). *Puruṣa* is defined as pure consciousness, while *prakṛti* encompasses both the human body, the material world with its elements, and various mental components of a human being such as ego, intelligence, and emotions, which are different from the eternal, unchanging spirit. In Sāṃkhya philosophy, both the physical world and the physical and mental parts of a human being evolve out of *prakṛti,* or matter. Matter consists of three different strands (*guṇas*): *sattva* (light), *rajas* (passion), and *tamas* (dark inertia). In its initial state, the *guṇas* are in perfect balance and matter is unmanifest, but due to the presence of the eternal consciousness of *puruṣa, prakṛti* begins to evolve. The first parts of the manifest world to evolve out of the primordial matter are *buddhi* (intelligence), followed by *ahaṃkāra* (self-awareness), and the five *tanmātras* (subtle elements, i.e., sound, touch, form, taste, and smell). From these evolve *manas* (the mind), the five *buddhīndriyas* (sense organs, i.e., hearing, feeling, seeing, tasting, and smelling), the five *karmendriyas* (organs of action, i.e., the capacity to speak, grasp, walk, excrete, and generate), and the five *mahābhūtas* (great elements, i.e., water, air, earth, fire, and ether). In this intricate psycho-physiological evolutionary model, it is worth noting that intelligence is primary, and that the objects of our senses precede both the sense perception and the sense organs themselves and the physical world, which is the latest evolutionary stage. This model implies, intriguingly, that the physical world emerges out of our own perception. A human being, then, contains an eternal consciousness, *puruṣa,* as well as intelligence, self-awareness, the ability to sense, and our physical bodies, which are made up of the same elements as the rest of the physical world.

After the age of the Upaniṣads, Hindu philosophies do overall, as Koller has demonstrated, draw a distinction between the immaterial and eternal *ātman* on the one hand and a body-mind continuum on the other.[18] The mind (which includes thoughts and emotions) is not, as in Western thought after Descartes, regarded as something distinct from the body but rather a part of it, and something radically different from the entirely transcendent self. Significantly, many mental functions such as emotions and thoughts are classified as parts of the body, rather than the self, in Hinduism. While Sāṃkhya is a dualist school of thought, its dualism does not align precisely with the Cartesian dualism; the mind is here a part of nature, closely tied to the body, and separate from the eternal consciousness. In the Sāṃkhya worldview, it is the full understanding of this dualism that leads the *puruṣa* to liberation. While *puruṣa* is in some sense bound to *prakṛti* and strives to be free, the mind-body continuum of *prakṛti* is not a prison for the consciousness; *prakṛti* is said to strive tirelessly for the liberation of *puruṣa*.

The Yoga tradition, which is Sāṃkhya's "sister school" in the system of Hindu philosophies, adopts the notion of a radical dualism between *puruṣa* and *prakṛti*, but it adds a set of bodily practices (breathing techniques, bodily postures, etc.) in order to facilitate the ultimate liberating insight into the difference between *puruṣa* and *prakṛti*. There is more to the human body in Yoga, however, than merely a cluster of physical elements. The Yoga system maps the body as a "locus of spiritual energies and points of graduated spiritual awakening."[19] Patañjali's *Yogasūtra* (ca. 250 CE[20]) outlines the famous *aṣṭāṅgayoga* (eight-limbed yoga), an eight-part approach to enlightenment, which includes abstinences, observances, bodily postures, breath control, withdrawal of the senses from external objects, concentration, meditation, and spiritual absorption. In classical Hindu Yoga the body becomes an essential tool for the liberation of the spirit/self.

The Advaita Vedānta school of Hindu philosophy, which is based on the teachings of the Upaniṣads, accepts the Upaniṣadic idea of the absolute unity between the individual *ātman* and the cosmic *brahman* (divine force) but introduces the concept of *māyā* (illusion). According to the Advaita Vedānta philosophy of the well-known eighth-century philosopher Śaṅkara, everything other than the ultimate reality of *ātman-brahman* is an illusion, including the material world and the human body. In this system of thought, the human body is far less useful in the quest for enlightenment than in Sāṃkhya and Yoga.

In Tantric Hinduism, however, the body is again seen as an instrument for salvation, as in the Yoga tradition. Tantra is an esoteric tradition with Hindu, Buddhist, and Jain iterations, flourishing from the eighth century onward. While many of the Tantric texts describe antinomian practices, Tāntrikas themselves often saw their own practices as based on Vedic, Buddhist, or Jain orthodoxy, but adopting more radical methods suited to the less-than-ideal state of the world in the *Kali Yuga*. Padoux defines Tantrism as "an attempt to place *kāma,* desire, in every sense of the word, in the service of liberation . . . not to sacrifice this world for liberation's sake, but to reinstate it, in varying ways, within the perspective of salvation."[21] In this Tantric quest for liberation, the human body plays a significant role.

Hindu tantra teaches that a human being has both a coarse (*sthūla*) body and a subtle (*sūkṣma*) one. The coarse body is purely physical and made up of the five elements: earth, water, wind, fire, and ether. The subtle body (*sūkṣma śarīra*) is made up of energy channels (as many as seventy-two thousand of them, according to some texts) running through the physical body. The subtle body is androgynous, consisting of both the female serpentine energy known as *kuṇḍalinī* and a male principle that is identified with the god Śiva.[22] The subtle body contains six wheels (*cakras*) associated with self-realization and the attainment of enlightenment,[23] along with "veins" or energy conduits called *iḍā, suṣumnā,* and *piṅgala,* along which the *prāṇa* or life-breath travels.[24] Some Tantric texts contain speculations about the supernatural powers (*siddhi*) of the body. Secrecy is an important part of Tantrism; the most important teachings of the tradition should only be transmitted from trained teachers to initiated students. In order to keep these secret doctrines from outsiders, Tantric texts and artworks are often rich in cryptic symbolism that is only meant to make sense to those initiates whose teachers have explained the symbols to them. While many Tantric texts are therefore quite difficult to interpret, the emphasis on the body as the ground for higher realization is quite clear.[25]

Yantras and *maṇḍalas* are of particular importance in Tantra precisely because these diagrams mediate between the macrocosm and the microcosm, the divine and the human, the cosmos and the body.[26] In Tantric Śāktism, the *yantra* is one of the three forms of the goddess herself: the goddess is worshipped as a *mūrti* (icon) in the temple, as the sacred sound of a *mantra,* and in the form of a *yantra* or *cakra.*[27] Here, the *yantra* is identical with the goddess herself and with her creation. But the Tantric *yantra* can also represent the devotee's progressive stages of meditation, from the gross material reality represented by the square enclosures of the Śrīcakra with four gates opening out to the four directions, toward the highest stage of perfection represented by the *bindu* in the center.[28]

The construction of *yantras* is especially important in Tantric initiation rites.[29] Through the *dīkṣā* ritual, the body of the initiate is transformed into a cosmic *maṇḍala*, and the self of the person is dissolved into the absolute while the initiate's body becomes—like a *yantra*—a site for the revelation of the universe and its deities.[30] While there are no tales of androids or automata in Indian Tantric texts, Tantric ideas of a human body becoming a *yantra* diagram inhabited by divine forces are very much present as a subtext in Bhoja's *Samāraṅgaṇasūtradhāra*, as we have seen in the previous chapter. It is possible to read the android *yantras* in Bhoja's text as stand-ins for the real human body as a cosmic *yantra* and site for the unfolding of divine power.

Some of the Tantric ideas about the transformative power of the body are picked up in the alchemical Hindu tradition, which flourished from the tenth century CE onward. While the ostensible goal of Hindu alchemy, like that of its Western counterpart, was the transmutation of base metals into gold, the production of elixirs of immortality is also described in Tantric texts. Mercury (*rasa*) played a significant part in these elixirs, and Indian alchemy as a whole is often referred to as *rasāyana* (the path of mercury). Swallowing mercury was regarded as a way for the alchemist to become transformed into a "second Śiva" and become immortal.[31] Ultimately, the immortal body of the alchemist represents perfect control over the physical elements, just like the body of the automaton. When the *Samarāṅgaṇasūtradhāra* dwells on the possibility of mercury-powered *yantras*, these automata are as much symbols of alchemical perfection as they are of actual mechanical possibility. It is worth noting that the term *yantra* is often used for an alchemist's chemical apparatus, and that some of these *yantras* are specifically said to be humanlike in form. On a symbolic level, any *yantra*—whether it is an alchemist's apparatus, an android, or a mystical diagram—fulfills the same desire for absolute control over the physical elements of the world. While Indian alchemists speculated about the possibility of physical immortality, most other ancient Hindu philosophers argued that immortality is a quality that belongs only to the self and not to the physical body.

There did, however, exist one school of Hindu philosophy, the Cārvāka school, which taught that immortality was nothing but wishful thinking. The Cārvāka philosophers taught that there is no such thing as an eternal *ātman*, and that upon death, both the body and the consciousness that inhabits it temporarily will cease to exist.[32] In fact, nothing at all can be said to exist except material objects. The notions of gods and souls are dismissed in the Cārvāka school as mere human fancies.[33]

How are these varied and shifting notions of the relationship between body and self reflected in ancient Hindu robot tales? If a self can be separated from one body and enter into another, through a process of reincarnation, could the self also enter the body of a robot? And if so, could a robot become a real person? The marionette Pinocchio was able to become a "real boy" through the intervention of a fairy in Carlo Collodi's classic children's book. But what about the wooden body of the Hindu automaton? Can it become a real human being?

The Body as *Yantra*

The notion of the human body as a machine has deep roots in Western thinking.[34] While Eliot Deutsch argues that this view is grounded in seventeenth-century mechanistic science,[35] we have noted earlier in this book that the metaphor of the body as a machine is far older than that.

The notion that the body can be viewed as mechanical is highly significant, but this metaphor must be interpreted differently in different cultural contexts. It means something very different to say that a human being is like a machine in industrial England and in ancient India.

In European thought, the notion that a human being is like a machine has often been associated with materialism, the complete absence of an immortal soul. In ancient Hindu texts, however, the body is like a machine *until* it is imbued with an eternal self. The *Kaṭha Upaniṣad*'s metaphor of the body as a chariot is significant; a chariot is a mere mechanical contraption, unable to move in the absence of the charioteer, in this case *buddhi*, or intelligence. In Hindu texts, the animation of the body requires an animating entity such as the *buddhi* or *ātman*.

The seventh-century author Daṇḍin, known both as a grammarian and as an author of prose romances, writes in one of the introductory verses to his incomplete romance *Avantisundarī* (The Lovely Lady from Avanti):

> He who placed intelligence into us mortal machines
> through the wisdom of the *Mahābhārata* in a former age,
> homage to that sage![36]

Daṇḍin is here praising Vyāsa, the legendary author of the great Hindu *Mahābhārata* epic. Intriguingly, he is comparing that text's audience to "mortal machines" (*martya-yantra*), who are animated through the intelligence that comes from reading or listening to the *Mahābhārata*. Here, the lifeless automaton is the reader, brought to life through great literature. By referring to humans, before intelligence is imparted to them by literature, as "mortal machines," Daṇḍin implies that *yantras* are comparable to the mortal part of humans, the body, but that this body can be animated by something eternal.

The relationship between the body and the self is shown in a striking way in Somadeva's eleventh-century collection *Kathāsaritsāgara* (The Ocean of Stories), where a young prince comes across an entire city populated by *yantras*:[37]

> In due time, he arrived at an enormous city by the sea shore, filled with tall buildings resembling mountain peaks, with streets and arches, and adorned with a palace as golden as Mount Meru, and it looked like a second earth. He entered the city by the market street, and saw that all the inhabitants, vendors, women, and citizens were wooden automata, moving as if they were alive. But he realized that they were lifeless by their lack of speech. This caused a great wonder in his mind. He eventually arrived along with Gomukha at the king's palace, and he saw that all the horses and elephants were of made of the same material. Then, full of wonder, he entered

> that magnificent palace, shining with seven ranges of gold buildings, along with his minister. Then he saw a man of great splendor sitting on a jewel-studded throne, surrounded by guards and women, all machines made of wood. He was the only living being there, and he made these things move, just like the *ātman* reigning over the senses. That man saw that the hero Naravāhanadatta was of noble appearance and stood up and welcomed him. Then he made him sit down in his own seat, and he sat down before him and questioned him: "Who are you, and how and why have you come to this deserted land with only one companion?" Then Naravāhanadatta told his own story from the beginning . . .

The sense of wonder (*adbhuta*) in this tale is followed, as so often in ancient Indian texts, by a deeper insight into the nature of reality. This text introduces a religious element into the fantastic tale of an android city by suggesting that the relationship between the animated *yantras* and their maker is symbolic of the relationship between the human senses and their animating *ātman*. By implication, then, the human body can be understood as automaton of sorts, as lifeless as a figure carved out of wood until it is brought to life through the agency of the *ātman*.

Although this tale from the *Kathāsaritsāgara* does not mention how the *yantras* got to the faraway city in the first place, the answer is given in a different part of the story collection. The young man who had to flee after his brother's mechanical geese had stolen jewels from the king was the maker of these robots:

> When my brother Prāṇadhara, who was correctly named,[38] had gone away, I assumed that in the morning I alone would face danger at the hands of the king. So, I climbed into another mechanical chariot, which I had made myself, and quickly traveled two hundred *yojanas* away from there. Then I got back in the flying chariot and traveled another two hundred *yojanas*. To my terror, I discovered that I was close to the sea, and I left my chariot behind. I continued on foot, and in due time reached this empty city. Out of curiosity I entered this palace, which was filled

> with clothes, jewels, and couches and all the other luxuries fit for a king. In the evening I bathed in the water of the lake in the garden, ate some fruit, and climbed into the royal bed all by myself. I thought to myself that night: "What am I going to do in this deserted place? Tomorrow, I will leave this place and go somewhere else, for surely there is no need to fear King Bāhubala any longer. After I had thought this, I went to sleep. In the later part of the night, I had a dream, and a hero of divine radiance, sitting on a peacock, spoke to me: "You must live here, sir, and you must not travel anywhere else. When it is time for meals, you must go to the central court of the palace and wait there." When he had said this, he vanished, and I woke up and thought: "No doubt this heavenly palace is made by Kārttikeya, and he has granted me this dream because of good karma from my previous lives. I have come here because I am meant to be happy living in this city." So I thought hopefully, and I got up and said my daily prayers. When it was mealtime I went to the central court, and while I waited there, golden dishes appeared in front of me, and food fell onto those dishes from heaven: butter, milk, rice, boiled rice, and other things. All the sort of foods that I thought about came to me as fast as I could think about them. After I had eaten it all, I felt comforted by the deity's grace. So, my lord, I began to live in this city, with royal luxuries coming to me every day just as quickly as I could think of them. But you can't get wives or companions just from thinking about them, so I crafted all these people out of wood. Even though I am a craftsman, I have enjoyed all the pleasures of a king since I have come here, through the power of fate, and my name is Rājyadhara.

Here, the wooden *yantras* are presented as substitutes for humans, created by a man who longs for a wife or a companion. This idea that a mechanically fashioned android serves as an emotional stand-in for an actual human being is familiar from numerous other android tales around the world as well, from the story of Descartes's mechanical daughter to the android child in the film *A.I.*

The story about of the city of *yantras* suggests that, on a symbolic level, robot tales as a story genre in Hindu literature are about the relationship between the human body and the *ātman* that animates it. The simplest form of *yantra* animation is represented by a person sitting inside the *yantra* and controlling it, just like the simplest image of *ātman* in Hindu philosophy is that of a little person inside the physical body.[39] Often, the animator is also the creator of the *yantra*, just like the animating *ātman* is sometimes perceived as a creator.[40]

But the idea that bodies fashioned from wood can be imbued with life is not just found in Hindu fairy tales; it is an integral part of Hindu theology overall. It is impossible to read tales of *yantra* bodies made of wood without also drawing parallels to the Hindu concept of *mūrtis*, or icons of the divine.

Gods and Androids in Hinduism

In classical Hinduism, the worship of deities plays a central role in daily life. Gods and goddesses, in the form of images (*mūrti*, literally, "form"), made of wood or metal or stone and fashioned into the likeness of one of Hinduism's 330 million gods, are found at the vast majority of Hindu shrines. Ritual worship, *pūjā*, involves the worshippers entering into the physical presence of the *mūrti*, seeing it with their own eyes, and letting the gaze of the statue or image meet theirs in return. This mutual gaze, the sacred exchange of vision between the deity and the devotee, between image and human, is central to the Hindu religious experience.[41] Hindus are not worshipping images; they are worshipping *with* images. It is the god, not the god's image, which is worshipped, but the image is the site for the encounter between god and devotee.

An image of a god, carved out of wood or stone, is nothing but a lifeless object until it is animated through ritual. A *mūrti* is ritually "brought to life" through the ceremony of *prāṇapratiṣṭhā* (the placement of the life-breath). This consecration ceremony transforms the artist's statue of the deity into the embodiment of that deity. The ritual "opening" of the eyes of the image is particularly important, since this is the moment when the statue is thought to come alive, in a spiritual sense.[42] To the worshippers, the images *are* alive. When the divine being enters into the statue, the physical material, wood or metal or stone, from which the image is made, changes into *śuddhasattva,* a supernatural "pure substance."[43]

The very notion that a body carved out of wood or stone or sculpted out of metal can be imbued with self and possess agency presages the idea that androids can be made to move and act and speak in Hindu texts. The Hindu *mūrtis,* like the Hindu *yantras,* are not entirely immobile; during many festivals, the image of the deity is taken out of the temple and shrine and transported around the city so that the worshippers can interact with the deity. As Vidal has observed, when a divine image is taken out of the temple and driven around in a village or town on an elaborate chariot or palanquin, worshippers often insist that it is the deity that is guiding the movements.[44] Vidal describes a ritual from Himachal Pradesh where the deity is brought out from the temple and asked questions by the worshippers. The movements of the deity are interpreted as answers to the question asked by the villagers,[45] similar to how a statue's movements were seen as answers in ancient Egypt (see chapter 1).

There are also devotional tales in Hinduism of deity statues miraculously coming to life and interacting directly with the devotee. The seventh-century Tamil poet-saint Campantar (Sambandar), for example, is said to have visited the temple of Śiva and Pārvatī at the age of three, and to have drunk milk directly from the statue of the goddess herself. Davis recounts a legend that a Muslim sultan's daughter kept a statue of the Hindu god Viṣṇu in her bedroom. Each night, the statue came alive and revealed itself to the princess in its full glory. When the statue was eventually returned to India, the princess died of sorrow.[46] More recently, a famous Hindu "milk miracle" attracted a great deal of international attention. On September 21, 1995, it was rumored that statues of the elephant-headed deity Gaṇeśa began to "drink" milk offered to the deity all over India. Videos soon surfaced showing the milk offered to the deity vanishing from the spoon held up to the statue.[47] Some Hindus believed firmly that they were witnessing a miracle, and that the deity actually consumed the milk offered, and milk sales skyrocketed all over India. Indian scientists soon stepped forward, however, and offered a rational explanation for the curious phenomenon of the vanishing milk: capillary action, the ability of liquid to flow into narrow spaces. But from the perspective of this study, the most fascinating part of the "milk miracle" is the widespread belief that the statue of the deity had agency and could affect a change in the physical world. This notion, as we have seen, is not at all alien to Hindu thought; if deities exist and inhabit their earthly images, why would they not be able to move and act through the image?

Conceptually, the idea that an object made by an artist could have the ability to move, act, and even speak is not too far removed from what unfolds in Hindu *yantra* tales. Significantly, the Hindu *yantras* require their own form of *prāṇapratiṣṭhā*; we will see an example of a deity (Garuḍa) entering into a *yantra* and imbuing it with life. But what of those *yantras* that are not directly conceived as imbued with divine spirit? Perhaps a spark of the divine is present even there; the *Samarāṅgaṇasūtradhāra* speculates that *sūta*, mercury, could be the material that causes *yantras* to move. Mercury is, especially in the alchemical texts of Hinduism, equated with the life-giving seed of the god Śiva himself.[48] Vidal has argued that there are similarities between robots and religious images of gods; both gods and robots function as "social partners" for the humans who interact with them, they often have humanlike appearance, both can seem unpredictable, and both have an unclear ontological status vis-à-vis human beings.[49] A *mūrti* is far more than an artifact; it is a living thing. That which distinguishes between the living and the nonliving in Hinduism is the presence of an *ātman*, rather than the organic or nonorganic material out of which something is made. If an *ātman* enters into a stone image—or a *yantra*—then that object becomes a living thing.

Vaucanson's Duck and Caṇḍamahāsena's Elephant

In addition to tales about mechanical men and women, there are also ancient Indian tales about mechanical animals. As we have seen in the first chapter of this book, there are many references to mechanically constructed animals—actual and imaginary—in European literature as well, from Polybius's mechanical snail to Vaucanson's defecating duck. But while the European mechanical animals are attempts to reproduce the natural world mechanically,

I argue that Indian tales of animal *yantras* do something quite different.

Vaucanson's duck, as we saw in chapter 1, is an attempt at replicating a real duck, down to its system of digestion. The mechanical duck caused such a sensation among Vaucanson's contemporaries precisely because it seems to suggest that animals *are,* on one level, machines, and that they can be accurately reproduced by mechanical means. The Indian animal *yantras,* on the other hand, are not purely automated machines, however; they are always animated by something or someone. The tales of Indian animal *yantras* imply that animals, like humans, can only be brought to life through the animating presence of a self.

In one well-known episode from the eleventh-century folktale collection *Kathāsaritsāgara,* a mechanical elephant roams through the forest.[50] While this may at first sight seem like an extraordinary feat of engineering, it is immediately revealed that the elephant is in fact moved by people who are hiding inside it. In this tale, King Caṇḍamahāsena wants to trick the king of Vatsa. He has a mechanical elephant constructed that resembles his own elephant, and he hides his soldiers inside of it. The soldiers then parade this artificial elephant around in the forest by the Vindhya mountains, where the king of Vatsa likes to hunt. When the king of Vatsa sees the elephant, he advances toward it, and the soldiers inside quickly jump out and capture him.

The mechanical elephant is here an Indian Trojan horse, but while the Trojans know perfectly well that the horse was an artificial wooden animal constructed by the Greeks, in the Indian story, the king of Vatsa believes that the mechanical elephant is a real live elephant. In that sense, the mechanical elephant is a parallel not only to the Trojan horse but also to the Mechanical Turk, von Kempelen's chess player automaton (see chapter 1), which turned out not to be a true automaton at all but rather a contraption operated by someone hiding inside it.

The Sanskrit story of the king who owned a mechanical elephant must have been circulated for centuries before its inclusion in the *Kathāsaritsāgara,* however; a (possibly) mechanical elephant belonging to a king named Mahāsena is also mentioned very briefly in the sixth chapter of the seventh-century Sanskrit biography

Harṣacarita, which tells the story of the king of Vatsa, who liked to sport in "elephant forests," who was captured by the soldiers of king Mahāsena, who came "out of the body of an illusory elephant" (*māyā-mātaṅgāṅgāt*).[51] The same story is also found in the Pāli canon of Theravāda Buddhism, although the characters have different names. In this version, King Caṇḍa Pajjota is jealous of King Udena, who seems to possess a greater splendor than Caṇḍa Pajjota himself. He therefore resolves to capture his rival by means of an elephant *yantra,* since King Udena is very fond of elephants:

> So the king had a mechanical elephant made of wood, wrapped about with strips of cloth and deftly painted, and turned it loose on the bank of a certain lake near the country of his enemy. Within the belly of the elephant, sixty men walked back and forth; every now and then they loaded their shovels with elephant dung and dumped it out. A certain woodman saw the elephant, and thinking to himself, "Just the thing for our king!" went and told the king, "Your majesty, I saw a noble elephant, pure white even as the peak of Kelāsa, just the sort of elephant your majesty would like." Udena mounted his elephant and set out, taking the woodman along as a guide and accompanied by his retinue. His approach was observed by spies, who went and informed Caṇḍa Pajjota. The latter straightaway dispatched armies on both flanks of his enemy, allowing the space between them to remain open. Udena, unaware of his enemy's approach, continued to pursue the elephant. He recited his spell and played his lute, but all to no purpose. The wooden elephant, driven with great speed by the men concealed within its belly, made as if it failed to hear the charm and continued its flight. The king, unable to overtake the elephant, mounted his horse. On and on sped the horse, galloping so rapidly that by degrees the army of the king was left far behind and the king was quite alone. Then Caṇḍa Pajjota's men, who were posted on both flanks, captured Udena and turned him over to their king.[52]

Here, the artificial elephant is only capable of movement because of the living men hidden inside it. The purpose of this artificial elephant is not to make a point about animals being machines but simply to deceive and gain a military advantage. Deception is a recurring theme in many Indian tales of animal and human *yantras*. One of the most striking and elaborate ancient Indian tales about an animal automaton involves several forms of deception. This story is from the folktale collection *Pañcatantra* (ca. 300 CE[53]):

The Weaver and the Mechanical Bird[54]

> In a town there lived two friends, Kaulika and Rathakāra. The two were childhood companions and loved each other dearly, and they always spent their time together. One time there was a great festive procession in a temple in the town where they lived. The two friends wandered about in a crowd of actors, dancers, and performers, with people from many regions. And then they saw a princess, riding on a female elephant. She displayed all the auspicious marks. She had come along with her chamberlain and a eunuch to see the deity. When Kaulika saw her, he was like a man struck by poison, or a man under the influence of an evil planet. Wounded by the arrows of love, he fell to the ground.
>
> When Rathakāra saw his condition, he was pained by his friend's torment. He lifted him up with the help of some trustworthy men and brought his friend to his own house. Kaulika was treated with spells and soothing remedies prescribed by the physicians, and after a while he regained consciousness. Then Rathakāra asked him: "My friend, why did you so suddenly lose consciousness? Tell me about it in your own words!" . . .
>
> Then Kaulika said: "My friend, when I saw the princess riding on the female elephant at the festival, the God of Love put me in this condition. I cannot stand this suffering!"
>
> But when Rathakāra heard this, he said with a smile: "Friend, if God is willing, we have a plan that will succeed! You may have the princess today!"

Kaulika said: "But the royal harem is watched by guards, and nobody enters alive. How can I be united with her? What false assurances are you deceiving me with?"

Rathakāra said: "My friend, just you see how clever I am!" And when he had said that, he immediately constructed a Garuḍa bird, which could move by means of wooden pins. It had a pair of arms, a conch, a discus, a mace, and a lotus flower, as well as a diadem and a jewel on its breast. Then Rathakāra made Kaulika climb into it. He marked him with the mark of Viṣṇu and showed him the art of steering the bird with the pins. He said: "My friend, go off dressed as Viṣṇu, and woo the princess at night in the harem with false and deceitful speeches, and love her according to the rules set forth by Vatsyāyana. The charming girl will be alone on the roof of that seven-storied palace, and she will think that you are Viṣṇu!"

Kaulika listened, and he went there in secret, in the form of Viṣṇu. He said to her: "Princess, are you asleep or awake? I have come here for your sake from the ocean of love, and I have left Lakṣmī! So make love with me!"

When she saw him, with his four arms, seated on Garuḍa, with his weapons and the jewel on his chest, she got out of bed and whispered, astonished: "Lord, I am but a mortal woman, an impure worm! You, my Lord, are holy in all these three worlds, and you deserve to be worshipped! So how would it be appropriate to make love with you?"

Kaulika said: "You have spoken the truth, you charming girl. But you see, the shepherdess Rādhā who used to by my wife has been incarnated in you! That's why I've come here."

When she heard that, she said: "My Lord, if that's how it is, then please go and ask daddy. He will make the wedding arrangements and give me to you."

Kaulika said: "You charming girl, I don't roam about in the full sight of humans like that! Oh, what's the point of this chatter! Just give yourself to me in a more informal marriage, and if your father curses us, I'll pulverize him and his family!" He stepped off his Garuḍa and grabbed her left hand. He led the shy and quivering girl to bed, and then he made love to her for the rest of the night according the precepts of Vatsyāyana. At dawn he returned to his own house.

And from then on, he spent his time constantly serving her. But then at some point the chamberlains saw that she had a love-bite on her delicate lower lip, and they said in secret: "Oh, look at that! The body of the princess seems to have been enjoyed by a man! How can such a thing happen in this well-guarded house? Let's tell the king!"

Then they all went to the king and said: "We don't know how this happened, Your Majesty, but someone has entered the well-guarded harem. Your Majesty must be the judge!" When the king heard that, he was alarmed, and thought: "The birth of a daughter always makes you anxious. One is so perplexed: Who should she be married to? When she marries, will she be happy or not? It is difficult to be the father of a daughter! As she is born, she afflicts her mother, and then when she grows up, all her relatives are tormented! Given in marriage to another, she commits a sinful deed! It is difficult to separate a daughter from misery."

He worried a great deal, and then he spoke to the queen, who was sitting apart: "My queen, you should know what the guards have said. Imminent death is upon him who did this."

The queen became alarmed when she heard this, and she hurried to the harem. There she saw her daughter with a bruise from a love-bite on her lower lip and nail marks on her body. And she said: "Oh, you sinful girl! You bring disgrace to your family! Why this breach of morality? Who is this death-marked man who has ventured into your presence? You have gone this far, now tell the truth!"

The princess, bowing her head in shame, told the whole story about Kaulika in the shape of Viṣṇu. When the queen heard the story, she hurried to the king. There was a smile on her face, and every hair on her body stood erect. She said to the king: "Congratulations, your Majesty! It is the Lord Viṣṇu who comes to the girl at night. She is married to him in an informal marriage. You and I will go up to the roof terrace at night and see why he doesn't talk to anyone." When the king heard that, he was delighted, and the day seemed to him as slow as a hundred-year fast.

At night the king and the queen hid on the roof terrace. The king's glance was fixed on the sky, until he saw Viṣṇu descending from the sky, mounted on Garuḍa, and with conch, discus, mace, and lotus flower in hand, as described before. It seemed to the king that he was drenched in a stream of heavenly nectar, and he said to the queen: "Darling, there is nobody in the world more fortunate than you and I. Out daughter is loved by Viṣṇu! All our wishes will be fulfilled! Through the power of my son-in-law, the entire earth will be under my rule!"

So confident was the king that he crossed the boundaries of all the kings along the border. When the other kings saw that he crossed the boundaries, they all got together and waged war on him. In the meantime, the king sent a message to his daughter through the queen: "My girl, since you are my daughter, and Lord Viṣṇu my son-in-law, how can it be suitable for all these kings to wage war against me? Let your husband know how my enemies are destroying me!"

So at night, the princess addressed Kaulika timidly: "My Lord, it is not fitting that my father is surrounded by enemies when you are his son-in-law! Could you please be so kind as to slay all the enemies?"

Kaulika responded: "My charming girl, trifling are your father's enemies, trust me. I'll break them into little pieces in an instant with my discus."

But as time went by, the whole country was laid waste by the enemies, and the king had only his ramparts left. Since the king did not know that Kaulika was just dressed up as Viṣṇu, he sent him camphor and light musk and other perfumes, and clothes and food and drink, and he said to him through his daughter: "My Lord, it seems that the place is now in ruins, and the fodder and the firewood are destroyed. My people's bodies have become old from all the hits. They are unable to fight, and many are dead. So, now that you know this, ordain what should be done."

When Kaulika heard that, he thought without worry: "I'm leaving her now! I'll get up on Garuḍa and showed myself all armed in the sky. The enemies will think I am Viṣṇu, and they will be struck by fear and killed by the king's weapons. For it is written:

Even a snake who is poisonless should
be hissing and spitting and puffing its hood.
It isn't the venom that kills, people say,
but rather the serpent's ferocious display.

And if I were to die in defending this place, all the better! For it is written:

The man who heroically lays down his life
for country, or master, or even for cattle,
or priests, or of course, for his own dear wife,
will go straight to heaven's realm after the battle.

After he made his resolve, he went and brushed his teeth, and then he said to the princess: "My charming girl, I won't have anything to eat or drink until all the enemies are slain. Enough of this talk—then I'll sleep with you! But go tell your father that you think the whole army should leave the city and go to war. I will stand in the sky and make the enemies powerless, and then they can easily be killed. I can't slay them myself, you see, or those wicked people will go straight to Viṣṇu's heaven. They have to be destroyed in such a way that when they flee and are killed, they won't go to heaven."

When the princess heard that, she went and told it all to her father. The king believed what she said, and he got up at dawn and went out to war with his well-equipped army. Kaulika, resolved to die, took his bow in his hand, climbed up on Garuḍa, and flew out for battle.

In the meantime, the real Garuḍa, who had been plagued by a long separation from the Lord Viṣṇu, laughed out loud because the Lord remembered him. Viṣṇu said to him: "Oh, Garuḍa, did you know that Kaulika dressed up as me and climbed up on a wooden Garuḍa and courted a princess?" Garuḍa answered: "Everything is known, my Lord, and everything is as desired. What do we do now?"

The Lord answered: "Today Kaulika has entered the battle, firmly resolved to die. He wishes to die, wounded by the arrows of some excellent warrior. But then when he is dead, everyone will say that a large flock of warriors killed Viṣṇu and Garuḍa! Then people won't worship us anymore! So go enter into that wooden Garuḍa immediately! I myself will enter into Kaulika's body and destroy the enemies. When the enemies are slain, our glory will increase!"

"Right!" said Garuḍa, and Viṣṇu entered the weaver's body. Kaulika stood midair through the greatness of the Lord, with his characteristic conch, discus, mace, and bow, and in an instant all the excellent warriors were made powerless. Then the king and his army slew all the enemies in battle. And then people started to whisper that the king had slain the enemies with the help of his son-in-law Viṣṇu. When Kaulika saw the slain enemies, he descended happily from the sky. But then the king and the ministers and the townspeople saw that it was Kaulika, a man from their city, and they said: "Hey, what's this?"

Then he told them the whole story form the beginning. The king was delighted by Kaulika's courage, and since he had been glorified by the slaying of his enemies, he decided to give Kaulika the princess in marriage in front of all the townspeople, and give him the kingdom. And Kaulika spent his time happily with his bride. It was what one calls a well-planned fraud.

In this intriguing tale, deception and ingenuity are rewarded, and there is no punishment, karmic or otherwise, for the fraud perpetrated on the princess, the king, and the kingdom. Indeed, both the Hindu caste system and reverence for the gods are thrown out the window as the low-caste weaver impersonates a god and succeeds in winning the princess and the kingdom. Significantly, it is the *yantra* that makes this radical reversal of social roles possible; without a convincing flying "Garuḍa," the weaver's impersonation of Viṣṇu would have been far less convincing, and his access to the well-guarded palace almost impossible. In a way, then, this is a profoundly subversive tale, celebrating human ingenuity by showing that a cleverly made machine can force both royalty and gods to elevate a lowly weaver. In the story's most dramatic turning point, the god Viṣṇu himself is forced to *become* the weaver impersonating him, while the real divine bird Garuḍa "enters into" the *yantra* and gives it true life. This story suggests that *something* has to enter into a machine to make it into a human being, but also that humans are capable of making *yantras* that imitate life so well that they force the hands of the gods themselves. The Indian blogger Aadisht Khanna draws a humorous parallel between the weaver of the *Pañcatantra* story and Goldman Sachs: "The moral is that you should conduct your affairs in such a way that if you fail, it will lead to someone or something even bigger or more powerful failing too. This lets you get away with anything."[55]

In the *Pañcatantra* story, there are two different entities animating the mechanical Garuḍa. First, the weaver sits inside the mechanical bird and flies it, but later the real Garuḍa enters into it, and the *yantra* becomes one with the divine bird. The mechanical bird, assumed to have been the real Garuḍa, actually becomes so, and the illusion in the story becomes reality.

What happens at the story's end to the automaton who has become a divine bird and the weaver who has become a god? Are they still animated by their divine counterparts, or do they go back to being a wooden *yantra* and a human being? The story doesn't tell us; the *Kathāsaritsāgara* simply informs us that the weaver marries the princess and lives happily ever after. But is he still a human weaver? And is his bird still an automaton? There is no way to know.

This is a tale of radical transformations: from powerless weaver to powerful prince, from lifeless wood to living bird, and from human to god. While the conclusion of this tale is somewhat reminiscent of the ancient Greek tale of Pygmalion, it is also worth noting the differences: Ovid tells us that Pygmalion was a sculptor who fell in love with a lovely ivory statue of a woman that he himself had carved. The statue eventually becomes a living woman (called Galatea in later literature) through the intervention of the goddess Aphrodite, as a reward for Pygmalion's piety and devotion to the goddess. The mechanical bird in the Indian story also becomes real through the power of a deity, but in this case, there is absolutely no piety involved; Viṣṇu and Garuḍa have no choice but to make the bird *yantra* come alive in order to save their own reputations.

Several ancient Greek and Latin tales suggest that humans are ill advised to try to imitate the gods. Icarus dies from flying too close to the sun, and the weaver Arachne is transformed into a spider for bragging that her weaving is better than Athena's.[56] Intriguingly, no such punishments are meted out to ancient Indian characters who dare compete with the gods themselves. Rather, the weaver's tale suggests that human creation can have powerful consequences; the wooden Garuḍa and the fake Viṣṇu are themselves transformed into *mūrtis* imbued with divine presence.

A similar lack of expected karmic consequences can be seen in a tale from the *Kathāsaritsāgara* where a clever, but dishonest, artisan (Rājyadhara, the one who later creates the city of *yantras*) constructs two mechanical geese (*yantrahaṃsa*) that fly through the window of the king's treasury and steal royal jewels:

> There is an excellent city named Kāñcī, and it adorns the lovely bride of the earth like a girdle. There was a famous king there called Bāhubala, who won a fortune by the might of his arms, and imprisoned this fortune in his treasury, although she is a restless lady. We were two brothers in his kingdom, artisans by trade, skilled in making *yantras* out of wood and other materials, the kind that Maya first invented. My older brother was by name Prāṇadhara, and he was maddened with love

for a capricious woman. I myself, my lord, am called Rājyadhara, and I was constantly devoted to my brother. My brother used up all my father's money as well as his own, and some of what I had given him out of affection. Then he, completely infatuated with this woman and wanting to steal money for her sake, crafted a pair of geese out of wood, with a mechanism and strings attached to them. He sent the pair of geese out at night by pulling on the strings. By means of the machinery, they entered the king's treasury through a window, and they took jewels from there with their beaks, put them in a basket, and came back to my brother's house. My older brother sold the jewels and spent the money he received with his beloved, and in that way, he robbed the king's treasury every night. Although I tried to stop him, he would not give up that improper way of acting, for who, when blinded by love, can tell the difference between right and wrong? Then the keeper of the treasury started looking into the matter for several days in succession, since the king's treasury was being plundered night after night without the bolt moving, although there were no mice in there. At first, he did not speak of it because he was afraid, but then he got annoyed and went and told the whole thing to the king as it was. Then the king stationed him and some of the other guards in the treasury at night and commanded them to stay awake and find out the truth. The guards went to the treasury at midnight, and while they were there, they saw my brother's two geese coming in the window, controlled by strings. The geese moved around by means of their machinery and took the jewels. But then the guards cut the strings, and they took the geese to show the king in the morning. Then my older brother was confused and said: "Brother, my two geese have been confiscated by the guards of the treasury, for the strings have become slack, and the pin of the machinery has dropped. So, you and I must both leave this place immediately, for the king, when he hears about all of it in the morning, will punish us for being thieves, since everyone knows that we are skilled at making mechanical devices. But I

> have a mechanical chariot that will quickly travel eight hundred *yojanas* if you press a spring. Let us escape in it today to a faraway foreign land, even though exile may be unpleasant. How can an evil deed done in spite of good advice bring joy to anyone? This is the ripened fruit of my wickedness in not heeding your advice. It has now extended to you, who are innocent, as well as to me." After saying this, my brother Prāṇadhara immediately wanted to put his family and me in the flying chariot. But though he urged me, I would not get in it because it had so many people in it. So he flew it up to the sky and went off to some faraway place.

In this case, the birds are programmed (by means unspecified) by the artisan to return to him with the stolen jewels. Here the animator is located outside of the robots. The artisan seems to control the birds with some kind of remote control, but no further details are given in this story. As in the *Pañcatantra* tale of the mechanical Garuḍa, the automata allows the maker/owner to commit a dishonest act. It is intriguing that the theft, like the fraud in *Pañcatantra,* is directed against the king. Perhaps these tales of human mechanical ingenuity are also fantasies about machines giving power and wealth to those who are disenfranchised by the social hierarchy.

We should note that mechanical birds subsequently became very popular throughout Asia. A wooden Garuḍa bird, similar to the one from the *Pañcatantra,* is encountered in a Mongolian story, *The Stories of Siddhi-Kur,* a translation of the Sanskrit text *Vetālapañcaviṃśati.* This story of the mechanical Garuḍa is not found in the extant Sanskrit versions of the *Vetālapañcaviṃśati,* however, although it is likely that the Mongolian narrative is based on a lost Sanskrit text. In the Mongolian tale, the son of an artisan makes a Garuḍa out of wood. When a person sits inside this Garuḍa bird and knocks on the top side, it goes up, if one knocks on the bottom, it goes down, and if one knocks one side, it goes to that side.[57] The more elaborate plot involving the automaton becoming real is, however, lacking from the Mongolian version.

Mechanical geese occur frequently in popular Khmer literature, likely due to Indian influence.[58] In the popular verse novels *Brah Jinavaṃs* from 1856 and *Haṃs Yant* from the eighteenth to nineteenth centuries, the heroes are traveling to the heavenly realm (as heroes in Khmer literature often do) on a mechanical goose.[59] The Indian influence is clearly demonstrated by the term used for the mechanical goose: *haṃs yant* is a borrowing from Indic *haṃsayantra*. The *Brah Jinavaṃs* story is extremely popular and is often enacted in traditional shadow theater performances. Even though magical birds of all kinds often appear in Khmer literature, the *haṃs yant* is not a purely magical creature but rather an ingenious machine. With the aid of this wonderful flying machine, Brah Jinavaṃs manages to find his lost wife and reunite with her. The *haṃs yant* is made from metal and studded with precious stones.[60] In the story entitled *Haṃs Yant*, the hero Suvaṇṇakumar (a Middle Indic name meaning "The Golden Boy") wins the hand of a princess with the aid of his mechanical goose. In these cases, the mechanical birds allow the heroes to attain otherwise impossible goals, much like the weaver in the *Pañcatantra* tale.

It is perhaps significant that the mechanical birds in many of these tales are referred to as *haṃsa* or *haṃs*. The *haṃsa* in Sanskrit literature, mechanized or not, is a creature far from Vaucanson's duck, whose purpose is to demonstrate that animals and machines are not that different from each other. The *haṃsas* are not mere birds; they are also spiritual icons in ancient Indian culture and a frequent symbol for the *ātman*, or immortal self.[61] The vast Hindu *Mahābhārata* epic includes a tale of a lovely princess, Damayantī, and her suitor, the young king Nala.[62] The two fall in love long before they meet each other in person thanks to *haṃsas* carrying messages back and forth between them (likely literature's first instance of virtual dating). But in a symbolic sense, their frequent communication by means of *haṃsa* signals their souls communicating with each other, even at a distance. The very term *haṃsa* is even used in meditation as a mystical *mantra*, uttered to aid a person to reach enlightenment. A person's journey to liberation is often compared to a *haṃsa* taking flight. When we encounter mechanical *haṃsas* in Indian and other Asian literature, then, these birds are often not only machines; they are *yantras* whose name and form hint at the presence of a soul, and of that soul's capacity for enlightenment, a flight to a higher reality.

Chapter 5

Mechanical Gardens and a Craving for Flying Machines

Androids in Jainism

Jainism and the Living Cosmos

Among the religious traditions that have arisen on the Indian subcontinent is Jainism. According to Jainism, the path to liberation from the cycle of death and rebirth has been taught by *tīrthaṅkaras* (ford-makers) or *jinas* (conquerors), who are omniscient teachers. The twenty-fourth *jina* of this world age, Mahāvīra (literally, "Great Hero"; his original given name was Vardhamāna) lived in the fifth century BCE and is usually regarded as a slightly older contemporary of the Buddha.[1] Like the Buddha, Mahāvīra was born a prince but left his royal life behind and chose to become a wandering ascetic before attaining enlightenment. Mahāvīra is not, however, regarded as the originator of the Jain teachings, but just the last in a long line of spiritual teachers who have conveyed the same message about the path to salvation since times immemorial.

One of the most central religious tenets of Jainism is nonviolence, *ahiṃsā,* toward all living beings, which is defined as refraining from actions that cause unnecessary suffering to living beings.[2] For Jain mendicants, the practice of *ahiṃsā* translates into strict vegetarianism as well as prohibitions against harming even the tiniest insect. For laypeople, there is more leeway in this regard, as it is not always possible in the course of ordinary life to avoid harming simple, one-sensed life-forms. But even for laypeople, it is a goal to avoid harming complex life-forms such as animals and humans, and vegetarianism is the religious norm.[3] But *ahiṃsā* is not just abstaining from physical violence toward others; hatred and a desire to harm are also contrary to the ideal of *ahiṃsā*. Jainism teaches that all living beings have an eternal soul, called *jīva* (literally, "life") or *jīvātman* (life-self), and that this soul is reborn until it reaches liberation, which is defined as a state of eternal bliss. There are two types of *jīvas*, those that move (including humans and animals) and those that do not (including plants). The *jīva* consists of pure consciousness and is by nature both blissful and omniscient, but both the bliss and the omniscience have become obscured by karma and need to be recovered through the annihilation of karma.

A *jīva* in Jain philosophy is classified as a substance (*dravya*), and it may possess qualities such as knowledge, energy, and bliss, in varying degrees.[4] The Jain view of life is far more expansive than what we find in other religious traditions; humans, animals, and plants are all classified as living beings, but so are rocks, raindrops, gusts of wind, and sparks of fire. Living beings are divided into four categories called *gatis*: gods, hell-beings, humans, and plants/animals. The plant and animal category is further subdivided into beings that are stationary (*sthāvara*) and those that are moving (*trasa*).

In Jainism, *jīvas* are further classified according to the number of senses that life-form possesses. A being who is *ekendriya-jīva* has a single sense through which to experience the world, that of touch. These beings include plants and trees, but also things like stones, lumps of clay, water, fire, and air, which can be considered life-forms in Jainism.[5] The complicating factor here is that air, water, fire, and earth can both be embodied souls, in which case they are living, or mere elements, in which case they are not.[6] All stationary life-forms have a single sense, that of touch, but they are capable of experiencing pleasure and pain. Included in this category of single-sense life-forms are the *nigodas*, which are invisible microscopic life-forms with brief life spans.[7] A *be-indriya jīva* is a life-form that has two senses, taste and touch, and these beings include worms, snails, and leeches, which are mobile.[8] Ants, bugs, and moths are life-forms with three senses (*tri-indriya jīva*), namely taste, touch, and smell.[9] The more evolved *corendriya jīva* add the sense of sight and therefore have four senses. These beings include wasps, scorpions, flies, and butterflies.[10] Humans belong to the class of life-forms who have five senses (*pañcendriya jīva*), including hearing, but so do animals, hell-beings, and demigods. Humans do not, therefore occupy a particularly unique role in the Jain cosmos, and reincarnation can cause any being to be reborn as a higher or lower life-form according to karma. Significantly, Jainism views the world as imbued with life of many kinds, and all these life-forms, from raindrops to trees, are connected to humans through the process of reincarnation; even if someone is human in this lifetime, they may have been a tree in the past, or may be reborn as a raindrop in a later lifetime. Respect for all life is therefore not a question of "preserving resources" in Jainism, but rather a recognition that all things in the world, humans included, are of the same essence, even if some currently exist in a more developed form. But if a breath of wind or a pebble can be alive, then what are the nonliving things in Jainism? The nonliving are things like time, space, and karma.[11]

As we have seen in a previous chapter, the idea of the larger cosmos reflected in the human body is found in Hinduism as early as the *Ṛgveda* (ca. 1200 BCE). A similar view of the cosmos as a giant person is found in Jainism—although here, we can also find a notion of a cosmic woman as well as a cosmic man.[12] The cosmos is described in canonical Jain texts, beginning with the *Bhagavatī Sūtra,* as wide at the bottom, narrow in the middle, and wider again at the top. At some point, this suggestively shaped cosmos was interpreted as a "cosmic man" (*lokapuruṣa*). While illustrations of *lokapuruṣas* are commonly attested in Jain art and manuscripts from the sixteenth and seventeenth centuries onward, the term *lokapuruṣa* is attested in older Jain texts, and the concept seems to date back to at least the first to second centuries CE.[13] Umāsvāti, in his *Praśamaratiprakaraṇa* (Treatise on the Delight of Tranquility), writes that "living beings and lifeless elements [constitute] what is known as six-fold substance. That is the cosmic man. He stands in a posture of spread-out legs and with the pair of his arms resting on the hips."[14]

But if the human body can represent the cosmos in Jainism, what then of the mechanical body of the automaton? The idea that there exists a close correspondence between the human body and an inanimate structure (the cosmos) is echoed in some of the Jain narratives about mechanical beings. But before we can analyze the Jain stories about *yantras* as machines, we need to pause for a moment at the idea of *yantras* as sacred diagrams in Jainism.

Yantras in Jainism

Yantras, in the sense of sacred diagrams, are used in a variety of religious rituals in Jainism. These diagrams, which can be impermanent patterns made of colored powder or grains, or designs drawn on paper, painted on walls, engraved on metal, or embroidered on cloth, are understood to be the ritual equivalents of temple icons (*mūrtis*) as places where deities reside.[15] The principal deity is represented at the center of the diagram, and Gough observes that Jain texts describing *yantras* often explicitly connect the diagrams to the Jain depictions of the assembly (*samavasaraṇa*) of all beings in the universe gathered in concentric circles to hear a *jina* speak.[16] The Jain *yantras,* then, become not just representations of a sacred cosmos imbued with *jinas* and deities, but places where the worshippers can connect with both *jinas* and gods.

Particularly popular is the Śvetāmbara *siddhacakra* (the wheel of the liberated soul), also called the *navapada* (nine ideals), which depicts the entire Jain cosmos in symbolic form (fig. 5.1). Eight lotus petals surround a white-clad figure, that of an enlightened being (*arhat*). On the lotus petals are representations of other spiritual figures: liberated souls (*siddhas*), mendicant leaders (*ācārya*), mendicant teachers (*upādhyāya*), mendicants (*sādhu*), as well as the jewels of right faith (*darśana*), right knowledge (*jñāna*), right conduct (*cāritra*), and right austerities (*tapas*).[17] Worship of this *yantra* is said to lead to prosperity and the destruction of sin.[18] *Siddhacakras* can be sculpted out of metal, painted on fabric, or drawn on the ground with colored grain. During the biannual nine-day festival of *olī, siddhacakras* are created in temples, made out of colored grain.

But just like in Hinduism, the term *yantra* (*janta*) can also signify a mechanical device or an automaton in Jain religious texts. Description of machines that move on their own accord occur in several Jain texts, and the preoccupation with such machines in Jainism is especially interesting since the materials from which these

Figure 5.1. Jain Siddhacakra from Gujarat, India. *Source*: Public domain.

machines are made (wood or metal) can themselves be imbued with living soul in Jainism. From the Jain perspective, a mechanical bird made from wood may not be an actual bird, but the wood from which it is made could still be seen as an embodiment of a living soul. Just like the *yantra* diagrams are sites for connecting with the sacred in Jainism, so can the *yantra* machines ultimately turn into vehicles for knowledge and enlightenment.

Androids and automata of various kinds are featured in literature by Jain authors, who composed their canonical literature in the Middle Indic dialects of Ardhamāgadhī and Old Mahārāṣṭrī. Later, Jain texts were also composed in Sanskrit, from around the seventh to eighth centuries CE onward.[19] Occasionally, as in the case of Hindu texts, it is difficult to tell when a *yantra* is simply a well-constructed tool or simple machine, and when it signifies something more like an automaton. Mechanical devices of various kinds are described in the Jain *sūtras*, which are likely dated to around the sixth century CE. Here, we hear about self-moving chariots, such as the *ratha-musala*, a mechanical chariot that moves by itself in battle.[20] Raghavan, however, suggests that this sort of "self-moving" chariot may simply have been moved by a person hidden inside it.[21]

The Carpenter's Flying Machine

Machines much more akin to automata in a modern sense are described in the fourth- to fifth-century CE text *Vasudevahiṇḍī* (The Wanderings of Vasudeva) by Saṅghadāsa, which is a Jain story collection reminiscent of Hindu fairy tale collections like *Kathāsaritsāgara*. Like the *Kathāsaritsāgara*, *Vasudevahiṇḍī* is ostensibly a retelling of the *Bṛhatkathā*, a lost Indian literary work referenced by many later authors.[22] The *Vasudevahiṇḍī* is composed in Old Mahārāṣṭrī. Here, we find a description of Indian traders who travel by sea to the country of the Javaṇas (Yavanas, presumably Greeks or Romans), where one of them learns the art of making automata:

> There was a city by the name of Tāmralipti. There, a king by the name of Ripudamana ruled, and his wife was called Priyamati. This king's childhood friend was a rich merchant by the name of Dhanapati. There was also in that city a carpenter by the name of Dhanada. One day, he had a son. But Dhanada was very poor, and his wife had also lost her entire fortune, so both of them starved to death. But their son grew up in Dhanapati's house. He used to eat the chaff in the grain storage, and therefore they gave him the name Kokkāsa. And so he grew up.
>
> But the merchant Dhanapati also had a son named Dhanavasu, and he built him a ship to travel to the land

of the Yavanas. And the son said to his father: "Send Kokkāsa with me; he shall travel with me to the land of the Yavanas." And the merchant let him leave.

The ship sailed away, and following the winds of the ocean, it arrived at its destination. The ropes were tied on all sides, and after the sails had been lowered, the sea merchants and their servants disembarked. The cargo was unloaded, the gifts for the king were brought, and the sea merchants began doing their trade.

Kokkāsa went to the house of a carpenter who lived near the quarters of the land and sea merchants and spent the day there. That man's sons were just learning different sorts of crafts. Their father taught them, but they understood nothing. Then Kokkāsa said to them: "This is how you should do it! This is how it should be!" Astonished, the teacher said to him: "Boy, you must learn the craft! I will teach it to you." The boy responded: "As you command, sir!" Then he began to learn, and thanks to the good teaching of the master he learned the entire craft of woodworking. Trained and released by the master, he stepped aboard the ship again and went back to Tāmralipti.

But times were bad there. Then he created two doves in order to attract the attention of the king and to make a living. These doves flew through the air daily and fetched dry *kalama* rice that belonged to the king. Then the guards reported to King Śatrudamana that they saw how the grain was carried away. The king commanded his ministers to investigate. They were wise and experienced and discovered the truth and reported to the king: "Your majesty, a pair of automated doves takes the grain away and brings it to Kokkāsa's house." The king said to them: "Bring him here!" He was brought in and questioned, and he told the king everything without holding anything back. The king was delighted, gave Kokkāsa gifts, and said to him: "Build a machine that flies through the air; then we will both travel in it wherever we want." And Kokkāsa built the machine, just as the king had ordered. He and the king climbed into it, and they traveled wherever they wanted. And so some time passed.

When the king's main consort saw that, she said to him: "I too want to travel with you through the air to faraway places." The king sent for Kokkāsa and said to him: "The great queen shall come with us!" But Kokkāsa said: "It is not advisable for a third person to enter; this vehicle only carries two people." But the stubborn queen was firm in her resolve, and the foolish king climbed in with her. Then Kokkāsa said: "You will regret it. We will definitely crash." With these words he climbed in, pulled the rope, and pushed the lever of the machine, which made it fly through the air. They rose toward the sky. When they had traveled several miles on their journey, the ropes tore under the extra weight, the machine sank, the lever fell out, and the vehicle descended slowly to earth. The king and his queen, who hadn't wanted to listen, began to be plagued by regret. Then Kokkāsa said to the king: "Wait here for a moment while I go to the town of Tosali and look for tools to repair the machine." With these words he took off, and the king and the queen stayed behind.

Kokkāsa went to the house of a carpenter and asked him for a carving knife. The carpenter recognized that he was a craftsman and said to him: "I have to build a chariot for the king right away, so I don't have a spare carving knife." Kokkāsa said: "Give it to me; I will build the chariot." The carpenter gave him the carving knife. He took the carving knife and while the carpenter stood by in amazement, he put both wheels together in a moment. Then the carpenter understood that he was Kokkāsa. And he said to him: "Wait here a moment while I go to my house and get a different carving knife you can bring with you."

But the carpenter went to King Kākajangha and told him everything. The king had Kokkāsa captured and inundated him with gifts. The king asked him: "Where are you going?" He told the king everything.

> They fetched King Amitradamana and his queen, and Kākajangha threw the king in jail and put his queen in his harem. Then he said to Kokkāsa: "Teach the princes your craft!" But he replied: "What are the princes going to do with this craft?" In spite of his warnings, the king forced him to teach them. And he went and taught them. Then he built two mechanical horses, and he made them in such a way that they could fly. While the teacher slept, King Kākajangha's two sons climbed up on the mechanical horses and made them go up in the air by pressing the lever. When Kokkāsa came back, he asked: "Where are the princes?" People answered him: "The princes climbed up on the mechanical horses and flew away." Then he said: "What have they done? The princes are lost—they do not know the lever to bring them back." The king overheard this and said: "Where are the princes?" Kokkāsa said: "They went away with the horses." Angry, the king gave the order for Kokkāsa to be executed, but one of the princes told him. When he received the message, he built a machine as round as a circle. And he said to the princes: "Sit down on that! When I blow the conch, everyone push the lever in the middle at the same time. Then the vehicle will ascend to the sky." They agreed and sat down on the round machine. Then Kokkāsa was brought in to be executed. Just as he was about to meet his fate, he blew the conch. When the princes heard the sound of the conch, they pushed on the lever in the middle. Then they were all pierced through by spears, and Kokkāsa was executed. The king said: "Where are the princes?" A servant told him: "They are all speared on the round machine." Then King Kākajangha cried: "Oh no, oh no, what have I done?" and he died of a broken heart.[23]

At first sight, there is nothing particularly religious about the tale of Kokkāsa and his many flying *yantras*, which seems to be a straightforward adventure story. The moral of the tale seems to be that *yantras* should only be entered by those who are wise and worthy; tragedy always ensues when those who are ignorant and unworthy try to travel in the *yantra*. Śatrudamana's queen, who foolishly insisted on coming along on the flight even when told that she shouldn't, becomes part of a rival king's harem, and Śatrudamana himself imprisoned as a direct result of disregarding Kokkāsa's advice. King Kākajangha loses his foolhardy sons and dies himself after the princes insist on stealing the flying mechanical horses and enter the dangerous round *yantra* with the deadly spikes. The idea that a *yantra* represents a dangerous space, only accessible to those who are worthy, can perhaps be read as an echo of the other *yantras* of Jainism, the geometric diagrams; in both cases, *yantras* are sacred spaces and sites for encounters with supernatural powers.

There are several automata mentioned in this tragic tale: mechanical doves (*kapota-juvalaya*), a flying machine (*āgāsa-gamaṇa-jantaṃ*, literally, "a *yantra* that can go in the sky"), flying horses (*ghoṭaka-janta*), and a mysterious round flying machine. The automaton technology in the story originates with the Yavanas and is clearly greatly sought after, especially by royalty. Just like in the Hindu story about the flying mechanical Garuḍa, technological skill erases social differences in this tale; a poor craftsman who knows how to construct flying machines can become a king's friend. And while the evil king Kākajangha seems to have unlimited power over the poor craftsman, the brutal mechanical execution of the foolish princes demonstrates that the power of the machine-maker is equal to that of a king. A variant of this story is found in Budhasvāmin's Hindu text *Bṛhatkathāślokasaṃgraha* (ca. 9th c. CE), which is a compendium of material taken from the lost *Bṛhatkathā*; here, the science of creating flying machines (*ākāśa-yantra*, literally, "ether machine") is said to be known only to Yavanas, who keep this technology secret.[24] Yavanas are also featured in Saṅghadāsa Kṣamāśramaṇa's eighth-century CE commentarial work *Bṛhatkalpabhāṣya*, where we learn that mechanical images (*janta-paḍimā*) of humans, capable of walking and opening and closing their eyes, are frequent among the Yavanas in their country.[25]

The Mechanical Garden of Somadeva Sūri

The fullest descriptions of *yantras* in Jain literature are found in Somadeva Sūri's tenth-century *Yaśastilaka Campū*, which describes a mechanical fountain garden in great detail.[26] This dramatic prose text opens in a lovely city called Rājapura (the royal city), where a king called Māradatta lives an indulgent lifestyle, enjoying wine, women, and playing in the fountains of his gardens. But the king comes under the influence of a sinister Tantric teacher who tells him that there exists a magical sword that could be his if he would only sacrifice a pair of every living being, including humans, to the dread goddess Caṇḍamārī. The king agrees, and the text describes in horrifying detail all the atrocities committed by Hindu goddess-worshippers and Śiva devotees. When a boy and a girl, who are living as ascetics, are dragged in to become human sacrifices, it occurs to the king that they may actually be the children of his own sister, who had left the court as young children to live a pious ascetic lifestyle. The kings wants to be sure, so he asks the children to tell him their life stories, and they do so with great detail, covering memories from several previous incarnations as well as their present lifetimes. The children are indeed revealed to be the king's niece and nephew, and the king is so impressed with them that he decides to convert to Jainism and become a peaceful renouncer himself. The description of the mechanical garden is part of the nephew's recollections of the luxury he experienced during a previous life as a king.

At the end of the text, the author Somadeva tells the reader that he himself is a Jain monk, belonging to an order called the Devasaṃgha. The concluding verse of the poem tells us that it was composed in the Śaka year 881 (= 959 CE), in the month of Caitra (March), when a king by the name of Kṛṣṇa had vanquished the Pāṇḍya, Cola, and Cera kings, in an area that corresponds to the modern-day Dharwar/Dharwad in south India, and copied by a famous scribe called Racchuka.[27] The accuracy of the date Somadeva gives is confirmed by inscriptions that reference the Rāṣṭrakūṭa king Kṛṣṇa III's victory over the Cola prince Rājāditya, son of Parāntaka, in March 959 CE.[28] The text itself is composed in Sanskrit, in a mixture of prose and verse. Somadeva Sūri's Sanskrit is elegant and erudite, and he cites and mentions numerous literary and religious authors and their works, both well-known Indian writers like Bhavabhūti, Bhartṛhari, Vyāsa, and Kālidāsa and more obscure poets and philosophers. Somadeva Sūri seems equally well versed in Hindu legal literature, medical works, treatises on elephant lore, and the religious texts of the Hindus and Buddhists. As discussed in the previous chapter, the *Yaśastilaka Campū* may have influenced both the *Samarāṅgaṇasūtradhāra* and the *Śṛṅgāramañjarīkathā*, the well-known Sanskrit texts ascribed to King Bhoja.

Somadeva Sūri seems to have been associated with the court of the Vemuḷavāḍa Cālukya king Baddega II, an under lord of the Rāṣṭrakūṭas, who ruled large portions of south India from the sixth to the tenth centuries CE.[29] There is even a Jain temple in the Karimnagar district, which according to inscriptions was built by King Baddega in honor in Somadeva Sūri, who was his teacher.[30] Somadeva Sūri is also credited with converting King Baddega to the Jain faith.[31] In addition to the *Yaśastilaka Campū*, one other text ascribed to Somadeva Sūri has survived, the *Nītivākyāmṛta*, which is a treatise on political science, a topic the author may well have gained expertise in while living at the royal court. The *Nītivākyāmṛta* is, according to a commentarial text, written for King Mahendrapāla of Kanauj.[32]

It is perhaps no wonder that a text composed by a king's beloved teacher contains such stunning descriptions of royal gardens. The *Yaśastilaka Campū* describes a lovely mechanical fountain house (*yantra-dhārā-gṛha*, literally, "mechanical stream house"), which one commentator on the text calls an "artificial cloud pavilion" (*kṛtrima-megha-mandīra*).[33] This fountain house is said to be cooler than the Himalayan mountains themselves. There is also a mechanical cloud (*yantra-jaladhāra*),[34] an mechanical water bed (*salila-tūlikā*), artificial "wishing trees" (*kalpa-vṛkṣa*), mechanical crocodiles and monkeys spraying water, as well as "cloud damsels" (*payodhara-purandhrī* or *megha-puttalikā*) who emit water from their breasts, as well as other "water deities" (*jala-devatā*), presumably fountains in the shape of statues of deities, as well as lotus flowers made from moonstones.[35] Of particular interest are the "wind-damsels" (*pavana-kanyakā*),[36] who fan people, since they may have served as inspiration for the mechanical maiden in a tragic Buddhist love story we will encounter later in this book. Somadeva's text contains a strong Jain message about the horrors of religious sacrifices and the importance of nonviolence. But it is his stunning description of a garden filled with androids that likely inspired the Hindu king Bhoja to write about automata and fountains a century later. Although the *Yaśastilaka Campū* draws materials from many earlier sources,[37] the description of the automated garden seems to be original to Somadeva Sūri's work.

Intriguingly, Somadeva Sūri's dense and detailed description of the royal garden, with particular attention to the layout of the garden's artificial landscape, is evocative of the elaborate descriptions of the structure of the cosmos in Jain texts. Jain texts and illustrations map the precise layout of the universe in rich cosmographic detail, perhaps because knowledge of the architecture of the cosmos is believed to be essential for the process of the liberation (*mokṣa*) of the soul (*jīva*).[38] The verbal mapping of the world reminds the reader of a larger order and structure that exists beyond the apparent chaos of the visible world, and meditation on the architecture of the cosmos is believed to help remove karma from the soul.[39] There is a close connection between cosmography and *yantra* diagrams in Jainism, and the structure of the cosmos is often echoed in the layout of the religious diagrams. Meditation on *yantras* therefore becomes a meditation on the invisible structure of the cosmos as well.

Somadeva Sūri's detailed verbal mapping of the royal garden and its wondrous mechanical devices fuses the two types of *yantra* in Jainism; while describing the layout of the garden filled with mechanical *yantras*, the poet is simultaneously creating a verbal map of the garden that allows the reader to visualize it in structural detail, thereby transforming the garden of *yantras* into a yantric diagram.

A Craving for Automata

Automata are also described in later Jain narrative literature as well, such as the eleventh- to twelfth-century texts *Gadyacintāmaṇi* and *Kṣatracūḍāmaṇi* of Vādībhasiṃha.[40] These texts describe a *candrakayantra* (literally, "moon *yantra*"), with figures of three boars embedded in it, and the contestants of a bow-shooting contest have to hit the boars within the revolving wheel. It is quite likely that the description of the *candrakayantra* here is inspired by the *matsyayantra* in the Hindu *Mahābhārata* epic (see introduction). These same texts further describe a *yantramayūra* (peacock machine), an automated peacock-shaped chariot made for the pleasure of the pregnant queen Vijayā. The creation of the automated peacock chariot in the Jain texts is explained as a response to the queen's *dohada*, her pregnancy craving, which in this case is a craving to fly through the air in a mechanical chariot. While this episode seems to draw inspiration from the earlier tale from *Vasudevahiṇḍī*, where a queen insists that she, too, wants to fly in a mechanical flying machine with her husband, the queen's wishes are here explained as the result of her pregnancy, rather than an irrational whim. *Dohada* is a particularly important concept in Jainism, where it is believed that a pregnant woman's cravings are caused by the baby's karma from previous lives, and the characters in Jain stories always go to great lengths to make sure a pregnant woman gets exactly what she wants, whether it's a particular food or a ride in an automated flying peacock chariot.[41] This episode is quite similar to a passage from Budhasvāmin's (9th c. CE) *Bṛhatkathāślokasaṃgraha*, where the pregnant Vāsavadattā has a similar craving for a flying *yantra*; she insists that she must see the world from above in a flying *yantra*.[42] Although the *Bṛhatkathāślokasaṃgraha* is older than Vādībhasiṃha, it is still tempting to speculate that the trope of the pregnant woman craving an automated chariot originated in a Jain environment, since the emphasis on *dohada* as a motivating force in the story is so very familiar from Jain literature.

The insistence on seeing the world from above is significant here. The mechanical *yantra* becomes a vehicle for a larger vision of the world, and as mentioned above, an understanding of the very architecture of the cosmos is regarded as important for the process of enlightenment in Jainism. In this way, the mechanical *yantra* of the flying machine functions similarly to a yantric diagram that maps the cosmos; it allows the devotee to see the ordered universe as it truly is. Unlike the sons of the evil king Kākajangha, however, who craved a vision for which they were not prepared, the pregnant queen in this tale does get a satisfying glimpse of the structure of the world "from above." The flying *yantra* in Jainism is also a religious *yantra*, in that it allows those who step into it to see the cosmic architecture that removes negative karma from the soul, perhaps particularly pertinent for a queen who carries a child whose desires and karma, for the duration of her pregnancy, are closely intertwined with her own. This Jain narrative suggests, then, that the pregnant queen's seemingly random craving for flying is in fact a longing for an understanding—both hers and her child's—of the cosmos into which her child will be born.

Chapter 6

I, *Yantra*

Androids in Buddhism

What is the difference between a human being and an automaton? If an artificially created being looks like a human, speaks like a human, and displays human intelligence and consciousness, could we call it human? Or is our humanity inextricably tied to our biological bodies, our flesh and blood? Is there perhaps something else, something more intangible and abstract, like a soul or self, that defines our humanity?

These questions have preoccupied humans since at least the seventh century BCE, when an ancient Egyptian wrote about the magician Merire, who made a man out of mud and commanded it to burn the pharaoh and his men (see chapter 1). The ancient question of the distinction between the human and the near-human still haunts well-known science fiction films like *Blade Runner* (1982), *A.I.: Artificial Intelligence* (2001), and *Blade Runner 2049* (2017).

What if there is no essential difference between humans and automata? What if we are all androids, "dreaming of electric sheep"? What if we are all automata, deluding ourselves into thinking that we are real? One of the retellings of the most startling android tales in Buddhist literature, the story of the painter who falls in love with a mechanical woman, arrives at the conclusion that there is no difference between human beings and androids. This intriguing legend has traveled throughout Asia and been retold in many different ways, each time conveying a slightly different message to its audience. This chapter examines the various ancient versions of the tale of the man who loved a mechanical woman and the ideas each recension of the text articulates about what it means to be human and not-so-human. I will then compare these insights with the more abstract formulations of what it means to be human found in philosophical Buddhist texts, with particular attention paid to the idea that a human being is a sort of machine.

The Painter and the Mechanical Woman

The simplest version of the tale of the painter and the mechanical woman is found in the Tibetan translation of the *Mūlasarvāstivāda-Vinaya,* the monastic code of an early Buddhist school, and is likely based on a lost Sanskrit original:

> The Buddha told the astonished monks that things had been the same way in a previous life: "Once when a painter came to a craftsman, he was served by a young woman made of wood. He wanted to enjoy her, but then she broke, and he looked silly. As revenge, he painted a picture showing himself hanging from a rope on the wall. As the craftsman saw this, he thought that his friend had committed suicide because of his shame, and he reported this to the king. The king came and saw that it was only a painting. Then the craftsman looked silly. Śāriputra was the painter then."[1]

This all-too-brief version of the story of the painter and the mechanical woman leaves many questions unanswered: Does the painter know that the wooden woman is not human, or is she so lifelike that he is convinced that she is an actual woman? Is the craftsman deliberately trying to prank the painter by not telling him that the woman is not human? Is the painter upset because he was taken in by an illusion of humanity, or because his desires were frustrated when the mechanical woman fell apart? The story of the painter and the mechanical woman is here connected to the previous lives of the Buddha's two main disciples, Śāriputra and Maudgalyāyana, and is used to show the audience that even in a previous life, Śāriputra was the cleverer of the two. Since Śāriputra is often depicted as the wisest of all of the Buddha's disciples, it is no wonder that he is able to outwit Maudgalyāyana, who by implication was the craftsman in a previous reincarnation, in this text as well. The overall message of this brief narrative seems to be: Do not let yourself be taken in by an illusion, whether it is a mechanical woman who appears to be human, or a lifelike portrait on the wall. The painter's imitation of humanity through his art is even more impressive than that of the craftsman, since the painter is able to convince his friend that a two-dimensional painting is an actual human being, while the craftsman had to create a three-dimensional wooden woman to replicate humanity. It is not clear from this version of the tale, or from any of the other retellings, whether the craftsman actually intended to play a prank on his friend by introducing him to a lifelike automaton, but the painter's competing revenge illusion is certainly deliberate.

A more elaborate Tibetan retelling of the story, omitting the rivalry between the Buddha's disciples, but expanding on the rivalry between the painter and the craftsman, is also found in the Tibetan version of the *Mūlasarvāstivāda-Vinaya*:

> In an earlier age, there was a painter in Madhyadeśa,[2] who on one occasion traveled to the land of the *Yavanas*. There, he entered the house of a craftsman. The craftsman sent a mechanical woman he had made to serve the weary traveler. She washed his feet and then just stood there. He called out to her to step closer, but she did not respond. Because he believed that the craftsman had sent her to him so that he could make love to her, he grasped her by the hand and wanted to pull her to him. But then the mechanical woman fell apart and turned into a pile of wooden pieces. Since he had been made a fool, he thought: "I have been made a fool, and therefore I want the craftsman to be made a fool in front of the king." He painted his own form on the wall, as if he had hanged himself, and hid himself behind the door. When the time when he would usually get up had passed, the craftsman wanted to find out why the painter had not appeared, and he saw him hanged. As

> he wondered why he would have taken his own life, he saw the mechanical woman, turned into a pile of wooden pieces. Then he thought that the painter had hanged himself out of chagrin that he had been made a fool. In the country of the Yavanas, it was the custom that when someone died suddenly at home that the funeral not take place before the king had been notified. The craftsman therefore went to the king and announced to him that a painter from Madhyadeśa had come to his house, and that he had sent a mechanical woman to serve him, but that he had grabbed her hand and wanted to pull her close, upon which she had turned into a pile of wooden pieces. Out of chagrin that he had been made a fool, he had then hanged himself. He [the craftsman] then asked the king to inspect the dead man so that he could bury him. The king commanded his envoys to perform the inspection. The envoys arrived on the scene and pondered how to get the hanged man down, and some advised to cut the rope, and they got an axe. But as they wanted to cut the rope, they saw that it was a wall, and that the craftsman had been fooled. Then the painter came out of hiding and said: "My host, you have only made a fool out of me, but I made a fool out of you in front of the king's companions."[3]

Intriguingly, while the painter is here still identified as Indian, the robot-maker's home is relocated to a foreign land, Yavana country. It is not clear where exactly the author imagines Yavana country to be, but the association between automata and Yavanas is, as we saw in chapter 2, frequently made in Indian texts. The Indian painter, while momentarily outwitted by the clever foreign robot-maker, is here shown to be more than the foreigner's equal when it comes to creating lifelike art. In this version of the tale, it is clear that the painter believes the woman to be the craftsman's servant, sent to him by his host for his sexual enjoyment. While this rendition of the story still focuses on the theme of illusions, there is a disquieting subtext of sexual violence in the narrative as well. The mechanical woman may be read as a metaphor for an enslaved female servant who has lost her agency, her free will, and her very humanity by being treated like an object by her employer and a plaything for his guests.

An even more detailed version of the story of the painter and the mechanical woman, also emphasizing the wooden woman's lack of free will, is found in the Chinese translation of the *Tripiṭaka*, the Theravāda Buddhist canon. This version of the story ignores Yavanas altogether:

> Once in north India there was a craftsman who worked with wood. With great ingenuity, he fashioned a woman from wood; she was of an unrivaled beauty; with her clothes, her belt, and her beautiful ornaments she was not different from a real woman; she went, she came, she could also serve the wine and watch the beds; she was only lacking speech. At that time there was in south India a painter who was also very good at painting.

Again, the painter assumes that the mechanical woman is real until he attempts to take her to bed and discovers that she is made of wood. In order to get back at his host, he paints a picture of himself hanged, adding the realistic touches of "flies posed on his mouth and birds pecking at it." When the craftsman and the painter discover that they both succeeded in fooling each other, "the two men truly recognized what a delusion is; each renounced everything that he loved in order to leave the world and enter religion."[4]

This Chinese version, like the longer Tibetan one, signals its Indian origin by placing the story firmly in India. This version of the painter's tale culminates in an epiphany for both men, the craftsman and the painter: the world is full of illusions, and the truth can only be found in religion. The implied contest between the craftsman and the painter as to who can create the most realistic representation of a human form is somewhat reminiscent of the anecdote of the two painters Zeuxis and Parrhesius recounted by the Roman author Pliny the Elder. According to Pliny, Zeuxis painted grapes so lifelike that even the birds thought they were real. But Parrhesius did even better; he painted a veil so realistic that Zeuxis tried to look behind it to find his rival's painting.[5] In the Chinese rendition of the tale of story of the painter and the mechanical woman, however, the focus is not on the power of art to imitate life, but rather on the insight that only religion offers a refuge from the illusions of the world.

The Sanskrit *Bhaiṣajya-Vastu*, preserved in a manuscript from Gilgit in present-day Pakistan, contains a brief variant of the tale of the painter and the mechanical woman.[6] The Gilgit manuscripts, discovered in 1931, are among the oldest surviving Sanskrit manuscripts, dating back to the fifth to sixth centuries CE, although the contents are believed to be older. This version of the tale is rather abrupt, fragmented, and lacking in details.

> Previously, in Madhyadeśa, there was a master painter. [For the sake of wealth] he went to the land of the Yavanas. There he arrived at the house of a *yantra*-maker. He created a mechanical girl to serve him and sent her to him. She washed his feet and then stood there. Then he spoke at the time she was leaving. She remained silent. He observed that. "She was sent to me as a servant." Grabbing her by the hand, he began to pull her close. Then the chain collapsed. He appeared ashamed. "I was embarrassed by him [the *yantra*-maker]. I will embarrass him along with the king and his entourage." Then he painted an image (*pratibimba*) of himself hanging, facing the door. He hid in the doorway. So when it was time for him to get up, he had disappeared. Then the *yantra*-maker appears. He came from afar. "Why is that door not closed?" When he had entered, he saw him as if dead from hanging. "For what reason has he deprived himself of life?" He sees that wooden girl with the collapsed chain. He appears ashamed. This was suitable for the occasion.

This version is quite close to the longer Tibetan rendition but is lacking quite a few of the narrative details. As in the long Tibetan version, the *yantra* is this text can be read as a metaphor for a female servant whose lack of autonomy over her own body renders her a vehicle for a guest's pleasure. The painter feels entitled to a sexual encounter with the woman because "she was sent to me as a servant." The (artificial) servant girl's lack of control over her own body signifies a larger social control over the bodies of women, and especially female servants. Mary Douglas has argued persuasively that the body is always socially constructed: "The social body constrains the way the physical body is perceived. The physical experience of the body, always modified by the social categories through which it is known, sustains a peculiar view of society. There is a continual exchange of meaning between the two kinds of bodily experience so that each reinforces the categories of the other."[7] Douglas further argues that "bodily control is an expression of social control."[8] While Douglas here refers specifically to bodily control during ritual, I argue that we might see the control over the robot's body in android tales as a metaphor for the social control over human bodies as well. In all the versions of the story of the mechanical woman, the android servant is more or less explicitly stated to be under the control of her master and is made to serve the guest who has arrived. But chillingly, the guest who believes her to be fully human is still treating her like an object, given to him for his gratification by his host. It is not difficult to see a subtext of gendered violence and exploitation here. Perhaps any society that produces tales of indentured android servants must always be familiar with the concept of indentured humans. The mechanical maiden's silence represents mystery, inactivity, and a lack of agency; through her silence, the female becomes a blank canvas upon which the male protagonist can project his desires.

Another Sanskrit version of this tale preserved in the *Kaṭhināvadāna* also depicts the painter as feeling entitled to the servant girl's love, even if he does try to seduce her with compliments. The main focus on this rendition, however, is on the painter's embarrassment at having been tricked and on his subsequent revenge on the craftsman:

> Then he (the painter) said to her: "Come here!" She remained silent. He thought: "Surely, she has been sent here as a servant girl to serve me." He praised her: "Ah, the creator of women has made a jewel-daughter! In my view, I have been reformed due to my karma. Oh, pity the people born in Jambudvīpa,[9] who will not get to experience such a very charming young woman, so perfect in beauty and youth, through their eyes, or

> hands, or bodily touch!" After he honored her with this honeyed speech, he approached her in order to draw her close to him. "My darling, my beauty, come here!" When he realized that the mechanical wooden girl still did not speak, he went to her, his mind filled with desire. He reached for her hand and pulled her close. Then she turned into a pile of wooden rubble. He was blamed and looked foolish.[10]

As in most other versions of the narrative, the painter then paints himself hanged and gets his revenge on his host in the presence of the king. The story concludes by identifying the painter with Śāriputra and the craftsman with Mahāmaudgalyāyana. This elaborate Sanskrit rendition combines many elements that are present in the shorter versions of the tale: the android-makers association with the foreign Yavanas, the rival illusions of the mechanical woman and the painting, the arrival of the king's men, and the identification of the painter with Śāriputra and the craftsman with Maudgalyāyana, who here has the prefix Mahā- (the great) added to his name. The emphasis of this version of the tale is on the ingenuity of each of the two rivals, and on the superior cleverness of Śāriputra.

A Chinese version of the tale, preserved in the *Puṇyavantajātaka,* is quite close to the *Kaṭhināvadāna* story and may very well be based on it. As usual, the painter is fooled by the mechanical woman and paints himself dead:

> The host hurried to the king and said: "In Madhyadeśa there is a painter, who came as a guest to my house and stayed there. I have made a mechanical woman out of wood in order to serve him. He thought it was human and grabbed it by the hand; then the connection fell apart. That man was ashamed, hanged himself, and died. May the king be assured! I wish to hold his funeral rites." Then the king sent an envoy there to observe. The envoy said: "Cut down the rope and have him brought down. Then I will see if he hanged himself and died, or whether he was murdered by his host." At this time, the host took an axe in order to cut him down. But he

> only cut into the wall. Then the guest stepped forward and said: "Am I dead or am I alive?" Then the host was embarrassed in the presence of the royal envoy.
>
> The Buddha said to the monks: "What do you think of that?" At that time, the painter was Śāriputra, and the one who made the mechanical maiden out of wood was Mahāmaudgalyāyana. While he (Śāriputra) at that time possessed wisdom and managed to conquer the other, he will now yet again conquer through his supernatural power (*ṛddhi*).[11]

We should note a few intriguing details that stand out as unique in this particular recension: There is an additional little twist to the plot when it is suggested that the craftsman was briefly suspected of murdering the painter. The addition of supernatural powers ascribed to Śāriputra is also worth noting; apparently, his superior skills in creating a lifelike imitation of humanity is here associated with supernatural ability.

The most elaborate, and perhaps also the most interesting, version of the tale of the painter and the mechanical woman is preserved in Tocharian B, an extinct Indo-European language attested in sixth- to eighth-century CE manuscripts found at the Tarim Basin in what is now China. Many of the Tocharian manuscripts contain translations of Buddhist Sanskrit texts, although there are also translations of some Manichean texts and some commercial documents and medical texts preserved as well. The two related Tocharian languages, conventionally referred to as Tocharian A and B, were generally written in a modified form of the Indian Brāhmī script. The Tocharian version of the tale of the mechanical woman is preserved in the Tocharian translation of the *Puṇyavantajātaka,* a text found in many different recensions. The *Puṇyavantajātaka* likely originates in India but is also found in an Arabic version, four Buddhist versions (in Prakrit, Chinese, Tibetan, and Tocharian), and three Jain versions (in Prakrit, Sanskrit, and Old Gujarati).[12] The Tocharian translation is closely related to the other Buddhist versions of the text. But the Tocharian translation also includes a number of short tales, including that of the mechanical woman, that are not found in other versions of the Jātaka text.[13] The frame story of the *Puṇyavantajātaka* involves five brothers (or five friends in the Tocharian version) who each represents a positive quality or virtue: beauty, heroism, skill, wisdom, and merit. The wise man is the one who narrates the story of the mechanical woman, which is used to illustrate the superiority of wisdom over the other positive qualities his friends embody. Associating the tale of the painter and the wooden woman with wisdom is an interesting narrative choice; one would easily imagine that the story of a lifelike android could be used as an example of skill instead, since the craftsman who created the robot was supremely skilled. However, in the context of the tale, the creation of the mechanical woman serves to emphasize that while robot-making may be impressive, it is nothing compared to the ability to understand the nature of illusions. We should note, however, that at the end of the entire *jātaka,* the brother who is crowned king is the one who represents religious merit, which is even more important in the *Puṇyavantajātaka* than wisdom.

> Once, a long time ago, a painter from a country far away went as a guest to the house of a craftsman. Then the craftsman received the painter with great hospitality, and at night he made a bed separately for him in the house. He anointed him with sesame oil, and he put a mechanical woman at the head of his bed. She was an adorable beauty, and, as if with a show of respect, she grasped his hand and served him eagerly. She seemed embarrassed and looked down a little. She looked lovely, but seemed shy. She didn't talk or laugh. She reached out her arm, serving him, almost as if she were in love, and fanned the heat away from the painter's body.
>
> Then the painter in his ignorance got the idea that the wooden woman was a real woman, and he thought: "O, such beauty! Such shyness, such feminine modesty!" "She doesn't seem like a flirtatious woman, and she doesn't care for my esteem. She reaches out her hand, serving me, and then seems to pull it back into her lap." The necklace on her chest moved a little; and it heaved up at that instant.—"Even if she is demure, she still delights my heart with love," he thought. "Who is she? Is she the craftsman's sister, or daughter, or wife, or servant?

Or has she come here as a guest, like myself?—Oh, but as a guest she wouldn't have been ordered to serve another guest! The craftsman has shown me a great deal of trust, that he has let such a beautiful woman be alone with me!" Then the painter thought: "I will not afflict my passion upon her!" and he yawned and stretched.

Even so, when he looked at the woman, he thought: "Oh, no! The god of Love himself has come to life in her to confuse me! If she were just to sit there in my sight and adore me and fan me, the delicate woman would let no harm come to my dreams, as long as I do not adore her in my heart." And he thought: "Because of the danger involved, wise men are not permitted to show love to the following ten types of women: (So it was written!) You shall not make a pass at a royal woman, your father's wife, an officer's wife, a relative's wife, a teacher's wife, and (even more importantly) a woman who flatters men, a woman who's after your money, a woman who makes herself available to many men, and (most importantly) a very beautiful woman, or the wife of a man who's out to get you. Because she belongs to my relative (the craftsman) and is beautiful to look at, I should not show her love."

But then he thought: "But who is capable of holding himself back, alone with such a beautiful woman in such a place, at such a time! Why shouldn't I declare my love? Or maybe I'd better hold her hand first?" Then the painter grasped the hand of the mechanical woman with love. And the mechanism fell apart; rags and sticks and ropes fell to the ground, and there was no more girl. When he saw that, the painter leaped startled out of bed, and he examined her carefully. Then he said: "Oh, how badly I have been tricked by my teacher the craftsman! Oh, the power of passion! Oh, the horridness of ignorance, that a human being can be so firmly in love with a bunch of rags!" It is true what good people say: as far as the *ātman* (self) of human beings is concerned, it leaves no memory behind. And indeed, the *ātman* itself does not exist. Just like this thing I perceived was put together

> from rags, ropes, and sticks, so is also the perception human beings have of the *ātman* put together from bones, flesh, and sinews.[14]

The painter's conviction that the android is the perfect woman makes this story an interesting foreshadowing of E. T. A. Hoffmann's famous android story "The Sandman," in which the male protagonist falls in love with a female automaton precisely because he interprets her lack of speech and passion as charming female qualities. Like Hoffmann's story, the Tocharian tale articulates something vital about gender: the male gaze perceives the lifeless android as the perfect woman precisely because the android lacks the qualities present in living, breathing women. The painter experiences the automaton as so charming *because* she doesn't speak, which suggests that he is interested in (sexual) ownership of a woman rather than in dialogue with one. He finds the android perfect, precisely because she is not a real woman.[15]

Schelde has argued that literary depictions of men creating female automata represent a form of "womb envy," a man's desire to create life without the aid of a mother.[16] In tales of male robot-makers, females are robbed of agency and reduced to objects rather than creative subjects. Plank proposes that such fantastic stories express a desire to create without sexuality, to "purify" the act of creation by divorcing it from the sex act,[17] but we should note the creation of automata is not only an asexual creation but, in most cases, a form of creation devoid of female input, reducing the female to a form of male creation and the object of male desire. But in the tale of the painter and the mechanical woman, the desired female object is unstable and reveals itself to be a construct, perhaps an echo of the Buddhist idea that meditating on a female body in a state of decay is a powerful cure for physical desire.

It is interesting to note, however, that the painter, while drawn to the silent and demure female, is more respectful of "her" in this version of the tale than in most other recensions. The Tocharian version of the tale presents the painter's approach to the mechanical woman as more of an awkward attempt at courtship than an outright sexual assault.

The painter's moment of epiphany when the android falls apart sets this recension of the tale of the mechanical woman apart from the other versions and transforms a story of folly and illusions into a Buddhist meditation on the nature of humanity. The painter's disappointment when the woman falls apart leads to a moment of enlightenment. The painter's realization that she was nothing but a construct is followed by the unsettling insight that *he himself* is also nothing but a construct, a machine made up of "bones, flesh, and sinews." According to Buddhism, everything physical and mental is made up of aggregates of *dhammas*, or psycho-physical atoms. But all of these aggregates are impermanent and will eventually dissolve, just like the constituents of the mechanical woman fell apart. His shocking discovery of the "woman's" true nature leads the painter to a deeper realization of the impermanence and soullessness of all things, himself included. After the initial realization that the mechanical woman was a mere imitation of humanity follows the even more disturbing insight that the painter *himself* is no more real than she is. The painter's insight that he himself is, at least in a metaphorical sense, a robot foreshadows modern films like *Blade Runner*, where both Deckard and Rachael are androids convinced that they are human. From a Buddhist perspective, however, *all* selfhood is ultimately an illusion, and realizing that we are mere robots is the path to enlightenment. It is particularly fitting that the main character in this tale is a painter, adept at creating illusory human beings through his art. It is only when the mechanical woman falls apart at his touch, however, that he understands that he himself is as much a simulacrum as a portrait of a human painted on a wall, or as a woman created from wood.

Werner Winter proposes that several Tocharian Buddhist texts could have been performed as plays, and he sees the interchange of prose and verse in this Tocharian tale as well as the frequent descriptions of easily enacted actions in the present tense as markers of texts meant to be orally performed.[18] Beguš compares the type of Tocharian performance Winter postulates as something akin to the Chinese performance genre *pien-wen* (transformation texts), and she identifies several performance markers in the Tocharian *Puṇyavantajātaka*.[19] In this case, descriptions of things meant to be visualized by the audience are interspersed with verses meant to be recited.[20] If the Tocharian tale of the painter and the mechanical woman was indeed performed in front of an audience, even in a very simple form without any elaborate sets or props, such a performance would almost certainly help enhance the text's religious message. The performer would then create, through words and gestures, a simulation of the painter and the mechanical woman, and reveal them both to be nothing more than illusions. The performance itself would then add another layer to the already complex series of simulacra described in the text and convey the message that human identity is a mere illusion to a Buddhist audience.

Beguš has examined the relationship between the different versions of the story of the painter and the mechanical woman and concludes that the tale was likely a folktale prior to its sacralization and inclusion in the Buddhist canon.[21] As evidence, she points to the brief and anecdotal form of what she finds to be the original version of the tale, as well as the lack of religious aspects in the basic plot of the tale. She argues that the folktale was later adapted to Buddhist ideology. Beguš sees the Sanskrit version preserved in the *Mūlasarvāstivāda Vinaya* (preserved in the Gilgit manuscripts) and the *Kaṭhināvadāna* as original.[22] She stresses the importance of wisdom in the different versions of the tales and argues that all versions of the tale conclude that the wisdom of the sage is superior to the magical skill of seeming to bring inanimate objects to life.[23] The Sanskrit versions both contrast Śāriputra's wisdom and Maudgalyāyana's magic power.[24] While Beguš argues that the Tocharian version "never turns to Buddhist ideas," I find that the text's emphasis on the automaton as a symbol for the selfless human being is, in fact, a summary of the most essential teaching of Buddhism, that of *anattā*.

Mechanical women are also attested in several other Indian texts, such as the long poem *Yaśastilaka Campū* by the tenth-century Jain author Somadeva Sūri, as mentioned in the last chapter, which details all the wonders of a park with mechanical fountains, an artificial waterfall, and wind-maidens (*pavana-kanyakās*) who create little breezes by fanning. Somadeva Surī specifically mentions a *yantraputrikā* (mechanical girl) placed near the king's bed to fan him.[25] In this case, however, the mechanical woman is simply a charming garden ornament rather than a vehicle for enlightenment, as in the Tocharian text. While all of the versions of the tale of the painter and the mechanical woman illustrate different aspects of the Buddhist doctrine, the Tocharian recension points to the idea that lies at the heart of the Buddhist view of humanity: *anattā*, "no-self."

What Is a Human Being in Buddhism?

Buddhism originated in India around the fifth century BCE. The life story of the historical founder of Buddhism parallels that of Mahāvīra, the most recent *jina* of Jainism, in many ways. Siddhattha Gotama, the man who was to become the Buddha, was born as a prince in Lumbini in what is today southern Nepal. Like Mahāvīra, he left his palace life behind and became a wandering ascetic. After several years, he reached enlightenment, and was from then on known as the Buddha (The Awakened One). The Buddha encapsulated his spiritual insights into four simple theses, which he called "The Four Noble Truths":

1. All this is suffering
2. The root of suffering is desire
3. Suffering is extinguished when desire is extinguished
4. This is accomplished by following the eightfold path

The eightfold path to the extinction of suffering includes right understanding, right thought, right speech, right action, right livelihood, right effort, right mindfulness, and right concentration. An essential part of this eightfold path, right understanding, is grasping the impermanence of all things: everything that exists will eventually cease to exist. According to the Buddha's teachings, there is nothing eternal in this world, and therefore also no such thing as an eternal self or soul (*attā*). This lack of self is immensely difficult for humans to accept; we yearn for eternity and permanence and delude ourselves into thinking that we have an eternal soul, but this delusion is ultimately just another cause of suffering. Freedom from suffering can only be reached once humans realize that all things are fleeting and without any eternal substance.

Although Buddhism shares several important concepts with Hinduism and Jainism, such as the ideas of karma and reincarnation, the insistence that there is nothing permanent or eternal sets Buddhism apart. But if mechanical *yantras* in Hinduism represent, as we have seen, temporarily soulless bodies that *could* be imbued with an *ātman* or self, what then of Buddhist robot tales?

Unlike Hinduism, which teaches that all living beings have an eternal *ātman*, Buddhism claims that the idea of a self is nothing but wishful thinking. According to Buddhism, the idea of the self is a mere illusion born from our longings for permanence, while both the body and more abstract aspects of humanity, such as our consciousness, are ultimately temporary constructs.

The idea of *anātman* (Sanskrit) or *anattā* (Pāli), or "lack of self," is central to Buddhism. Simply put, according to Buddhism, living beings do not possess a soul or self that lives eternally after the death of the physical body. Instead, Buddhism teaches that all things are made up of psycho-physical atoms (*dhammas*); physical objects are made up of physical atoms, while mental aspects of our existence are constructed of mental atoms. These atoms cluster together into temporary constructions. A human being is in its totality made up of five such clusters or aggregates (Pāli: *khandhas;* Sanskrit: *skandhas*) of *dhammas*: physical form (*rūpa*),[26] sensation (*vedanā*),[27] perceptions (*saññā*),[28] mental formations (*saṅkhāra*),[29] and consciousness (*viññāna*).[30] Consciousness must not be confused with an eternal self, however; consciousness is merely a temporary formation that may last through several reincarnations but will eventually be dissolved. The five aggregates are all marked by impermanence. The physical form that constitutes a body will be dissolved into its constituent parts when a person dies, and while the other *dhammas* may continue to hold together as aggregates through several reincarnations and attach themselves to a series of other physical forms, they too will eventually be dissolved into *dhammas* when a person reaches final enlightenment.

So what is the human body according to Buddhism? The Theravāda Buddhist tradition, which traces its origins back to the teachings of the historical Buddha, does at times view the body (and especially the sexual body) as problematic, a distraction from the journey toward spiritual liberation,[31] and refers to the body in terms like "a heap of corruption."[32] One canonical Buddhist text even associates *rūpa*, physical form or body, with suffering through an elaborate play on words: "And why, monks, is it called body (*rūpa*)? It suffers (*ruppati*), O monks. That is why the word body (*rūpa*) is used. What does it suffer from? It suffers from cold, heat, hunger, thirst, from the touch of bugs, mosquitoes, wind, sun, and serpents. It suffers (*ruppati*), O monks. That is why it is called body (*rūpa*)."[33] Sue Hamilton argues, however, that a profoundly negative view of the body is not found in the very earliest Buddhism, where the attitude toward the body is more analytical than negative. She proposes that the influential fifth-century commentator Buddhaghosa and his contemporaries, who began to write about the body in very negative terms (comparing it, for example, to a stinking toilet), diverges from the original Buddhist material.[34]

Although the human body is associated with decay, impermanence, and suffering in some forms of early Buddhism,[35] the earthly body of the Buddha himself is nevertheless preserved in the form of holy relics enshrined in *stūpas* and temples. As we will see in the next chapter, one Buddhist tale even shows a killer robot eagerly defending the holy relics of the Buddha; in this case, the permanence of the relics in an otherwise impermanent world is echoed in the permanence of the android, buried in a former age with the holy relics themselves and ready to be reactivated.

Some Buddhist texts describe the human body as something akin to an automaton or a machine; the body is just a "collection of feet and toes, legs, chest, loins, belly, navel, backbone, heart, ribs and flanks, hands, forearms, upper-arms, shoulders, neck, jaw, forehead, head, skull, accumulated by the action that causes existence, the abode of sundry passions, ideas and fancies."[36] Buddhist texts deconstructing the human body by making it into a list of components, physical and mental, presage texts like the tale of the painter and the mechanical woman from the *Puṇyavantajātaka*, where the human body and its constituents are explicitly equated with a machine and its parts. Like the automaton, the human body is a construct, a cultural artifact. The android in Buddhist texts serves, then, as a metaphor for the constructed and impermanent human body. Meditation on the human body in a state of death and decay is an important practice in many forms of Buddhism,[37] and this form of meditation is regarded as helpful both in overcoming physical desires and in grasping the concept of impermanence.

But even though the body and its desires generally tie humans to an unsatisfactory existence, there is also, especially in Mahāyāna Buddhism, the notion that the body can be a tool for enlightenment. The eighth-century CE Indian scholar-monk Śāntideva famously prays:

For as long as space endures
And for as long as living beings remain,
Until then may I too abide
To dispel the misery of the world.[38]

The successive bodies of an enlightened *bodhisattva,* while not permanent, must last long enough to enable them to exist in the world until all human suffering is alleviated. We see a contrast, then, between the ordinary decaying human body on the one hand and the body of a Buddha or *bodhisattva* on the other. As Mrozik points out, the Buddhist fascination with the ideal body of the Buddha is widespread.[39] Many Buddhist texts list the thirty-two bodily marks of a Buddha, which include things like long fingers, level feet, dark eyes, a ten-foot halo, golden skin, a deep voice, and white teeth with no spaces in between them. Mrozik argues that there is a range of "virtuous bodies" described in Buddhist literature, bodies that are healthy, beautiful, and free of flaws, their beauty signaling the person's positive karma from past lives.[40]

The well-known *trikāya* (three body) doctrine of Mahāyāna Buddhism postulates that a Buddha has three different bodies:

1. A Truth Body (*dharmakāya*), a limitless body that encapsulates enlightenment itself. This is not a physical body but rather the very nature of reality, of the world as it truly is.
2. An Enjoyment Body (*saṃbhogakāya*), a body of bliss. This is a subtle, nonmaterial body, the form in which a Buddha can appear to a practitioner during a visionary experience.
3. An Emanation Body (*nirmāṇakāya*), a physical body manifested in space and time. This would be the earthly body of the historical Buddha, Siddhartha Gautama, a form that is accessible to all sentient beings.

Additionally, the Dzogchen tradition of Tibetan Buddhism operates with a "rainbow body" (*'ja' lus*), a body of pure light, attained by those who achieve a level of awareness that transcends the physical world.[41] This state is described as "the dissolution of the physical body at death into a state of rainbow light,"[42] although it is also believed to be possible to achieve this rainbow body in this lifetime.

Although the Emanation Body of the Buddha is a physical one and subject to decay, as all human bodies are, the veneration of relics in Buddhism, which are bones, strands of hair, or other bodily remnants of the Buddha or other enlightened beings, suggests that the Buddha's Emanation Body is still, in some essential way, different from all other decaying mortal bodies. Even in its state of decay and dissolution, the Buddha's Enjoyment Body becomes a sacred artifact, a tool for meditation and a vehicle for enlightenment. Although these relics are, on an abstract theological level, mere reminders of mortality and impermanence, they are nevertheless in practice regarded as holy talismans, powerful and transformative for those who are in their presence.

The Robot as a Metaphor for Humanity

The idea that a robot may serve as a metaphor for a human being is found in Buddhism as early as the *Laṅkāvatārasūtra*, a Mahāyāna Buddhist text from the third century CE. Here, the Buddha compares all humans to androids, *yantra-puruṣa*: "This world is like an automated water-powered wheel or a *yantra*; it goes on rolling the cycle of reincarnation, carrying varieties of bodies and forms, resurrecting the dead like *vetālas* (magically reanimated corpses or zombies),[43] causing androids (*yantra-puruṣa*) to move about as if a magician moves them. O Mahāmati, a thorough understanding of these things is called comprehending the selflessness of persons."[44] Here, the android or mechanical man is a metaphor for the selflessness of human beings, just like the other startling image in this passage of the reanimated corpse or *vetāla*, moving but devoid of true self. Since the *Laṅkāvatārasūtra* is arguing that all phenomena are ultimately devoid of essence and that only consciousness is real, the automaton here becomes an apt metaphor for the ultimate soullessness of all things.

A similar idea can be seen in Buddhaghosa's fifth-century Pāli text *Visuddhimagga* (The Path of Purification):

> Therefore, just as a wooden *yantra* is empty, lifeless, and motionless, and yet it walks and stands through the combination of wood and ropes, and seems as if it has activity and occupation, so too is this name and form (*nāmarūpa*) empty, lifeless, and motionless, and yet it walks and stands and seems to have activity and occupation through the combination of interrelated things. This is how it should be seen. Therefore the Ancient Ones said:
>
> Name and form are really here.
> But there is really no human being to be found.
> It is empty and fashioned like an automaton,
> a pile of suffering, like a pile of grass and sticks.[45]

The idea that human beings are themselves machines in one sense or another may be familiar to some readers from European literature, particularly the fantastic fiction of the Romantic era.[46] Similar ideas are encountered in Buddhist robot tales, but the cultural context and, ultimately, the meaning of the human-as-robot metaphor is entirely different in Indian and European literature. The European stories representing humans as robots are dark tales of estrangement, alienation, and lack of meaning. The Buddhist tales, on the other hand, present the idea that we are all robots as an illuminating insight that can ultimately lead to salvation.

While the Hindu robot tales from India articulate a vision of the body as *mūrti*, lifeless material brought to life by the entry of a divine soul, the Buddhist robot stories present robots as our soulless doubles. Androids are a form of simulation, in that they feign what they do not have: humanity.[47] But humanity is in itself viewed as a simulation in Buddhism, a feigning of the nonexistent soul.

The Buddhist androids, then, are the sort of simulation that the French philosopher Jean Baudrillard (1929–2007) calls "hyperreal"; they are simulacra or "models of the real without origin or reality," references without any referents.[48] The notion of a hyperreality, a condition where the real and the virtual are so intermingled that there is no longer a clear distinction between them, is particularly relevant at this moment in time where internet bots can mimic humans, gain Twitter followers and Facebook friends, and become powerful political and social influencers. The signifier and the signified, the real and the mere representation of the real, have collapsed in on each other; copies become a reality unto themselves, and "reality TV" is perceived as capturing something that is "real." But even though the term *hyperreality* is quite recent, the concept is as old as Buddhism. According to the fifth-century CE Buddhist philosopher Vasubandhu, our mental consciousness, *manas*, processes all our sense impressions and projects a coherent, completely simulated model of reality. We create our own false picture of reality, but this pleasant simulacrum needs to be discarded in order for a person to reach enlightenment. Our ego, our sense of self, is a part of this false reality. What does it mean, then, when androids imitate us, when our own selves are just a part of this mental simulation?

The androids may be imitating us, but in a Buddhist sense, we are no more real than they are. The artificial is imitating something equally artificial; there is nothing to separate the "real" from its artificial simulacra. Buddhist robot tales are a play of illusions that reveal that ultimately, even the humanity that the robots imitate is not real; it is all artifice and construction, and this insight is itself true enlightenment.

Chapter 7

The Buddha, the Emperor, and the Killer Robot

Aśoka: The Emperor and the Legend

One of the most striking Buddhist legends of automata involves the well-known historical figure of Aśoka, the emperor who was instrumental in spreading Buddhism far beyond India. Aśoka (Asoka in Pāli) was the grandson of Candragupta Maurya, who founded the Maurya dynasty in India in the fourth century BCE. Aśoka expanded the borders of his grandfather's empire and promoted Buddhism but also introduced many new nondenominational ethical ideas that had profound influence on later Indian culture. Although it is notoriously difficult to assign precise dates to ancient Indian rulers, the dates of Aśoka's reign can be determined with some degree of accuracy to around 270–232 BCE. In one of his edicts, carved into rock, Aśoka mentions communication with five foreign kings, Antiochus, Ptolemy, Antigonus, Magus, and Alexander. These kings have been plausibly identified with Antiochus II Theos of Syria (r. 261–246 BCE), Ptolemy II Philadelphus of Egypt (r. 285–247 BCE), Antigonus Gonatas of Macedonia (r. 276–239 BCE), Magas of Cyrene (r. ca. 258–250 BCE), and Alexander of Epirus (r. 276–255 BCE), which places the date of the rock edict around 256–255 BCE and helps determine the dates of Aśoka's rule.[1] Aśoka's known communication with kings from realms to the west may even have served as inspiration for the later claims in the *Lokapaññatti* that there was contact between the court in Pāṭaliputta in India, and the royal court in Rome.

Buddhist texts construct an image of Aśoka as an ideal world ruler and the very embodiment of the ideal of a *cakravartin*, a benevolent ruler who fuses spiritual and political power in his global reign. The term *cakravartin* literally means "turner of the wheel" and is closely connected with the image of the Buddhist doctrine as a wheel set in motion by the Buddha at the time of his first public sermon, a metaphor that itself conveys a sense of mobility and expansion.[2] A *cakravartin* is, per definition, someone who is instrumental in keeping the wheel of Buddhism moving (fig. 7.1).

While Buddhism began as a small movement in northern India, it expanded into a transregional culture under Aśoka, who

Figure 7.1. Emperor Aśoka. Relief from Amaravati, India. *Source*: Wikimedia Commons, CC BY-SA 3.0.

was himself a convert to the tradition from Hinduism. Through his public edicts, carved into rocks and pillars throughout his empire,[3] Aśoka constructed an overarching imperial ideology around the significant Buddhist term *dhamma* (Sanskrit: *dharma*), which occurs over one hundred times in his brief edicts.[4] This Middle Indic term, which can be translated as "duty," "righteousness," or even "the teaching of the Buddha" is not, however, in Aśoka's edicts associated with uniquely Buddhist ideas such as the Buddha's four noble truths. It is possible, therefore, that the *dhamma*-centered ideology Aśoka was advocating should not necessarily be identified with Buddhism itself, but rather that it constituted a new nondenominational Buddhist-inspired ideology that was meant to transcend religious differences. Out of Aśoka's edicts, we can see a new form of identity emerging, an identity defined more by adherence to a new common ethos than by sectarian or local affiliation.

In one of his edicts, Aśoka expresses deep regret for the loss of life in the battle he had won against the rebellious Kaliṅga people.[5] Rather than celebrate his recent victory, Aśoka mourns his fallen enemies and laments the devastating effects of war. In other edicts, Aśoka advocates for new ethical ideas, such as pardoning prisoners sentenced to death,[6] banning the killing of animals,[7] planting fruit trees to benefit the public,[8] promoting tolerance toward all religions,[9] and providing necessary medicines for both humans and animals.[10]

In addition to his edicts, Aśoka established numerous *stūpas*, or Buddhist shrines containing relics of the Buddha, throughout his empire. Alongside the royal edicts, the *stūpas* served to establish the emerging religion of Buddhism as a physical, monumental imperial presence throughout the Indian landscape. Pious Buddhist legends claim that Aśoka built a staggering eighty-four thousand *stūpas* in India, but the impossibly high number is likely a way of indicating the significance of relic cult as religious worship under Aśoka.[11] While the construction of *stūpas* containing relics appears to be a pre-Buddhist practice as well, Aśoka appropriated this local form of worship as part of an imperial ideology. So effective was Aśoka's *stūpa* construction as a reminder of his status as a *cakravartin* that many later Buddhist monarchs took to building *stūpas* precisely as a way to imitate Aśoka in an attempt to establish themselves as *cakravartins* as well.[12] Aśoka soon became a figure of legend as well as history, and his life story is told in great detail, embellished with several supernatural elements, in texts like the second-century CE Sanskrit *Aśokāvadāna* (The Story of Aśoka).

In the following pages, we will see Aśoka appear as a main character in a medieval Buddhist legend about killer robots guarding the Buddha's relics. What are we to make of Aśoka's role in this curious narrative? I argue that Aśoka's presence in the *Lokapaññatti* signals to the Buddhist reader that the text will involve both royal power and Buddhist piety, two qualities associated with the famous ruler. The killer robots in the tale are part of a larger narrative about kingship, power, relics, and sacred structures, and this framework is essential for understanding the seemingly bizarre narrative about Rome and Pāṭaliputta competing over robot-making technology.

While the narrative begins in Rome (*Romavisaya*, "the region of Rome"), the Rome of the *Lokapaññatti* is a vaguely conceived faraway Otherworld that has little to do with actual ancient Roman civilization. The association of robot-making technology with Rome may, however, hint that the author of the text was familiar with the medieval European legends about the Roman poet Vergil as a creator of automata, as we will see later in this chapter.

The *Lokapaññatti*

While the Indian *yantra* tales we have examined so far in this volume have been infused with a sense of wonder—amazement at the lifelike qualities of an automaton, delight in the skill of the engineer—this chapter is devoted to a medieval Buddhist text that introduces a darker and more sinister element into the Asian *yantra* literature, while still conveying an essentially Buddhist message. Why is the tale of killer robots so different from other *yantra* tales included in this volume? Part of the answer may lie in the text's time of composition, its sources, and its historical context.

The *Lokapaññatti* (The Description of the World or The Image of the World), a Pāli text attested in manuscripts from Myanmar, is generally regarded as a medieval composition. Eugène Denis, in his definitive edition and translation of the text, dates it to the eleventh or twelfth century, a date that has been generally accepted.[13] The *Lokapaññatti* is ascribed to a Saddhammaghosa of Thaton in Lower

Burma, but not much is known about this author.[14] The Pāli text may have been based on a Sanskrit original, the *Lokaprajñapti*, which has been preserved in a Chinese and a Tibetan version, as well as some small Sanskrit fragments in Śāradā script.[15] Sankarnarayan and colleagues date the Sanskrit fragments of the *Lokaprajñapti* to the ninth century CE and the Chinese translation to the eleventh century. Some passages of the *Lokapaññatti* also have parallels in Assaghosa's *Cagatidīpanī*.[16] The portions of the *Lokapaññatti* that deal with the legendary emperor Aśoka and the killer robots from the kingdom of Rome—our topic for this chapter—are, however, only found in the Pāli version from Myanmar.

Denis's edition of the *Lokapaññatti*, which is a revision of his doctoral dissertation, is based on two twentieth-century manuscripts in the Tham script, one from the National Library in Bangkok and one from L'École Française d'Extrême-Orient.[17] Denis also writes that he became aware of a nineteenth-century manuscript from Mandalay but was not able to get it in time to use it for his edition. He also used a Chinese translation (from 588 CE) of a lost Sanskrit *Lokaprajñapti* to restore some corrupted passages, although about 35 percent of the Pāli text has no parallel in the Chinese translation.[18]

Denis proposes that the Pāli *Lokapaññatti* was composed in Burma (Myanmar), based on a reworking of older Sanskrit sources. He dates the text to the eleventh to twelfth centuries CE "for grammatical reasons" but does not specify what these grammatical reasons are. I find it reasonable to believe that the Pāli text may be several centuries later than Denis's estimation, in part because it seems to draw heavily on one of the Pāli versions of the *Thūpavaṃsa*, a text that can be dated with reasonable certainty to the thirteenth century.[19] If the *Lokapaññatti* is dated to the thirteenth to fifteenth rather than the eleventh century, this would place the text's composition at a time period when Thaton, where the text likely originated, was under the rule of the Hanthawaddy Kingdom, which blossomed during this era. The Hanthawaddy Kingdom is associated with a revival of Buddhism, close contacts with Sri Lanka, and an upsurge in religious construction projects. The *Lokapaññatti*'s focus on *stūpa* construction would make perfect sense if the text were indeed composed in a later time period characterized by massive royal building projects. The *Lokapaññatti* is mentioned as one of the texts donated to a particular monastery in a Burmese inscription dated to 1442,[20] although it is not clear that the version of the text referred to here is the Pāli version attested in the manuscripts Denis consulted or a different variant.

The *Lokapaññatti* deals with a wide range of subjects, from descriptions of the human world and its continents, divine realms and hells, to legends of well-known Buddhist characters such as the emperor Aśoka and the legendary monk Upagupta (Pāli: Upagutta). At the heart of the text's complex narrative of Aśoka lies a *stūpa*, discovered by the king himself, containing an unspecified relic of the Buddha. King Ajātasattu, Aśoka's ancestor, comes into possession of this precious relic and builds an elaborate structure to house it, and this *stūpa* is later hidden and rediscovered. Particularly notable is the curious legend of the mechanical men guarding relics of the Buddha, which is unattested elsewhere in Buddhist literature, and the text's insistence that robot-making technology originated in the "kingdom of Rome":[21]

> How is it that in the kingdom of Rome there are many machine-makers who know the art of magic? Their instruments of protection are magical machines with which they accomplish different sorts of actions: commerce, harvesting crops, capturing and executions, and so on. Those skilled in (making) spirit-vehicle-machines (*bhūta-vahana-yanta*) must register their names every month in a book. If one of these experts is not seen, or if he goes away for a long time, one should follow him and kill him with a spirit-vehicle-machine. Thus, there are experts in spirit-vehicle-machines, and they do not seek to leave for another kingdom.

The Rome of the *Lokapaññatti* has very little to do with the historical Roman civilization; the Rome of this narrative functions as a literary counterpart to India. Rome is here a faraway land with highly developed technology but with strange social customs and ruthless possessiveness about its technology. The *Lokapaññatti*'s depiction of the Roman registry of robot-makers and the state-sanctioned execution of those who do not sign in at the correct time has no parallel whatsoever in Roman sources but seems to represent the author's fantasy of a European "Other."

In contrast to the cruel culture of Rome in this narrative, Indian society emerges as humane and enlightened, and ruled over by benign kings. The idea that foreigners keep their android-making technology secret is one encountered elsewhere in Indian literature; we lean in the *Bṛhatkathāślokasaṃgraha*, for example, that Yavanas are particularly anxious to keep the secret of creating flying machines to themselves.[22] But being secretive about one's technology and executing those who access the information without having the proper authorization are of course two entirely different things, and I am not familiar with any other depictions of Rome as a high-tech "police state" of sorts.

It is worth noting that the *Lokapaññatti* differs from many of the other android tales we have encountered in the book in several ways: not only are the androids in this particular tale far more menacing than those in other Asian robot narratives, but they are also associated with magic rather than with just advanced technology. While Higley observes that the killer androids in the text are attributed to "scientific, not necromantic engineering,"[23] there is nevertheless a supernatural element to the androids in the *Lokapaññatti* that is notably absent in other Buddhist robot tales. The *Lokapaññatti* specifically associates the Roman robot technology with magic and refers to the androids created by the Romans as *bhūta-vahana-yanta*, or "spirit-vehicle-machines." A *bhūta*, in both Hinduism and Buddhism, is a spirit. Sometimes *bhūtas* are associated with *pretas*, or ghosts, but although the two types of beings are often identified in modern India (*bhūt-pret* often signifies ghosts in general), there does seem to be a distinction between the two in older texts. It is not at all clear what exactly a *bhūta* signifies in this particular text—is it simply an animating supernatural entity, or a malevolent spirit?—but its presence signals to the reader that the construction of the killer androids requires a knowledge of magic in addition to just technical expertise. We never learn precisely how these "spirits" animate the androids in this story, however. The magical element is quite unusual in the context of Indian robot tales, and it is possible that the uncharacteristic insertion of *bhūtas* into the androids may be an indication of the tale's Burmese origin. The worship of powerful nature spirits (*nat*) has been a significant part of the Burmese folk religion long before the arrival of Buddhism, and even after the conversion to Buddhism, the belief in *nats* still lingers. The spirits that haunt the killer androids in this tale may, then, be a local flourish by the text's Burmese author rather than an idea of Indian origin. While the other supernatural touches in the story are familiar from other Buddhist texts—prophecies uttered by monks or written in ancient texts—the presence of spirits in androids seems to be a distinct local touch.

After this description of Rome, the narrative of the *Lokapaññatti* turns its attention to a young man from India:

> There was a young man born in the city of Pāṭaliputta.[24] He had heard about this fact by popular rumor, namely that in the kingdom of Rome there was a great spirit-vehicle-machine. Then he made a plan and died while saying to himself: "I will make as many such machines as there are people in Pāṭaliputta." Reborn in the kingdom (of Rome), the man from Pāṭaliputta made a home with the daughter of the master of the spirit-vehicle-machines. Later, the master gave to his son-in-law the secret of the spirit-vehicle-machines out of respect. And the latter acquired the knowledge. A little time later, he had a son, and this was in truth a chance for him. While he himself possessed the secret of the spirit-vehicle-machines, out of respect he had never given it either to his son or to other people. Now he said to his son: "I will return to the city of Pāṭaliputta. When they learn of my departure, they will pursue and kill me with a spirit-vehicle-machine that moves through space. After that, you shall go to my country, the country of Dhamma,[25] remove the written sheet concerning the spirit-vehicle-machines hidden inside my thigh, in the middle of the flesh, and take it. Then you shall go to the city of Pāṭaliputta and inquire about my family. You will then win your life with the spirit-vehicle-machine." Having thus given his instructions to his son, he (the machine-maker) ran away. Then the people of Rome discovered during the night that no-one had seen him and understood that he had run away. They met, and then they did pursue him with a spirit-vehicle-machine and kill him. When he (the son) heard that he (his father) was dead, his son pulled out

> the sheet of writing placed inside the thigh of his father, performed the funeral rites for his father, and went to Pāṭaliputta and lived there.

The narrative unfortunately skips over the precise details of how the man from Pāṭaliputta was able to control his next rebirth and end up in Rome. It is also entirely unclear why our twice-dead hero needed to smuggle the instructions for making Roman machines to Pāṭaliputta in such an elaborate and inconvenient way, rather than simply teaching his son the technology, but we should note that the *Lokapaññatti* has a fondness for hidden treasures, and that the machine-maker's instructions hidden inside his dead body may be seen as another such treasure to be discovered. A few years later, an Indian king needs to hide a treasure of his own, and he calls upon the machine-maker's son to help him guard it:

> When King Ajātasattu received a part of the relics of the Blessed One,[26] he asked a monk who possessed supernatural powers: "What should be done now, Venerable One?" The monk, who had looked into the future, said to King Ajātasattu: "O great king, in the future, you will have a descendant named Asoka, king according to *dhamma,* a powerful universal king. So, place the relic in a box made of jewels; this will be contained in a box made from silver. To find a place for this latter box, you need to make a statue of a horse the size of Kaṇṭhaka, the Buddha's own horse, and place the relic in the belly of the horse, using the box to contain it. You shall worship it with great ceremony. Then you must dig the earth below it to the depth of a palm tree in order to obtain a circular area of half a *kosa*[27] surrounded by seven walls. Among these seven walls there will be a brick wall, then inside that a mortar wall, then inside that a wall of good *sal* wood, then inside that a wall of sandal wood, and inside that a wall of aloe tree, then inside that a wall of the most precious woods possessing all perfumes, then inside that a wall made of copper, next to the circular area surrounding the horse Kaṇṭhaka. You will construct, inside of this circular area, a small temple of one story

> made with the seven precious jewels[28] in the form of a pavilion. Inside the temple, on top of level soil and studded with precious jewels, you shall see the statue of the horse Kaṇṭhaka, a precious stone receptacle for the relic. On the four sides of the temple, that venerable monk Mahākassapa, who possesses supernatural powers, will place four lamps, making the following mental vow: *Until someone removes the precious relic, these lamps will not be extinguished, on that subject I make a mental vow.*"
>
> Then the king, in great majesty, presided over a great offering ceremony and placed inside the seven walls, at the interval of one fathom, machines assembled by the man who has come from Rome, which had the form of humans carrying a sword and swirling around. These statues of mechanical men, sword in hand, will slay anyone who poses danger. When he had built that (temple) in order to protect the precious relic, the king had it covered with seven roofs, above the circular area where the temple was found. Then, he covered everything with natural clay and surrounded it by a wall and planted a garden inside the wall. Then the four assemblies[29] came there and made a great ritual offering.

This hidden treasure of the relic, guarded by *yantras* made by Roman technology, is eventually discovered by Aśoka, Ajātasattu's grandson.

> A little time later, King Ajātasattu had a son named Bindusara. He [Bindusara] had a son called Asoka.[30] Asoka read old tablets written in gold and vermillion and saw his name there. He said to himself: "I am indeed the powerful universal king who is called Asoka, king according to *dhamma*, sovereign of Jambudīpa.[31] I will recover the precious bodily relic, and then I will construct eighty-four thousand stūpas[32] in Jambudīpa. But how will I know the place where the precious relic is found?"

An old abbess, who is 120 years old, recalls accompanying her mentor to a sacred mound when she was a young child, and she is eventually able to lead Aśoka to the correct location. But inside the mound, he encounters a problem:

> Having removed the lowest roof, King Asoka, surrounded by a large crowd, saw the whole circular area where the temple was, made from precious stones, surrounded by seven different walls, with different sorts of statues of mechanical men, carrying a sword in the hand, who whirled around the circular area and attacked everything, endowed with life or not, which was within their reach.
>
> Having seen the mechanism placed right in the middle of the seven roofs and seven surrounding walls, King Asoka was frightened and said: "How is it possible to get to the precious relic? With such protection, how is it possible to enter and get the relic?" For seven days the king was content with making ritual offerings to that which was visible.
>
> Then the king, seeking a man clever enough to destroy the mechanism, attached a thousand coins to the forehead of an elephant and had it paraded around with a proclamation made with the sound of drums: "He who is clever enough to destroy the mechanism, he will get the thousand coins." So he paraded it around. The man who was the son of the one who had gone to the kingdom of Rome and who had acquired knowledge of spirit-vehicle-machines, heard the proclamation, and said: "I will destroy the mechanism."

The story does not comment on the fact that the machine-maker's son must be over 120 years old himself, but simply notes that he was able to disable the *yantras* so that Aśoka is able to approach the sacred relic:

> Then the king entered, along with the community of monks and his entourage of ministers. When he saw the relic, he walked three times in a clockwise direction around the circular area where the temple was.[33] The four lamps, about which the venerable Mahākassapa, who had made a mental vow, had spoken due to his supernatural

> power, had not gone out yet. At this sight, the king, full of awe, entered the temple with the community of monks, saw the silver statue of the horse Kaṇṭhaka, walked around it three times clockwise, opened the mechanical door in front of the statue, and saw, placed inside of the horse's belly, a silver box, and inside that the precious bodily relic that shone like a diamond.
>
> Then the king and the community of monks celebrated the relic for seven days with dances, songs, and music, and all sorts of appropriate tributes. They honored it with ritual offering; then they brought out from the temple in the circular area the statue of the horse Kaṇṭhaka, and they returned to the city by a road that was all decorated, nicely cleaned, and adorned with banners and fluttering flags. They went around the village three times clockwise and placed it (the relic) in a great temple.

It is tempting to speculate that the *Lokapaññatti*'s depiction of deadly mechanical men guarding a hidden underground chamber associated with a revered historical figure, a chamber lit by eternally burning lamps, may be inspired by medieval European legends about the tomb of the Roman poet Vergil, which may help explain the text's curious insistence that robot-making technology originates in Rome.[34]

The idea of deadly mechanical men guarding the tomb of an important historical figure—a parallel to the robots guarding the relic of the Buddha—is found in numerous European medieval legends about Vergil.[35] There is no evidence that Vergil was ever associated with automata in antiquity, but from the twelfth century onward, beginning with John of Salisbury's *Policraticus* (ca. 1159), medieval European poets began to claim that Vergil had created several automata, including a bronze fly and a mechanical knight. Not only was Vergil himself frequently evoked as a brilliant inventor of automata in the Middle Ages, but the poet's tomb also features prominently in several legends of automata. Gautier de Metz's thirteenth-century encyclopedic poem *L'image du monde*, for example,[36] describes copper men guarding Vergil's own tomb and attacking those who dare trespass,[37] an idea quite similar to that of the metal men guarding the relics of the Buddha in the *Lokapaññatti. L'Image de monde* was immensely popular throughout Europe during the Middle Ages and translated into several languages, including the well-known English version *The Myrrour of the World,* printed by William Caxton in 1480. It is not inconceivable that the idea of automata guarding a tomb could also have reached the author of the *Lokapaññatti*.[38] Another point of similarity between the European Vergil legends and the Pāli text may be seen in the *Lokapaññatti*'s description of the tomb of the monk Upagupta. While the legendary character of Upagupta recurs in many Buddhist narratives, the *Lokapaññatti* is the only Buddhist text that asserts that this wise monk never died but dwells in a palace made of brass at the bottom of the ocean. The location of Upagupta's palace recalls that of Vergil's tomb in the *Itinerarium cuiusdam Anglici* (1344–1345): "On the eastern shore of the city of Naples rises a very high mountain in [or on] which Vergil is buried. No-one who has any wish to return dares visit the place. Sometimes the storms which rise there to beat upon the city makes its inhabitants think that the whole town is shaking and on the point of being engulfed in the rising waves."[39] But Vergil's burial in a castle under the sea is described even earlier, in an 1194 letter written by Conrad von Querfurt, who was a chancellor of Emperor Henry VI.[40] While burial in a palace under the sea may be a coincidental similarity, the presence of automata, an undersea metal castle, and a metal horse (the Buddha's and Vergil's, respectively) in both texts is intriguing. Furthermore, the association of a tomb, automated guards, and an ever-burning lamp is also found in both the *Lokapaññatti* and the medieval European Vergil legends. Comparetti, in his comprehensive study of Vergil in medieval literature, cites medieval legends of a tomb containing an eternal fire and an automated archer.[41] Comparetti also cites a legend of St. Paul's visit to Vergil's tomb, where the saint finds Vergil seated between two lit candles, next to a mechanical archer with a drawn bow.[42] If he were indeed familiar, directly or indirectly, with the European legends of the Roman poet Vergil, who was himself believed to be an inventor of androids in the Middle Ages, it is perhaps not surprising that the author of the *Lokapaññatti* ascribes the origin of robot-making technology to a vaguely conceived "Rome." We should note that in addition to a constellation of similar motifs, the

Lokapaññatti and *L'Image de monde* even have similar titles; while *Lokapaññatti* is usually translated as "The Description of the World," the *paññatti* of the title could equally well be rendered "reflection" or "image" rather than "description."

How could the European Vergil legends possibly have influenced a text composed in faraway Myanmar? If the *Lokapaññatti* was indeed composed during the Hanthawaddy rule in the thirteenth to fifteenth centuries as I have suggested earlier in this chapter, rather than a few centuries earlier, European influence on the Pāli text would not be difficult to explain. Foreign trade was flourishing in Myanmar during the Hanthawaddy Kingdom, and several European travelers, from Spain, Italy, and Portugal, among others, are known to have spent time at the Hanthawaddy courts. Although direct influence from Europe cannot be proven, the many points of similarity between the Vergil legends and the *Lokapaññatti* are suggestive. But even if one may suspect some influence from the European legends in some of its motifs, this robot tale from the *Lokapaññatti* is very much a Buddhist narrative with a Buddhist message.

The building of *stūpas* features prominently in the *Lokapaññatti*. Following the uncovering of the relic, Aśoka goes on a building spree:

> Then the king had built, in the eighty-four thousand villages of Jambudīpa eighty-four thousand *stūpas* for the sake of humans and earthly deities. He then put aside one part of the relic, divided the rest of the bodily relic into eighty-four thousand parts and sent them on purebred horses to be enshrined in the *stūpas* of Jambudīpa. Then, in the city of Pāṭaliputta, on the banks of the Ganges, he and his court erected a great *stūpa* that had the size of one-half *kosa,* and the floor of that *stūpa* was as flat as the palm of the hand. The *stūpa* was decorated with all sorts of precious stones and surrounded by many banners, flags, parasols, and three-layered parasols. It shone like the hair of the Buddha. With great pomp, the king, accompanied by the community of monks and a great gathering of people, placed inside that *stūpa* the part of that precious relic that he had previously put aside.

But at this point, rumor of the relic guarded by mechanical swordsmen reaches Rome, which leads to complications:

> At that time, Asoka, king according to the Dhamma, had become famous in all regions. The king had unearthed the bodily relic buried by his ancestor King Ajātasattu. He had constructed numerous *stūpas* and dedicated eighty-four thousand *stūpas*. His fame gradually extended and eventually reached the kingdom of Rome.
>
> The king of Rome, having heard tell of him, called together his machine-makers and asked them: "Tell me, by whom were they made, the mechanical men of King Asoka, which carry a sword in the hand and swirl around the circular area where the temple of the bodily relic is?" They answered: "Your Majesty, there is a machine-maker who escaped our king, your ancestor. It is he who has built these machines, and it is by him that they are now destroyed. And everything was done according to the rule in the book of the machine-makers." The king said: "I really wonder how a man who has knowledge of the spirit-vehicle-machines can be in the city of Pāṭaliputta. You, makers of machines, will make a metal chest outfitted with a mechanism. Inside it you shall place a statue of a man, a spirit-vehicle-machine who carries a sword. Then place a secret mechanism outside that and send the chest via messengers to Asoka in the city of Pāṭaliputta as a present filled with precious jewels, in homage to the king's meritorious deeds." The machine-makers agreed and said: "Very well, your majesty." They quickly made the metal chest as it should be made and sent it.

The narrative of the *Lokapaññatti* plays out in two real-world geographical locations, Pāṭaliputta and Rome, but its history is pure fiction. The tale ostensibly begins during the reign of the Indian kings Ajātasattu (Ajātaśatru) and Asoka (Aśoka), around the fifth to third centuries BCE. The faraway land of Rome is identified as a kingdom with a reigning king, although Rome did not have a king after 509 BCE, and certainly not during the reign of Aśoka. It is unclear how much knowledge the author of the text has of

Rome and of Roman civilization, but assigning a king to Rome makes this distant land a parallel and foil to the realm ruled over by the righteous Indian kings Ajātasattu or Aśoka. The king of Rome does not play a great part in the story, however, apart from sending a deadly gift to Aśoka, which signals his deceptive nature. Aśoka is pleased to receive a gift from Rome but wise enough to ask the *yantra*-maker's son for advice:

> Then the mighty king looked for the machine-maker. He arrived quickly, and the king said to him: "Master, open this metal chest filled with precious stones of an inestimable value. We wish to see them." The machine-maker examined the chest and divined that a spirit-vehicle-machine was hidden inside it. He examined it closely, and then he knew the truth. Then he thought: "This is not a chest of precious stones. In reality, this is a plan to kill me. There is for sure a statue of a man inside that is a spirit-vehicle-machine carrying a sword. The instant I open it, it will cut off my head."
>
> When he had discovered this, his hair stood on end, and he said to the king: "Your majesty, believe what I'm saying. A man like me, who has knowledge of spirit-vehicle-machines, is hard to find. My father, who was reborn in the kingdom of Rome, lost his life in pursuit of this science; and I who have acquired this knowledge have now come to your majesty's kingdom. Your majesty will want to save my life." The king asked: "Why do you speak like this?" He answered: "In truth, your majesty, I know that this precious chest is not filled with precious stones of inestimable value; rather, it contains a spirit-vehicle-machine carrying a sword to kill me. Thus, if I open the chest, at the very moment I open it, the spirit-vehicle-machine will come out of the chest and cut my head off. After he has cut it off, he will leave through the air and go back to the kingdom of Rome." When he heard these words, the king became terrified, and he asked anew: "How do you know that a spirit-vehicle-machine is found inside with a sword in the hand and that it will come out and cut your head

> off?" "Sir, thanks to my seven powers, I know that it will do so."
>
> The king asked his ministers: "What should be done?" The ministers answered him: "Sir, do not believe his words. It is a chest of precious jewels." The machine-maker said: "It is not a chest of precious stones; it is a chest destined to kill me." Then the minsters asked him: "Then what is to be done?" He answered: "Make a great fire and burn the chest. That is what should be done." The ministers said to the king: "Sir, the machine-maker has this deadly fear and he said something or other, imagining things that are not true. Sir, open the chest!" Then the king commanded him (the machine-maker): "Open it, master, I command you, do not be afraid." He responded: "Sir, if your majesty commands me with determination, I will open it. But sir, kindly permit me to go home first, to give a gift to my wife and children and bid them my farewell, and then I will return and open the chest on your majesty's order." The king let him go.

The machine-maker's son had no choice but to put his affairs in order and obey the king:

> He went, did everything that needed to be done at home, returned rapidly, gave his homage to the king, and entrusted his family to him. Then, turning his face toward the chest, he meditated on the three jewels[43] and opened the chest. At the very moment he lifted the lid, the mechanical man came out, cut his head off as one cuts off the bud on a stick of bamboo, disappeared through the air, and went back to the kingdom of Rome. Frightened the king said: "Alas! That mechanical man was indeed a spirit. As he said, the precious stones were nothing but a mechanical man who cut off his head and left. The king's ministers were reprimanded. Then the king Asoka ruled according to the law until the day when he made a final offering of splendid *amalaka* flowers and went to heaven.

While this narrative may at first glance seem very different from the other Buddhist *yantra* narratives we have encountered so far, I argue that this tale, in spite of its focus on buried treasure and killer robots, is still primarily a Buddhist text about religion and kingship.

Panikkar reads this text as one dealing with the future of human civilization, a warning about technology run amok. He interprets "Rome" in the story as a "symbol of the Western spirit,"[44] and of dangerous technology in general. The West in this narrative becomes, for Panikkar, the villain of the tale, introducing to India a soulless technology, and he ends his analysis poetically: "In sum, the destiny of the technological civilization is death."[45] Is this tale of the killer robots from Rome a warning against developing technology that cannot be controlled, machines that will end up controlling *us*? While Pannikar's reading is appealing in many ways and certainly resonates with a modern audience, it is also very obviously ahistorical; the message about the dangers of modern Western technology is likely not one intended by a medieval Buddhist author from Myanmar.

The *Lokapaññatti* is a tale of two kingdoms, one ruled by a tyrant and one by an enlightened Buddhist monarch. Significantly, they use the dangerous technology of the "spirit-vehicle-machines" entirely differently. While the Romans use the technology for practical purposes such as trade or agriculture, they are also quick to use their technology for destructive purposes, such as killing rogue robot-makers who might reveal their secrets or decapitating the king of a rival kingdom. The Indians in the story, in contrast, only use the androids to protect the sacred relics of the Buddha, and no harm comes to anyone in the process.

Significantly, there are two jeweled boxes in this story: one containing the relics of the Buddha, and the other a mechanical man programmed to kill. The parallel between the two treasures, the relics and the robot, are underscored at several points in the narrative: the secret of how to make robots is as closely guarded as the location of the relics, but both secrets are revealed in documents found by a worthy heir (the robot-maker's son and the emperor Aśoka, respectively). But the two jeweled boxes also point to a significant difference between the two kingdoms and their rulers: while the pious Indian kings Ajātasattu and Aśoka are primarily interested in the spiritual treasure that is the relic of the Buddha, the king of Rome treasures his marvelous technology over all things. For Ajātasattu, the *yantras* are not the actual treasure; they are just a means to protect the true treasure, which is the religious relic. But for the Romans of the tale, the deadly *yantra* is the treasure that must be jealously guarded. The Roman jeweled box containing the robot and the Indian jeweled box containing the relic therefore represent two sets of values in the story, and perhaps even two forms of kingship, one focused on worldly power and the other on religious piety. Both the jeweled boxes are associated with death, but the Roman box is associated with deception and violent death at the hands of an android, while the Indian box is associated with the blessed relics of the Buddha.

The *Lokapaññatti* and the Hanthawaddy Kingdom

If we assume that the *Lokapaññatti* was indeed composed in Thaton in the thirteenth to fifteenth centuries, many aspects of the text become even more meaningful. Kingship plays a significant role in the *Lokapaññatti*; the two Indian kings Ajātasattu and Aśoka are both ideal Buddhist kings, ruling according to *dhamma*, preserving the Buddha's precious relics, and building appropriate structures to house them. The Hanthawaddy kings modeled their kingship specifically on Aśoka and claimed to be new *cakravartins* and preservers of the *dhamma*. The *Kalyani* inscriptions from the Hanthawaddy Kingdom, for example, explicitly identify the Hanthawaddy king Dhammazedi (1472–1492), who was an ordained Buddhist monk prior to his appointment to the throne, with Aśoka.[46] The Kalyani inscriptions further claim that the region of Burma ruled over by the Hanthawaddy kings was part of Suvannabhūmi, the "Golden Land," to which Aśoka's monks had brought both Buddhism itself and Buddhist relics from Pāṭaliputta.[47]

If the version of the Pāli *Lokapaññatti* available to us was composed during the reign of King Dhammazedi, the text's preoccupation with the discovery and restoration of an ancient religious site housing the relics of the Buddha would be particularly meaningful. One of Dhammazedi's main accomplishments was the restoration of the famed Shwedagon pagoda, which today remains one of Myanmar's most well-known landmarks. This pagoda, which was likely constructed during the sixth to tenth centuries and rumored to contain relics of four different Buddhas, including several strands of hair from Siddhattha Gotama himself, the historical founder of Buddhism, had fallen into disrepair. Its rebuilding had begun under the Hanthawaddy king Binnya U (1323–1384), continued under Queen Binnya Thau (1453–1472), and was successfully completed under Dhammazedi.

The emphasis on Aśoka's piousness and that of the monastic order in the *Lokapaññatti* might also be of particular concern during the reign of Dhammazedi, when the king was troubled by the lack of monastic rigor among the Burmese monks and insisted that twenty-two senior monks accompanied by junior monks and other attendants travel to Sri Lanka to be trained properly and reordained in the traditional manner.[48]

The *Lokapaññatti*'s preoccupation with written texts also makes sense in the context of the Hanthawaddy era flourishing of Buddhist literature and frequent importing of significant manuscripts from abroad (such as Pāli texts from Sri Lanka). There is an unusual number of written texts in the *Lokapaññatti,* ranging from the Roman robot-maker registry, via the robot-maker's instructions for how to build automata, to the ancient manuscripts read by the young Aśoka in the text. While the vision of Aśoka poring over ancient gilded-leaf manuscripts is historically unlikely—Falk, in his historical overview of writing in India proposes that Aśoka may have invented script in India[49]—Aśoka is himself deeply connected with writing in the popular Buddhist imagination due to the numerous rock and pillar edicts he had carved around his empire. One may wonder why the initial robot-maker in the *Lokapaññatti* narrative has to come up with such a very complicated way of transmitting his knowledge of automata to his son. Surely, it would have been simpler to convey the information orally and in secret, rather than sewing the manuscript into one's thigh and arranging for one's own death? But the *Lokapaññatti* privileges written texts and manuscripts as media for conveying essential information, something that makes perfect sense for a text composed in a highly literate culture that treasures written manuscripts, especially those that are old or imported from faraway lands. The ancient text that Aśoka reads in the *Lokapaññatti* is, however, anachronistically Burmese in appearance; manuscripts written on gold leaves are not at all common in India, while several lovely examples have been found in Myanmar.[50] Vermilion is also frequently used in the production of ornate Burmese manuscripts.

The construction of *stūpas* is a particularly important theme in the *Lokapaññatti*, and it must have resonated deeply with an audience in thirteenth- to fourteenth-century Thaton, who would have seen new and magnificent structures being erected by the Hanthawaddy kings (1287–1539). The *Lokapaññatti*'s narrative provides a good explanation for how one could possibly have relics associated with the historical Buddha in places far from India; the original relic belonged to Ajātasattu, who lived close enough to the Buddha's own lifetime to make his possession of a relic plausible, and Aśoka's subsequent rediscovery of the original relic explains both how he came to build so many *stūpas*, and how original relics came to be associated with them all.

Although the *Lokapaññatti* narrative unfolds in Pāṭaliputta in India—with a brief detour to Rome—it is very understandable that Higley, in her discussion of the text, assumes that the young robot-maker in the text is from Burma.[51] While this character is explicitly identified as an Indian from Pāṭaliputta in the text, I would argue that the narrative's Pāṭaliputta is discursively equated with the Burmese kingdom familiar to its audience, an identification implied by references to familiar Buddhist building structures and materials, models of kingship, and the ornate form of gold-and-vermilion manuscripts. The Pāṭaliputta of the narrative is made familiar to the Burmese audience; at a time when dilapidated Buddhist structures were restored by the Hanthawaddy kings, the tale of Aśoka's discovery and restoration of the shrine that houses the Buddha's own relic would surely resonate in powerful ways. In contrast, the land of Rome in the text is depicted as ruthless and unfamiliar, a land terrorized by robots. The only action we see the king of Rome take in the story is deceptive; he pretends to send the king of Pāṭaliputta a gift, while the gift actually contains a robot programmed to kill. Blackburn observes that Buddhists in the region that we would now call Southeast Asia "placed themselves in a sacred geography they understood to have been constituted in the 3rd century BCE when the Indic king Aśoka . . . , following his conquest of the Kingdom of Kalinga in coastal Orissa, was said to have renounced violence and sent monks out from his capital at Pataliputra on the Ganges."[52] Blackburn's insight finds support in the *Lokapaññatti,* where the city of Pāṭaliputta and its pious kings are narratively presented as the story's "here," its familiar center, in spite of the text's composition in Burma many centuries after the reign of Aśoka. The message of the *Lokapaññatti,* then, seems to be that a mechanical *yantra* can serve as a protector of both the Buddha and the *dhamma,* but only if it is employed in the service of an enlightened Buddhist monarch, such as those of Pāṭaliputta or Thaton.

Chapter 8

Interpreting Indian Robot Tales

Robots, Fantasy, and Science Fiction

How should we classify the Indian robot tales we have examined in this volume as literature? Are they early fantasy literature, science fiction, religious myths, or something else?

Modern fantasy literature is often classified as a subgenre of that which we may call the fantastic. The most seminal modern work on this genre is Tzvetan Todorov's *The Fantastic: A Structural Approach to a Literary Genre.*[1] Todorov defines fantastic literature as works "in which events occur that cannot be explained by rational laws, and in which the reader hesitates to the very end as to whether these events have rational explanations or are the product of rational forces operating in everyday reality."[2] Todorov differentiates, however, between the fantastic and the uncanny. In fantastic stories, the premise is that there are irrational forces at work in the universe, whereas in stories of the uncanny, the seemingly supernatural events have a rational explanation. He draws a distinction between the fantastic and the marvelous; the fantastic is characterized by a hesitation—in the characters as well as in the reader—about whether certain events are supernatural or not, while stories that introduce entirely new natural laws different from those of the ordinary world belong to the genre that Todorov defines as "the marvelous."[3] He writes: "The fantastic is that hesitation experienced by a person who knows only the laws of nature, confronting an apparently supernatural event."[4] Todorov's definition of "the fantastic" fits many Western android narratives, such as Hoffmann's "The Sandman," or Gustav Meyrink's *The Golem*, but the Indian android tales do not fit as comfortably into this category. The painter who falls in love with the mechanical maiden experiences no hesitation over the status of the servant girl; he is convinced that she is fully human until the moment when she is revealed to be a machine. The reader of this tale, however, knows from the very beginning of the story that the girl is an android, since the narrator obligingly tells us so, so there is no hesitation on the reader's part either. Similarly, there is no hesitation on the part of the princess who sees the weaver flying in the mechanical Garuḍa as to whether she sees a divine bird or a machine, a god or a man. The robots in the Indian texts are perfect illusions of reality, causing no doubt or hesitation in their audience as to what their true nature may be.

But there are other definitions of fantasy literature that go far beyond Todorov's rather narrow definition of the fantastic. In his essay on fantasy literature, "On Fairy Stories," Tolkien defines fantasy as a genre characterized by an "arresting strangeness"[5] that takes the reader out of her everyday world and brings her into the realm of the imagination. Taking traditional fairy tales as his starting point, Tolkien defines "Fairy Stories" in the widest possible sense as narratives that take place in an enchanted Otherworld he refers to as "Faerie" or "The Perilous Realm,"[6] a secondary world that is defined in contrast to the primary world of our ordinary everyday existence. Tolkien writes: "Fantasy, the making or glimpsing of Other-worlds, was at the heart of the desire of Faerie."[7] This enchanted Otherworld of fantasy operates according to laws of its own, which may be quite different from those of our own world. Tolkien's own *Lord of the Rings* trilogy clearly fits into this definition of fantasy; while Middle Earth may resemble our everyday world in some ways, it is also filled with hobbits, elves, dwarves, dragons, and magic.

Echoing Tolkien, Mobley argues that fantasy requires the readers to enter "an Other World and following a hero whose adventures take place in a reality far removed from the mundane reality of the reader's waking experience. This world is informed by Magic, and the reader must be willing to accept Magic as the central force."[8]

James and Mendlesohn, in their introduction to *The Cambridge Companion to Fantasy Literature*, also build on Tolkien's understanding of the distinction between the everyday world and the enchanted Otherworld when they define fantasy as "the construction of the impossible," as opposed to science fiction, which is about "the unlikely," but scientifically possible.[9]

Do these definitions of fantasy fit our Indian robot tales? Do the *yantras* of ancient India inhabit an Otherworld? No, not quite. The robot tales in this volume may include supernatural elements, divine intervention, as well as occasional magic, but they are not set in an enchanted Otherworld different from the realm of everyday life. Gods and spirits may at times play parts in these narratives, but the tales are nevertheless set in the realm of humans, in a world populated by carpenters, artisans, weavers, and kings, a world recognizable to the audience as their own.

In Indian literature overall, there is often little distinction between *this* world and a radically different Otherworld. There may be an occasional exception; the *Kathāsaritsāgara* tale about the princess and the demon's daughter depicts princess Kaliṅgasenā's brief visit to the home of the demons in the Vindhyā mountains, a place that "looked like another and marvelous world." But even the home of the demons, with its waters of immortality, magnificent gardens, and shifting walls is not a true Otherworld in Tolkien's sense; it has a known, mundane geographical location and is created by the demons' power of illusion.

There are certainly other worlds besides the human one in the Indian worldview, distant places where gods or demons dwell. But the robot tales do not usually take place there; robots are part of the realms of the humans. But the human world where *yantras* are built and move about is not entirely devoid of enchantment in Indian literature; this world is frequently visited by superhuman agents of different kinds. Hindu gods can be incarnated as humans, ghosts and demons can threaten the human world, and all kinds of supernatural entities can curse and bless the humans they meet on their way.

In Western literature, fantasy is often contrasted with realistic literature, whose aim is to depict the world more or less as it is, or at least, as it could be. Realistic literature tells us what *could* have happened, in a world indistinguishable from the real one in which we live. Fantastic literature, on the other hand, defies the conventions of the real world; it is concerned with events that could not ever take place in the real world, but only in the realm of the imagination. But this distinction between the realistic and the fantastic becomes meaningless in ancient India, whose vast literature does not differentiate between a secular "realistic" realm and a supernatural one.

It is quite impossible to view fantastic literature as a separate genre in ancient India, since elements of the fantastic are encountered in almost all literary forms of classical Indian literature. Ancient Indian literature is (with some notable exceptions) rarely defined by an absolute realism. While Tolkien defines the Otherworld as a perilous land, ancient Indian literature is based on the radically different premise that it is *this world* that is the perilous and mystical land of Faerie, where the inexplicable and supernatural can easily happen, which explains the prevalence of *adbhuta* in the Indian tales.

Rosemary Jackson, in her important study *Fantasy: The Literature of Subversion*, argues that fantasy literature expresses the fundamental desires and anxieties of a culture, impulses that are normally suppressed. She defines fantasy as that which "traces the unsaid and unseen of culture: that which has been silenced, made invisible, covered over and made absent."[10] Drawing on psychoanalytical theory, she sees fantasy as a genre that expresses unconscious drives and anxieties. Significantly, she does not associate fantasy with a Tolkienian Otherworld; rather, she sees fantasy as "inverting the elements of this world, re-combining its constitutive features in new relations"[11] and articulating hidden desires. In a similar vein, Ursula K. Le Guin writes that "fantasy, like poetry, speaks the language of the night," of things ordinarily kept hidden.[12]

While such a reading of early European tales of automata is quite possible, can we also read Indian robot tales as stories of hidden or suppressed desires, a reversal of the ordinary world? This approach is fruitful when applied to some of the Indian android stories; a few of these tales do articulate hidden longings and culturally repressed desires. In a hierarchically structured society where such things are normally impossible, automata allow a weaver to marry a princess, and a craftsman and a king to travel to faraway lands together as friends. But I do not think that Jackson's reading of fantasy literature as naturally subversive, as a way of articulating that which has been repressed and glossed over by mainstream culture, necessarily applies to all the Indian android tales in this volume. On the contrary, the tale of the killer Roman robots in the *Lokapaññatti*, for example, is not at all politically subversive; rather, it seems to be a celebration of a specific form of Buddhist kingship and power, serving a particular political and ideological purpose at the time of its composition. Likewise, the texts that describe the delights of all the automata in the royal pleasure gardens are clearly in favor of both royalty and lavish spending on their palaces and gardens.

In general, I do not find it useful to read these ancient Indian texts as fantasy literature. The categories of "fantasy" and "the fantastic" are useful analytical tools in the study of European texts because there exists a large body of realistic literature with which the fantastic can be contrasted. In ancient Indian literature, on the other hand, no such contrast is possible; *all* ancient Indian literature contains realistic and supernatural elements interwoven into a seamless whole. Ancient Indian texts, in all preserved genres, describe a world where humans, gods, demons, spirits, and enlightened teachers interact with each other, where natural laws operate, and where higher forces may intervene at will. The contrast between the "real world" and the Otherworld that we find in Western literature does not exist in ancient India; it is all one world, where anything can and will happen.

Can we then classify the ancient Indian robot tales as early science fiction instead? These tales are certainly based on "imagined development of science," which Davenport identifies as a crucial aspect of science fiction.[13] These narratives are fantasies about flying machines, artificially constructed humans, and automated animals, all of which are perfectly possible, even if the technology to create such inventions was not yet available in ancient India. But while much of modern European and American science fiction is set in a world that only differs from the "real" one in one aspect, that of an imagined superior technology, the ancient Indian tales of *yantras* include many supernatural elements as well. In the tale of the weaver and the princess, for example, the flying Garuḍa bird is a mechanically constructed flying machine that *could* exist in a technologically advanced society. But the presence of an actual divine Garuḍa that can enter into a machine and bring it to life introduces a supernatural element that is often absent from European or American science fiction.

Science fiction is a relatively recent genre, although Fredericks has argued that science fiction elements can be identified in texts as early as Lucian's second-century *True History*, which involves a flight to the moon, alien life-forms, and artificial life.[14] Others have traced the beginnings of science fiction to Mary Shelley's *Frankenstein* (1818), or to the works of Jules Verne. What many of these tales have in common is that they depict events that are not possible *yet*, but which could conceivably be possible in the future. Although religious science fiction does exist and even though many science fiction stories may deal with religious themes, explicit references to gods and other supernatural entities are often absent from Western science fiction, however.

But what about contemporary Indian science fiction? Does the science fiction genre as it exists in modern-day India incorporate as many supernatural aspects as the ancient robot tales? Science fiction as a genre has enjoyed limited popularity in modern India, but it is increasingly recognized as a legitimate and valuable form of literature. Modern Indian science fiction explores many of the same themes as Western science fiction: advanced technology, space travel, time travel, and robots. But intriguingly, Indian science fiction often incorporates elements of traditional Hindu or Buddhist mythologies as well. Dr. Srinarahari Mysore, the general secretary for the Indian Association for Science Fiction Studies, points to the frequent "mythical elements" in contemporary Indian science fiction when he traces the historical origins of Indian sci-fi back to the Hindu epics, with their flying chariots.[15] He sees modern Indian science fiction as a genre beginning with Jagadananda Roy's 1879 Bengali short story "Śukra Bhramaṇ" (Journey to Venus) and Ambika Dutt Vyas's 1884 Hindi serial *Āścary Vṛttānt* (The Strange Tale), which features a journey to the center of the earth. Hemlal Dutta's 1882 Bengali short story "Rahasya" (Mystery) features a fully automated house, complete with an automatic doorbell, a burglar alarm, and a mechanical clothes brush. According to Dr. Mysore, the first Indian robot story is Durga Prasad Khatri's "Lohe ke ādmī" (The Men of Iron), which features a robot-maker, Professor Gamat, whose robots end up rebelling against him.[16] Dr. Mysore suggests that this story may be inspired by Čapek's *Rossum's Universal Robots,* which features a similar plot line. Although Indian science fiction writers may draw inspiration from foreign science fiction classics, they also frequently cite ancient Sanskrit texts such as the *Ṛgveda* or the *Bhagavadgītā* and incorporate familiar themes from Indian myths as well.

Raminder Kaur differentiates between two strands of contemporary science fiction in India: one strand with an optimistic faith in modern science and technology, which produces the sort of narratives where the technology may itself assume a mythological character, and a different strand, akin to that identified by Mysore, which draws on ancient mythology as a source for a sort of "proto science fantasy."[17] I would argue that we see the technological optimism and belief in the boundless possibilities in science in several ancient Indian robot tales as well, alongside the mythical elements. And as we have seen in Bhoja's *Samarāṅgaṇasūtradhāra,* a faith in technology and science can still be part of a larger religious worldview.

This blending of mythology and science is particularly popular in modern Bengali language science fiction from India. In Bengali literature, *kalpavigyan* (literally, "fantasy science") is a recognized local form of science fiction. Debjani Sengupta traces the origins of the Bengali *kalpavigyan* genre to a subversive reworking of the colonially imposed science education and neo-enlightenment ideology.[18] *Kalpavigyan* blends fantasy, Indian mythology, and science, but in doing so it creates a new and local alternative to the imperial imaginary.[19] This fusion of modern science and traditional Indian mythology is not limited to Bengal, however, even though it remains particularly popular there. Traditional mythological elements are found in almost all contemporary Indian science fiction narratives, from short stories and novels to films. It may be possible, then, to see the ancient Indian *yantra* tales, which fuse scientific and religious elements, as precursors to a particular kind of modern Indian science fiction, more mythologically oriented than its European or American counterparts.

Even though science fiction as a genre has been somewhat marginal in modern Indian literature until very recently, interest in science fiction books, television shows, and films is on the rise. The first Indian robot film was the 2002 Kannada-language movie

Hollywood, directed by Dinesh Babu. The film's main character is the socially awkward nerd Surendra, an Indian living in California, who pines for his lovely neighbor Manisha. Manisha, however, is more interested in Surendra's dashing twin brother, Upendra. Surendra brings his problems to his engineering professor, who decides to help his protégé out by creating an android copy of Surendra to woo the girl for him. This android, U47, is programmed with human skills, including seduction skills, but also human emotions. While the android turns out to be much better than its human counterpart when it comes to flirting, U47 is carried away by its programmed human emotions, falls in love with Manisha, and wants her for himself. The professor tries to solve the problem by creating a robot Manisha as a suitable mate for the robot Surendra, but then the American mafia kidnaps them all. While audiences liked the idea of a human man and his robot double competing for the same girl, the film received only mediocre reviews.

A similar plot resurfaced in an Indian film eight years later, but this time in a far more polished form. The fantastic critical and popular success of the 2010 Tamil-language science fiction film *Enthiran,* directed by S. Shankar, demonstrates that fascination with robots is alive and well in India. The Hindi version of the film was renamed *Robot,* which conveys the idea that the film is about an android but unfortunately loses the religious resonance of the original Tamil title; *Enthiran* is the Tamil term for *yantra*.[20] This science fiction/action/comedy film pays lighthearted homage to numerous classic European and American science fiction films; *Enthiran* is filled with visual allusions to *Metropolis, Star Wars,* the *Terminator* films, and several others. One of the messenger droids in the beginning of the film is actually called R2—a nod to the beloved *Star Wars* droid R2D2—and in one of the robot dance scenes in the film, a whole ensemble of golden androids that look very much like *Star Wars'* C-3PO, dances with the film's main robot star. But *Enthiran,* significantly, introduces an element of *adbhuta* as a tool for religious insight that is absent from its Western counterparts.

The main character of *Enthiran,* the obsessed scientist Vaseegaran, creates an advanced android by the name of Chitti (literally, "little brother") in order to assist the Indian army. Both the scientist and the robot are played by the same actor, the superstar Rajinikanth, who is so immensely popular that some of his fans actually refer to him as a god rather than a man.[21] The android Chitti has immense intelligence, superhuman strength, the martial art capacities of Bruce Lee, and fantastic dance moves. But just like the *golem* of Jewish legends, he sometimes takes verbal expressions much too literally; when a corrupt police officer offers to forgive a parking fine if Chitti will just "give him a cut," Chitti obligingly slashes the officer's hand. The film deliberately avoids marking Chitti visually or verbally as a machine, however, unlike Hoffmann's Olimpia with her stiff, unnatural movements and *Star Trek*'s Data with his inhuman pallor and artificially formal speech patterns, Chitti blends in easily among the humans. The only real difference between Chitti and his maker is that Chitti has better hair, cool sunglasses, and smoother dance moves. The boundaries between man and robot blur at several points in the film, especially when Vaseegaran himself is shown to be lacking in proper human emotions due to his absorption in his work, and his robot begins to bond with both his parents and his girlfriend in his stead. Chitti, as it turns out, performs humanity better than his maker.

At one point in the film, someone mentions God, and Chitti asks curiously what "God" is. When he is told that God is the creator, he exclaims with delight that then Vaseegaran must be God. This naïve remark illustrates the robot's lack of understanding of traditional religious concepts, but there is perhaps more to Chitti's remark than just a humorous misunderstanding. When Chitti points to the robot-maker played by Rajinikanth and declares him to be God, this is both an echo of the traditional idea that the robot-maker is "playing God" when creating an artificial human being and an ironic acknowledgment that, to the film's fans, the actor who brings the robot-maker (and the robot) to life is himself a god.

Trouble ensues when the robot falls in love with Vaseegaran's neglected girlfriend, Sana, and when the scientist's evil mentor, Professor Bohra, tries to co-opt the robot and sell him to European terrorists. At one point in the film, the villain installs a "red chip" in Chitti that transforms him from his sweet and well-meaning self into an evil double (cf. Maria's destructive double in *Metropolis*). This evil robot double sports a leather jacket, which signals to a devout Hindu audience that he is even associated with killing of cows, a powerful cultural taboo in India. This bad, leather-clad version of Chitti kidnaps Sana and tries to murder his own maker before Vaseegaran finally manages to remove the "red chip" (and the leather jacket). At the film's end, Chitti dismantles himself at his maker's command in a moment filled with great pathos.

While *Enthiran*'s plot may seem familiar—one can easily recognize plot elements from *Frankenstein*, *Terminator*, and *Metropolis*—one thing that makes *Enthiran* unique is the audience's response to the film's main star, Rajinikanth. Fan adoration of actors is of course nothing new, but Rajinikanth, who plays both the robot and its human maker, is actually the subject of religious worship, as a *Washington Post* headline announced: "India's biggest action-movie star isn't just an actor. He is god."[22] Indian movie star fandom is often particularly intense, but in the case of the south Indian actor Rajinikanth, his fans' fervor has literally turned into worship: Fans treat the release of his films as religious occasions, shave their heads and offer special prayers in temples, and throw coins and other sacrificial offerings at the movie screen when the actor appears. They treat the advertising cardboard cutouts bearing the actor's likeness as *mūrtis* and bathe them in milk as a religious offering.[23] As the producer of Rajinikanth's 2016 film *Kabali*, S. Thanu, observed: "Rajinikanth is not a human being. He is not an actor. He is [a] god."[24]

What does it mean, then, when a robot is depicted on-screen by an actor who is himself worshipped as a god? Intriguingly, Rajinikanth bringing the robot Chitti to "life" on the screen parallels the divine Garuḍa bringing the robotic bird to life in the tale of the weaver and the princess: the automaton, brought to life by a god, itself becomes a *mūrti*—which explains the sacrificial offerings thrown at the screen when Rajinikanth appears as a killer robot. Chitti's "divine" nature is visually illustrated in one of the film's many fight scenes. Chitti is attacked by a gang of street performers bearing daggers and swords, but he turns his metal body into a magnet and attracts all the weapons to himself. For a stunning moment, the android surrounded by a halo of swords and daggers, looks like the familiar image of the many-armed Hindu goddess Durgā bearing the weapons of all the gods. In the film, the stunned spectators even begin to chant "Mother Goddess" as Chitti approaches. While this scene is mildly humorous, it is simultaneously a reminder of the beloved Hindu text *Devīmāhātmya*, which tells of the origin of the goddess and her weapons. Later in the film, when Chitti turns evil due to the "red chip," Professor Bohra even quips, "He's an *asura* [demon] now." This demonic version of Chitti is still performing a familiar religious text for the audience, for when he kidnaps his maker's bride Sana, he chides her for crying like Sītā, the faithful wife who was kidnapped by a demon in the *Rāmāyaṇa* epic. Dr. Mysore's assertion that Indian science fiction is infused with mythology certainly holds true for this film as well.

The sequel to *Enthiran*, the 2018 film *2.0*, also features Rajinikanth in the double role of Vaseegaran the robot-maker and Chitti the android. This film is rich in echoes of the Hindu tale of the weaver and the mechanical bird, reinterpreted in the light of contemporary ecological concerns. The film begins with smart phones flying away all through the south Indian city of Chennai. The flying phones assemble in a bird formation and proceed to kill several people connected to the cell phone industry. With the help of Chitti, Vaseegaran discovers that the "bird" is powered by the ghost of an ornithologist significantly named Pakshi Rajan (Bird King), another name for Garuḍa. Upset that cell phone towers were killing birds, Pakshi killed himself and now haunts the city's cell phones. Pakshi's ghostly aura is eventually confronted by a flock of microbots, called Kutti 3.0, that look like miniature versions of Chitti, riding on pigeons. Pakshi's aura is destroyed, but Vaseegaran says at the film's end that people need to limit their use of cell phones so birds will not be harmed by cell phone towers. The film's ecological message is given a religious significance through the obvious visual resemblance of Kutti/mini-Chitti riding on the pigeon to the god Viṣṇu riding on Garuḍa. The fusion of religious and technological themes aligns the film in interesting ways with the ancient legends of automata explored in this volume. The film's advertising poster features a stunning bird made up of cell phones, but this futuristic image of the artificial bird bears a strong visual resemblance to traditional depictions of Garuḍa, which conveys to a Hindu audience that the bird's message in the film should be taken very seriously. In both of these films, robots and mechanical devices have the potential to become icons, in a very literal sense. While constantly changing shape, multiplying, and shifting through multiple forms, the robots have the potential to become *mūrtis*, as seen when the camera captures the moments when Chitti becomes Durgā, Kutti becomes Viṣṇu, and a stream of flying cell phones becomes the divine Garuḍa. In both films, the *yantra* becomes the site for the audience's encounter with the divine: an unexpected glimpse of a deity, in the form of a goddess, a bird, or a beloved actor.

Robot Tales as Myth

All the Indian robot stories we have examined in this volume are embedded in a religious context. The very term *yantra* is one that resonates with religious meaning; these are devices that demonstrate divine control over the material world, or the interconnection between matter and spirit, or the ultimate soullessness of all things. The automata of the king's pleasure garden are reminders that the cosmos itself is a *yantra* ruled over by Śiva, the sad remnants of a robot girl lead a man to understand the truth of the Buddha's message about the lack of permanence, and the automata brought to a princess by a demon's daughter for her amusement eventually lead her to the waters of immortality.

Sutton and Sutton propose that science fiction represents a "mythology for our time,"[25] and they regard science fiction as a "self-conscious form of myth in which man intentionally mythologizes scientific narrative."[26] They further observe that themes from earlier mythologies often serve as subplots for science fiction stories. Such a mythologization of science is very much present in recent Indian science fiction films like *Enthiran* and *2.0*, but I am not sure we can call the earliest Indian android stories mythologized science. In the *Samarāṅgaṇasūtradhāra*, for example, science and mythology are presented as parts of a seamless whole, the wondrous cosmic *yantra*, where the sun, the moon, and the elements are all controlled by Śiva, the invisible *bīja* of the threefold world. Science and myth are equally intertwined in the tale of the weaver's mechanical bird, the painter's mechanical crush, and the robots that guard the Buddha's relics. I do not think these are scientific narratives about automation, presented in the guise of mythology, but rather religious myths that articulate something essential about the very nature of humanity. How is a human being different from a mechanical one? The Hindu robot tales show us that life is made possible by an animating *ātman*, the Jain tales demonstrate that life is not limited to humans, or even to that which is traditionally regarded as animate, and the Buddhist narratives postulate that there is actually *no* difference between humans and machines. Taken together, these stories are a rich, nuanced, and inconclusive examination of the very nature of humanity.

Tales of Wonder

As we have seen, a notion of the uncanny is almost entirely absent from Indian robot tales, which are instead permeated by a sense of *adbhuta*, or wonder. While the audience of an Indian robot tale may share an experience a romantic love briefly during the painter's courtship of what he believes to be a lovely maiden, laugh at his folly, feel anger when the king orders Kokkāsa's execution because his sons flew off on the mechanical horse, compassion with the robot-maker who is forced to behead his mechanical son, disgust and terror at when Kokkāsa's flying machine spears the king's sons, and a sense of heroism when the weaver flies out over the battlefield on his mechanical Garuḍa, the prevailing mood in Indian robot literature is almost always *adbhuta*, or wonder: wonder at that which appeared to be human is after all only a machine, wonder at the robot-maker's cleverness, and wonder at the gullibility of humans.

Why is the revelation that a charming and talented young man who flirts with the ladies at the royal court is an android met with delight rather than repulsion in ancient India? Why is the painter who fell in love with a mechanical woman either annoyed at his own gullibility or inspired to reflect on his own lack of eternal soul, rather than creeped out when the woman's mechanical nature is revealed? Why do androids inspire wonder, rather than anxiety, in Indian literature?

Perhaps the answer lies, in part, in the relative permeability of the boundaries between the animate and the inanimate in Indian culture overall. If a deity or spirit can inhabit a tree, a stone, a river, or a mountain, and a god can be present in a *mūrti* (icon) and a Buddha (at least in the popular view) in his relics, the animation of an automaton is somewhat less unsettling than in a society where the animate and the inanimate are more strictly separated into rigid categories. Human exceptionalism is a cornerstone of much of Western thought,[27] and when inanimate objects begin to mimic humanity, the very notion of the human as exceptional and privileged, made in God's own image and likeness, begins to falter and causes a profound discomfort. Sanjukta Gupta contrasts the Christian notion of humans made in God's image with the Hindu view that it is not the physical form of a human being but rather "man's essence, his soul" that is "made of the same stuff as God, who is the soul of the world."[28] But sharing a divine essence with God is not something unique to humans in Hinduism; all living beings possess a self (*ātman*) that is of a divine nature, including animals, demons, and ghosts.

Automata do mimic humans, but so do many other entities in Indian mythologies: the human prince Rāma is a god in disguise, the beggar who visits his wife Sītā in the forest is a demon, and the housewife Yaśodā's young foster child is a deity who contains vast universes inside his mouth. To discover, then, that something that appears to be human is something else altogether is not quite as stunning—or as uncanny—in the context of mythologies where such imitations of humanity happen on a regular basis as in belief systems founded on the notion of human exceptionalism.

Any sort of fluid boundary between the human and the nonhuman is particularly troubling in a culture influenced by monotheistic religious traditions that place humans in a unique and privileged position. To be a human being, according to Judaism, Christianity, or Islam, is to serve a particular God-given role in the world, a role entirely different from that assigned to an animal, an angel, or a demon. The creation of a machine that is indistinguishable from a human being can easily be seen as a threat to the uniqueness of humans, a dangerous destabilizing of the divine order or the world.[29] In Hinduism and Buddhism, however, being human is not a permanent or divinely ordained condition, but the result of one's own karma from past lives. A person may be born as a human in this lifetime but could easily become an animal, a god, or a demon in a future lifetime, depending on that person's actions and their karmic consequences. Humanity is more fleeting in Asian religions than in Western ones, less stable and permanent, and this may be why an automaton hovering on the border between the human and the nonhuman becomes an interesting curiosity rather than an existential threat. As Halpern and Katz have demonstrated, followers of Judaism and Christianity are likely to show less positive attitudes toward robots than those who follow Eastern religions.[30]

Moreover, wonder in the ancient Indian robot tales is often associated with an unexpected revelation of reality, of a surprising truth hidden behind an illusory form. The mechanical woman reveals to the painter both the flawed nature of his perception of female perfection and his erroneous understanding of his own self. The weaver's mechanical Garuḍa reveals both the folly of trusting appearances and the ultimate power of the divine. The deadly automata of the *Lokapaññatti* reveal the superior nature of Buddhist kingship compared with the tyrannical rule of the imagined Rome. As the abstract *yantra* diagrams of Hinduism, Buddhism, and Jainism are sites for deeper insight into cosmic reality, so the mechanical *yantras* in the entertaining popular tales of these traditions point to larger realities beyond themselves. And in that lies the true *adbhuta* of these narratives.

The Egoless Robot and the Path to *Nirvāna*

Kang argues that automata and robots function as conceptual tools to explore the nature of humanity.[31] If so, what do our soulless doubles tell us about ourselves?

In the *Star Trek: Next Generation* episode "The Measure of a Man," the android character Data is put on trial. Is he merely a machine, the property of Star Fleet, to be disposed of at his owners' will? Or is he a sentient being with rights of his own? In the course of his trial, Captain Jean-Luc Picard introduces several arguments for why Data should be regarded as a person in the eyes of the law, including his self-awareness. Picard's opponent during the trail, Commander Maddox, argues that sentience requires "intelligence, self-awareness, consciousness,"[32] and Picard quotes Data in response: "'My rights,' 'my status,' my right to choose,' 'my life'—Well, that seems reasonably self-aware to me."[33] Is self-awareness truly what separates a sentient human being from a sophisticated intelligent machine? If so, what about those humans who lack self-awareness, such as infants, or those who are severely mentally ill? Are such individuals not fully human?

Self-awareness is often valorized in contemporary science fiction; it is what separates humans from machines, animals, or mere digitally constructed personas. But self-awareness has not always been regarded as a positive thing; self-awareness can also be associated with ego of self-absorption. In Buddhism, where the self is regarded as an illusion, to be self-aware is to be deluded, since the self of which one is aware is nothing but a construct. Buddhism strives to make us *less* self-aware, not more.[34]

Masahiro Mori, who coined the phrase "The Uncanny Valley," even claims in his book *The Buddha in the Robot: A Robot Engineer's Thoughts on Science and Religion*, that "robots have the Buddha-nature within them—that is, the potential for attaining Buddhahood."[35] How is it possible for a mere machine to attain Buddhahood? A robot is a constructed device, a collection of components—how could it have Buddha-nature within? As the story of the painter and the mechanical girl reminds us, this question does not merely apply to androids but also to us, the humans: Are we not also mere constructs, collections of physical components? How can *we* attain Buddhahood? Although Mori does not explicitly state this, from a Buddhist perspective, a soulless robot is not all that different from a soulless human being. The wonder—and discomfort—one may feel when seeing a robot that is humanlike in its appearance and actions may, from this perspective, be caused by the robots reminding us of our own mechanical nature, or our own *anattā*.

But the notion that the robot represents selflessness is not necessarily limited to Buddhism. In his lyrical meditations on fictional automata in Western literature and film, Wilson refers to two sides of the android: the android as a violation of natural law (Frankenstein's monster) and the android as the realization of spiritual potential.[36] Wilson refers to our cultural obsession with automata devoid of self as an "instinct for Eden," for a psychological state untainted by self-consciousness.[37] In Wilson's interpretation, androids represent a human longing for a state untroubled by self-awareness. He draws his inspiration, in part, from Heinrich von

Kleist's 1810 essay "On the Marionette Theatre," where puppets symbolize humans before the Fall, a state of innocence characterized by a complete lack of self-awareness. In this reading, automata are *us,* as we secretly long to be, blissfully unencumbered by ego.

Kakoudaki argues that androids are useful cultural fictions, and she writes: "One of the rewards of tracing the historical provenance and textual versatility of the artificial person is that it elucidates one of their chief cultural functions in modernity: their participation in a political and existential negotiation of what it means to be human."[38] I propose that this negotiation of humanity is not necessarily a modern phenomenon, however; tales of ancient androids function as mirrors where we can examine the "mortal machines" that are humans. Androids are proxies of the human body that allow us to theorize our own materiality and interrogate the relationship between the material and the spiritual in the makeup of a human being. Are we, as humans, purely material beings? Is our consciousness simply a byproduct of our biological composition? Or do we possess an immaterial component as well, something that distinguishes us from the material world?

Tales of artificial humans allow us to examine questions of humanity and selfhood and articulate ideas about our role as humans in the larger cosmic order of things. Hindu automata are distinguished from humans and animals by their lack of an eternal *ātman,* but they have the potential for animation and true life if an *ātman* were to enter the machine. Like all *yantras,* Hindu automata have spiritual potential; they are sites where cosmic and divine forces can unfold.

Jain automata break down the distinctions between human and nonhuman, between animal, mineral, and man. Humanity is not, in the Jain vision of the world, the only form of authentic life. The statues that come to life in the garden articulate the essential Jain belief that matter is also a living thing, and that humanity and machine are simply two different modalities of the same animated world; the world and the self are of the same essence.

In Buddhism, however, humanity itself is deconstructed and revealed to be nothing but artifice. Humanity is simply a human invention; we are nothing but an assembly of parts, robots made from organic materials, bewildered by our own erroneous belief that we possess some sort of selfhood. Tales of mechanical beings in Buddhist texts help destabilize the very notion of selfhood, which is regarded as a necessary step toward salvation.

The notions of humanity and identity embedded in these ancient robot tales are not mere curious intellectual artifacts from a distant past, however. These investigations into the nature of humanity and its boundaries foreshadow essential current and future debates in the fields of bioethics and technology ethics. If there is no fear of "playing God" in ancient Indian robot literature, is this fear also absent in modern Indian bioethics? Are Hindu or Buddhist scientists more accepting of genetic engineering, or in vitro fertilization treatments? If Hinduism defines life as the presence of an *ātman,* how does this play into debates over abortion or euthanasia in India? And what of those beings who possess an *ātman* but are not human, such as animals? Should they have the same rights as humans? And what if we develop machines that are so advanced that they may be regarded as sentient? Can a computer or an android in the future ever possess an *ātman*? If a deity inhabits a stone or metal image, could it also inhabit an automaton or a computer?

The Jain view of elements, stones, trees, and bodies of water as sentient clearly has vast implications for ecology and the need to treat the earth with the same respect as an animal or a human being. Jainism goes further than any other religious tradition in arguing for the sanctity of all life, but it also expands the definition of life far beyond what most religions do. How will Jainism articulate an ethics for the future if *ahiṃsā,* or nonviolence, should be applied to humans, animals, plants, water, stars, and perhaps even machines?

At first sight, the Buddhist notion of *anattā,* or no-soul, and the accompanying view of humans (and animals!) as mere assemblies of biological and psychological components might not seem to inspire great concern for the rights of individuals. After all, if humans are indistinguishable from robots, on what grounds do they deserve ethical treatment? And yet, Buddhist texts argue again and again that the greatest virtue is compassion (*karuṇā*) for all living beings. If those living beings are constructs, mere robots made of flesh and blood and sinew, without any eternal substance, why have compassion for them? Humanity itself may be a mere construct in Buddhism, but suffering is real. The goal of compassion, then, is to end suffering, whether that which suffers is human or automaton. In his insightful study of the Buddhist background of the Japanese roboticist Masahiro Mori's ethical philosophy, Kimura asks whether it would be ethically acceptable for an engineer to create a robot capable of feeling desire, suffering, and emotional pain. Based on Mori's work, he concludes that a robot could only be a true empathetic companion for a human being if it is capable of feeling suffering.[39] But one might even take this line of argument one step further and ask whether humans would not also be ethically obliged to feel compassion for a suffering robot and strive to relieve its pain.

The Dalai Lama, the spiritual head of the Gelug-pa school of Tibetan Buddhism, even proposed that in the future, a stream of consciousness might enter into a computer, and that a scientist may even be reborn *as* a computer.[40] This seemingly radical idea makes perfect sense in the context of Buddhist teachings, which do not ascribe any more selfhood to a human being than to a machine. The general openness to new technology, and robots in particular, in Asia may stem from a relative absence of the idea of human exceptionalism in Asian religions.[41] If a robot were to become sentient, or even to house a human mind in its mechanical body, this is not a problem in a worldview where humans are not unique and set apart from the material world.

Robot tales help us define humanity, both by delineating the boundaries between that which is human and that which is not and by blurring these very boundaries. In Hinduism, the difference between a human being and a robot is a question of *ātman*, but this also implies that robots have the potential to become human, if an *ātman* were to enter the machine. But in Jainism, the situation is more complicated; a *jīva* or soul can exist both in human beings and in the wood or metal components that make up a machine. Humans and robots are therefore not necessarily different by nature. And in Buddhism, the distinction between human and machine falls apart; humanity is itself presented as virtual, an artificial construct.

The title of this book—*I,* Yantra—is inspired by Isaac Asimov's famous short story collection, *I, Robot*. One of Asimov's characters says: "It is the obvious which is so difficult to see most of the time. People say 'It's as plain as the nose on your face.' But how much of the nose on your face can you see, unless someone holds a mirror up to you?"[42] This is what stories of artificial humans do; they hold up a mirror in front of us so that we can better see ourselves. In the final instance, robot narratives are about human beings. We read robot stories to find out who we are. And if we are lucky, our mechanical twins will smile at us, remove a limb or a head and reveal the mechanism inside, theirs and ours.

Appendix

Chapter 31 of Bhoja's *Samarāṅgaṇasūtradhāra*

Establishing a *Yantra*

1. The conqueror of the God of Love,[1] who is praised as the one who has set in motion the wheels (*cakra*) of the orbs (*maṇḍala*) of the sun and moon, the one who regulates all beings and who always moves the fundamental element (*bīja*), the threefold machinery (*yantra*) of the world, with its invisible center—may he come to our aid.

2. Now we will recite (the chapter called) "Establishing a *Yantra*" in order from the beginning. This is the only basis for *dharma, artha, kāma,* and *mokṣa*.[2]

3. When the elements (*bhūta*) spontaneously move along their own path, that which restrains and controls them is known as a *yantra*.

4. When the elements move along according to their own inclination and whim, it (the machine) controls (*yam*) them, and therefore it is called *yantra*.

5. There are four elements (*bīja*): earth, water, fire, and air. Because it is the basis of the others, ether is also mentioned.[3]

6. Some say that mercury (*sūta*) is a separate element, but they are not correct. Since mercury is naturally

of the earth, it should be treated as such (as part of the earth element).

7. Because mercury is earthly, it should not be regarded as separate from the earth element. But if its ability to produce fire is considered . . .

8. . . . then it is not different from fire. But because of its scent, it is different from fire and strongly connected with earth.

9. The Self (*ātman*) is indeed the fundamental principle of all things. It is one even though there are many selves.[4] There are differences between them, and many of these arise from mixing things together.

10. Machines may be automatic (*svayamvāhaka*), have wind-up mechanisms (*sakṛtprerya*), have hidden mechanisms inside, or have the mechanism far away.

11. Among these, the automatic is the highest, and the other three are inferior. They praise that one among them (the automatic) because of its remoteness, its invisibility, and its proximity.

12. That which has become invisible is the most effective one of all. They praise it because it causes wonder among men.

13. There is a motion characteristic of this wonderful mechanism, and another motion characteristic of the carrier. But in the case of an insect based on a wheeled machine pulling water from a well, one can see both (types of motion).

14. Because of the two kinds of motion, one can create variety. Because it is invisible, and because it causes amazement, it is praised among the machines.

15. Another type may be moved from the inside.[5] This second type of machine is of medium quality. By means of this second and the third types and so on, and in accordance with the four as well . . .

16. . . . because they are part of the elements, their number is great. He who truly knows that, that man becomes beloved . . .

17. . . . of women and kings and esteemed by the wise. Profit, fame, and worship, glory and honor and riches . . .

18. . . . what does the man not obtain, who knows this truly? A dwelling among coquettish women, a palace of the greatest wonder . . .

19. . . . a dwelling that is an abode of pleasure, a house of marvel, just like that of the gods, because of the beauty and activity seen there.

20. These things satisfy, and that satisfaction was known by the ancient ones as *dharma* (religious duty). Because of the satisfaction of the king, there will also be wealth (*artha*), and erotic love (*kāma*) is based on wealth.

21. Because of his accumulation of wealth, his renunciation and liberation (*mokṣa*) are not difficult to obtain.[6] The earthly/royal comes from the earth element,[7] and the earthly comes from those things born from water.

22. That again comes from things generated by fire, and that indeed from things engendered by wind. The watery element comes from the watery things, just like the windy elements come from windy things . . .

23. . . . by means of things born from fire, by means of those things that are born from wind, and by means of the earthly and the watery. The wind comes from the windy, the watery, the earthly, and the fiery.

24. In that which is born from fire, the element is mercury (*sūta*), and that is also in the wind. In the earthly things it is the element and in watery things the watery.

25. Thus, the elements of all things have well-known designations:[8] *sūtras* (texts) dealing with construction of walls, the weight of the pressing of the earth,

26. the dangling in the case of the activity of the measurer,[9] the different types of circles/wheels (*cakra*); the amalgam and crushing of iron, copper, silver, and tin.

27. Wood and fur and cloth relate to their own elements, and likewise measuring instruments (*urdaka*),[10] rods (*yaṣṭi*), spindles (*kartara*),[11] wheels (*cakra*), and spinning tops (*brahmaraka*).[12]

28. The array of water-engines (*śṛṅga*)[13] and iron arrows are the things whose constituent elements they know as coming from the earth (*aurvara*).[14] Heating is from fire, and torpor (*stobha*) and agitation (*kṣobha*) are born from contact with water.

29. Things like these are called the elements of earthly things. Streams and water reservoirs and whirlpools . . .

30. . . . and things like these are called the water-born things among the earth-born ones. Just like height, weight, and density (*nirandhratā*) . . .

31. . . . and upward movement are constituent elements of iron, the air born by its own nature is obtained by means of sturdy handles . . .

32. . . . by means of bellows, fans,[15] or flaps.[16] Shaken[17] and filtered, it becomes an element (*bīja*) in the case of the earth.

33. Wood and animal skin and iron may be earthly even when born from water. Otherwise, it may be classified as water, such as when something is horizontal, vertical, or low-lying.

34. In *yantras* that are generated by water, the element (*bīja*) exists on its own. The one propelled by heat

described earlier may be fire-born even in the case of that which is generated by water.[18]

35. Controlled, given, filled, and thrust back, the air is an element (*bīja*) even in the case of *yantras* generated from water.

36. In the case of those generated by fire, in the grasping of clay, copper, iron, gold, and so on, those who are well versed in elements declare that the element is earthly.

37. Fire may be the element of fire, and likewise water of water. By means of the bellows, among others, mentioned earlier, the wind becomes a fundamental element.

38. The fundamental principle born from the earth may be receiving and generating, setting things in motion, grasping and consolidating, by means of those things that are born from the air.

39. The fundamental principle born from water is likewise considered generated by wind when it sets things in motion and attacks, rotates, and turns.

40. Those things that are said to be seized by heat and generated by boiling, and so on, exist because of generation from air.

41. Set in motion, controlled, and generated, the air goes to its own element. In this way, one may construct another one.

42. One element is prominent and another inferior or secondary to it. Another is even more inferior because of better alternatives.

43. Many kinds of these (elements) exist. Therefore, who can discuss them in full? The earth has no activity; activity is in part innate in the remaining three (elements).

44. Thus, generally activity is generated in the earth by means of effort. It is constructed under the influence of the form of that which has been perfected.

45. It is not possible to determine the form of a *yantra* (machine) in this way. There is a combination of elements, well put together construction, and smoothness.

46. Inscrutability,[19] efficiency, lightness, soundlessness, or a great sound when intended, lack of looseness or stiffness . . .

47. . . . smoothness and evenness of motion, and lack of shaking in the movement, keeping rhythm in motion when made for entertainment purposes . . .

48. . . . displaying its objective when desired, and then again shutting down properly, verisimilitude (*anulambhanatva*) of form, firmness, softness . . .

49. . . . and endurance. These are the qualities ascribed to *yantras*. One *yantra* may do many things, and another may be operated by many people.

50. Well-made construction and inscrutability are the most important qualities of *yantras*. Here are the various actions of *yantras* in a systematic fashion:

51. We explain them now, neither in too much detail nor too succinctly. For some of them action is perfected, and for others time.

52. For some sound, for some height, for some form and touch. For movements have been declared endless due to activity:

53. Across, up, down, backward, forward on both sides, walking, running, or flying. These are the different types of movements generated.

54. Time is of many kinds due to divisions into *muhūrtas*,[20] *kāṣṭhās*,[21] and so forth. Sounds are also various: those that give joy, those that give pleasure, and those that are terrifying.

55. Elevation may be of water, and somewhere it is praised as being generated from the earth. Song, dance, instrumental music, kettle drum, and flute . . .

56. . . . and lute (*vīṇā*), cymbal, *tṛmilā*,[22] or drum, or whatever else is defined as a musical instrument . . .

57. . . . all of these are generated from a machine through the power of construction. In dance, it is drama and sprinkling,[23] both frantic and gentle.

58. The king's highway and the rural areas are all known because of *yantras*, and likewise the things that are in accordance with birth and the things that are contrary to birth.

59. These things are all accomplished by the proper application of *yantras*: the movement of earth-goers in the sky, and of sky-goers on the earth.

60. The various desired movements of earthbound mortals arise from the construction of *yantras* . . .

61. . . . just like the demons were conquered by the gods, or the ocean churned,[24] and just like the demon Hiraṇyakaśipu was killed by the Man-Lion.[25]

62. The running, battling, or letting loose of elephants[26]—there are many various movements, and many mechanical bathhouses . . .

63. . . . playing on hammocks of different kinds, and pleasure houses, different armies, huts, and automated servants (*svayaṃvāhakasevaka*) . . .

64. . . . halls of various kinds, constructed true illusions, and these other prominent things are made possible by the creation of *yantras*.

65. When five stories are constructed, the bedroom is placed on the first floor. In every watch of the night, it crawls along the others and goes to the fifth (floor).[27]

66. All these important and various things are properly accomplished because of *yantras*. Serrations gradually move three hundred wheels on a plate.

67. One should bring to life the automaton (*putrikā*) constructed in the middle of it once every half hour (*nāḍi*).[28] There is the appearance of fire in water, and from the middle of fire, water comes forth.

68. From insubstantiality comes substance, and from substance other things. By breathing it goes up to the sky, and by breathing it descends to earth.

69. A bed placed in the center of the ocean of milk has a serpent underneath, round and equipped with magnets in the opposite direction of the movement of the sun and so forth.[29]

70. Revolving day and night, it displays the movement of the planets. A man is moved in the shape of a charioteer, on top of the form of an elephant, and so forth.

71. Having moved for a *nāḍikā*,[30] it strikes a *yojana*[31] at the circumference. When an illuminated automaton has been created, it moves along quite leisurely.

72. Clapping makes the oil dance in the lamp in a clockwise manner, and until water is offered, it consumes water without cessation.

73. A moving elephant mechanically constructed is not recognized (as such). Constructed birds such as parrots obey repeated clapping of hands.

74. Causing wonder among men, they dance and recite: a mechanical girl, an elephant, a horse, or a monkey.

75. Dancing by gestures and spinning and clapping, it enchants the mind. Water is carried along by whatever path the field has.

76. From that it goes again from the canal into the lotus pools. The waters allowed through stop at a slab and then run on.

77. They (the automata) strike blows and fight without effort or exertion; they dance and sing and play the flute, and so on.

78. The movement of airs due to the power of being confined and released by the curves of the *yantras* are both divine and human, and do not only exist here.

79. Whatever is difficult to do is made possible because of a *yantra*. The construction of *yantras* has not been explained here, but that is because of secrecy, not because of any lack of knowledge.

80. In that case, the cause should be known. These things that are evident will not bring results. The elements have been explained here, but not the construction of the *yantras*.

81. Therefore, because these things have been explained, there should be no self-interest and no curiosity. In reality everything has been explained because the elements have been mentioned.

82. The working of the *yantras* can be logically deduced by the wise. The machines that are observed are illustrated here.

83. Therefore, those that give delight are to be known by instruction. This has been created in its entirety by our own intelligence.

84. First, we shall speak of that which was taught in the past. They say that the elements in *yantras* are fourfold: water, fire, earth, and wind. In each case, there may be many forms due to subdivisions. And it may go beyond these numbers due to mixed qualities.

85. What, then, is the highest wonder in the world? And what exists for the sake of satisfaction, and what is merely for the sake of curiosity? What becomes a vehicle for fame, and what an instrument of desire? What is religiously meritorious (*puṇya*), and what alleviates affliction?

86. The harnessing of the elements, controlled and generated by architects (*sūtradhāra*),[32] gives great pleasure. By rotation a painter (*citrakṛt*)[33] may create a wooden wheel or a hammock, or a *pañca*.[34]

87. A man knows how to create different *yantras* when he is equipped with traditional knowledge, skills, and instructions by those well versed in the discipline, and when his intelligence is complete and flawless . . .

88. . . . and he knows the subject of the science of *yantras* (*yantraśāstra*), which is fivefold through being endowed with various qualities. The fame of those who use all of this properly encompasses heaven and earth.

89. It is a thumb in length, and a quarter thumb in height, with two cavities, thin and round, made straight, with a hole going through the middle, joined together, and made of sturdy copper . . .

90. . . . among wooden birds, one which is like that on the inside, struck by the force of passing air, produces a sweet sound while moving and becomes a wonder for those who listen.[35]

91. It is made from two pieces well joined together, resembling a small drum with a hole inside, to be seized by means of two rings. A delicate hole should be made in its middle.

92. In the case of the previously mentioned *yantra*, as a rule it should be placed on the bed, with a hole drilled into it. Then it creates sound, love play, and passionate merriment due to its quivering.

93. Attached to the bed, it produces a specific melody. Alarm or anger are turned into the sounds of animals or children. What else should be mentioned when it comes to these machines? They bring about emotions on all sides, and things connected to love play lead to a great deal of growth.

94. A kettle drum (*paṭaha*), a drum, a flute, a lute, a large drum, a *damaru* drum, a cymbal (*ṭivila*),[36] or instruments that are sounded or struck—they generate sufficient sound—sweet, loud, or varied—that arises from the blocking and release of air in a regular way.

95. One can create a large bird of well-made construction formed of light wood in the cavity and add a mercury-machine (*rasayantra*) that is combustible and full of fire.

96. For those who are sleeping, the (mechanical) man mounted on that (mercury-powered bird) flies far into the air by means of the wind released from the flapping of the wings due to the power of the mercury, creating a marvel.

97. A wooden aerial car (*vimāna*), similar to a god's temple, moves about. One may place containers of mercury in the four corners of it in an orderly fashion.

98. Because it is born from a container heated by the slow fire placed in a jar, it instantly becomes an ornament in the sky, hot and roaring due to the power of mercury.

99. When one puts a very hot iron *yantra*, rounded and well made, whose interior is filled with mercury, in a high place, it produces a drum sound like a lion's roar.

100. Its vibration resonates like the greatness of the man-lion. When it approaches, elephants' temporal ducts release temporin.[37] Hearing that deep and

dangerous sound repeatedly, the elephants flee quickly in terror, shaking off the elephant driver's hook.

101. One may make an entire body with holes in its joints, the eyes, neck, soles of the feet, palms, forearms, arms, thighs, hands, and limbs.

102. It is made of wood, well made like a pillar and covered in discarded hide; made in the form of a man or a young woman, it is very charming.

103. When it has an iron arrow and threads in every hole, it creates the movement and stretching and contraction of the neck.

104. It shakes hands, spits betel juice,[38] bows respectfully, looks in the mirror, plays the lute, and so forth.

105. If something like this is seen, it produces a sense of wonder, because strings are drawn and released and opened regularly (seemingly) because of its (the automaton's) own intellect (*buddhi*).

106. When the form of a man is made from wood and placed by the door of the house, a bar fastened in his hands blocks the path of those entering.

107. It (the automaton) may be one that holds a sword, one that holds a bludgeon, or one that holds a spear. It strikes thieves entering in the night, closing the entrance forcibly.

108. Those machines that are bows and those that kill a hundred, those that are like camel necks,[39] and so on in order to make a fort difficult to access, and those that are for sport or the recreation of kings, they may all exist due to the suitability of their qualities.

109. Now we shall speak systematically of water *yantras*, both for amusement and for the purpose of work. People say that their movement is fourfold.

110. The water comes down from a wooden vessel placed high. Where there is a waterfall machine, it may be useful for gardens, and so on.

111. The one called *ucchrāyasamāpata* (even fall from an elevation) has high pipes, and *samanāḍikā* (with even pipes) should release water from a higher tank into a lower one.

112. Where there is water falling from a level height (*pātasamocchrāya*), then the water falls from a height, then goes horizontally and flows upward when it reaches the pillars with holes in them.

113. When the water has fallen from a great height and moves across high up because it reaches the pillars with holes in them, that is *ucchrāyasamāpata* (even fall from an elevation).

114. According to the rules, where there is water belonging to a pond or in a well, if that water goes up, that is known as *ucchrāya* (elevation).

115. That which has the form of a wooden elephant drinks water from a vessel. Its importance is defined as equal to its elevation.

116. The water is led in underground channels through low-lying paths to far away. It is made into a marvelous water place because of equal elevation.

117. An automatic bathhouse (*dhārāgṛha*) may be *pravarṣaṇa* (causing rain), or a second type may have pipes, or be immersed, and another one may be a *nandyāvarta*.[40]

118. This is not meant for common people but is suitable for kings. It is an abode for the auspicious ones, divine, and giving satisfaction and prosperity.

119. One should find a beautiful place near a reservoir of water and construct a pipe two or three times the height of the *yantra* . . .

120. . . . capable of carrying water, without holes on the outside and smooth on the inside. Where its water comes out, one should build a house at the auspicious moment . . .

121. . . . (a house) equipped with all the herbs of the Ābhīras[41] and with pots full of gold, with fragrant garlands, and made resonant by Vedic chanting . . .

122. . . . with pillars bright with gems or made from gold or silver or formed out of pine wood . . .

123. . . . or carved out of sandalwood or other excellent woods, such as *śāla* wood, with a hundred, thirty-two, or sixteen (pillars) . . .

124. . . . or with twenty-four, or with the number of the Sun (twelve),[42] all adorned with jewels, or even with four (pillars).

125. It should have lovely halls facing the east, with various lattice windows, and it should be surrounded by terraces and beautified by friezes.[43]

126. It should be made beautiful by mechanical birds, constructed from lovely *śāla* wood, and by monkey couples, and by gaping demons of many kinds.[44]

127. (The house should be) charming to look at due to *vidyādhāras*,[45] *siddhas*,[46] serpents, *kinnāras*,[47] and dancing celestial singers of the highest quality, and decorated with peacocks.

128. It should be covered by variegated clusters of vines and by wishing trees,[48] made charming by cuckoos, insects, bees, and rows of geese.

129. There should be a well-made tube in the middle, with all currents flowing, combined with a hollow tube that is lovely due to its many different forms.

130. In front of the well-made tube, accompanied by balanced pillars all around, one should make a proper mix with thick cement.

131. The cement should be a pulverized mixture of lac, *śāla* wood, pebbles, ash tree, and pongamia oil.[49]

132. For the sake of strong binding of the joints, these should sometimes be applied twice, along with a plaster made of hemp bark, sebesten fruit, and beeswax.

133. One should make that by means of an *ucchrāya* (elevated) *yantra*, which spreads water everywhere, equipped with different proportions, and then one should display it in front of the king.

134. One should add pairs of elephants all around, suitable for playing in water, (elephants) closing their eyes out of fear of the spray discharged from each other's trunks.

135. One (elephant) falls in love when it sees its own reflection in the shower. One should make water spray out from the elephant's eyes, temples, penis, and trunk.

136. One should make a (mechanical) woman with two breasts releasing streams of water and with water drops creating the semblance of tears of joy.

137. And one should make a woman with a stream coming from her navel or her heart, and one spraying showers from her fingernails.

138. With the support of the king, one may create wondrous things. One should make these main automata and their many delightful actions and control their movements . . .

139. . . . and in the middle of it all, one should create a lion throne fashioned from pure gold and jewels. That is where the king will sit, the lord of men, lord of the earth, the god who is the husband of Śrī.[50]

140. The king may take a bath in the fountain sometimes, his joy increased by auspicious songs, just

like the king of the gods himself is waited upon by those skilled in instruments and drama.

141. The king sits joyfully in the fountain house, the radiant dwelling place of streams, which is like clouds burst open, diving in tired from the heat.

142. Looking at the many different water features, he is not a mortal, but the king of the gods taking up dwelling on earth.

143. Equipped with an octet of different cloud types, this fountain house may be constructed like the earlier one. Because of its collection of showers, it is called *pravarṣaṇa* (causing rain).

144. When he has created these automata by means of a *yantra* with even height, or by means of a fourth one, the architect may fill them with pure water if they have curved tubes.

145. He should make the limbs of the automata entirely perforated with holes capable of releasing the waters, and then let them flow.

146. Those automata release the waters. Their tubes are curved, and by means of releasing the valves that block the openings when so desired, these marvelous machines create a wonder.

147. Whenever he wants to, the architect can make these water vessels rain forth water, in a twofold or threefold way. It is a great wonder.

148. This manifold family dwelling is the residence of Rati's husband,[51] full of marvelous artificial clouds, alleviating the heat of the sun's rays by sprays of water in the summer, but no happy sight for the sun's rays.

149. With one pillar or four, or eight, or twelve, or with sixteen, should one fashion this charming two-story house.

150. One should make a square in the form of a *puṣpaka*,[52] with four entrances, surrounded with walls, with a gate in the shape of a sword.

151. Over that, one should build a strong oblong courtyard reservoir in the middle. One should make a *karṇikā*[53] in the middle of that, embellished with lotus flowers.

152. In each of the four corners of that, one should make a charming wooden girl, her eyes fixed on the lotus in the center, with ornaments and with elegant dress.

153. By using the *yantra* described earlier, when the king is on the lotus seat, one may fill the courtyard reservoir with pure water from a golden pitcher.

154. When the reservoir is filled, the water held back in the middle of the platform, hidden in scented holes, rises everywhere.

155. The surface of the automaton's face is entirely perforated, and its limbs are made from beautiful, charming, and variegated components. It releases the water from its nostrils, ears, eyes, and so on.

156. The fountain house called *praṇāla* (drain) is a great marvel, and it is placed in the courtyard as the king's ornament. The architect creates it this way by means of his sharp intellect. These types of buildings are particularly praiseworthy among those with accomplished intellect.

157. One should make a sturdy and very deep reservoir with four corners, with a pavilion in the center of it with painted joints.

158. One should build a door with entrance and exit through a downward underground passage, made charming by showers from above.

159. In the way described in the chapter on paintings, the center should be adorned with paintings, like the abode of Varuṇa.[54]

160. It is illuminated by the rays of the sun that have entered the pericarp of the perforated lotus flowers, both lotus flowers coming out of the top and ones coming from the fibers and bulbs.

161. Then one may have them filled by pure water, when one has constructed a charming pavilion surrounded by flawless lotus flowers in the proper way.

162. The architect should create beauty by many means, with doors and arches and spacious chambers in all four directions.

163. He should create by an advantageous method a reservoir full of lotus flowers, filled with artificial fish and automated female sea monsters and birds and aquatic creatures.

164. The main officials, such as the vassals who are commanded by the king, and emissaries from other countries, should stand still there.

165. And then, when he has seen the water sports in the previously described ways and forms, the king should joyfully mount the palanquin.

166. Then the king, who is standing in the water-immersed chamber surrounded everywhere by courtesans, experiences a joy whose pleasure is like that of the serpent king himself in his underworld abode.[55]

167. In the middle of the oblong pond described previously, he should make a beautiful *puṣpaka,* built with four pillars and equipped with pearls and coral.

168. All around the pond, having filled the sturdy *puṣpaka,* which has well-made outlets, he should

make it beautiful by means of walls with *svastikas*[56] on the inside everywhere.

169. He fills it properly with water, as mentioned before, and the king goes to the *puṣpaka* and plays water games.

170. The king may play in the company of his playfellows and courtesans in the sprays emerging from the inside of the walls.

171. The king plays with his companions in the bathing pool, some sunken under water in one place, visible in another, and fallen when struck by water in another place.

172. The fortunate king looks at the multitude of the beloved (mechanical) women, standing at the bottom of the pool, bent down with shyness, and covering the buds of their breasts with sproutlike hands, the fastening of their clothes loosened by the sprays of water.

173. We shall correctly explain the construction of a wooden chariot or swing. The movement of the rotation of the *yantra* has been explained as fivefold previously.

174. Among them, *vasanta* (springtime) is the first one, and the ones called *madananivāsa* (dwelling of love), and *vasantatilaka* (ornament of spring), *vibhramaka* (moving to and fro), and *tripura* (the three cities), are the five types of swings.

175. The architect should construct four pillars, very strong and straight, fastened with a single rope, with equal space between, placed on well-made plinths.

176. In the aforementioned part of the palace, he should place a lovely ground floor the length of eight cubits[57] and half of that again in depth.

177. On the floor in the middle, he should make a pillar, with a base made of iron, with rotation and equipped with a plinth, surrounded by covering beams.

178. He should place a strong and ornate pot on top of the plinth, and surround that by *bhadras*[58] elevated one *dhanus*.[59]

179. If he wants, he can then create a pillar top with platforms, very straight and one floor above it. On the fence he may place a slab on top.

180. An elephant-headed *madalā*[60] should be made, to the point that it can pick up a diamond, very solid, created with effort, delightful to the mind, and lovely.

181. Above the platform, he should create if desired a set of four pillars or a courtyard, and over that a fastening with a firm foundation.

182. He should make an additional lovely floor in the corner, equipped with twelve beautiful pillars in that area.

183. In the middle of that he should make a rotator established on the central pillar. Because of the extent of that area, he may cover it with slabs in the back.

184. In the upper corners of a chariot placed on top of the platform, he should put five rotating wheels in the middle of the pillar.

185. On top of that, according to standards of beauty, he should make a structure in the shape of a lotus flower, whose plinth is a central pillar, ornamented with perfect pitchers on top.

186. On the pole rotating underneath there is a greatly rotating structure, equipped with a rotating mechanical rider by means of a wheeled *yantra*.

187. On the *vasanta*-type rider wheel, the king creates a whirling rider with a strong rotation, a delight for the eyes, which becomes an object of spotless fame in the abode of the gods in the springtime.

188. When he has built one firm pillar, built on the ground floor, and so on, with a height of four cubits, an upper floor should be built on top of it.

189. As stated before, he should make the rest in its entirety, endowed with a wheel, in the middle. He should make a *puṣpaka* that is loose on the pillar as far up as the pitcher.

190. And above that there should be a neck[61] equipped with four seats. And there, two powerful bell-shaped poles should be made by the pillar.

191. Thus, a person concealed inside the lotus-shaped structure will gradually and properly set in motion the multitude of wheels of moving *yantras* in this way. And thus those (mechanical women) with fawnlike eyes who stand in the chariot, their eyes wide open with desire or curiosity, swirl around.

192. Then the architect should build four pillars in the corners, straight, strong, and standing on well-built plinths, evenly spaced through the power of the earth (gravity?).

193. On top of that he should construct another floor. There the four riders spring to life, as described earlier, placed in the corners.

194. And on top of that he should build a half-floor, with joints of well-made wood, equipped with a wheel in the center, beautiful and attached to a tower.

195. There should be an outer lining, with many approved features of the *vasanta* type. Who is not amazed when they see the *vasantatilaka*, lovely due to the rotation of the riders on the wheels that are

swirling due to the mutual touching of the *yantras*, decorated like the temple of the gods?

196. Creating a stage for the establishment of *śāstras* (sciences), the first structure should be made square, beautiful, and with four cornices.

197. With faces in every corner, the wheels in the cornices are controlled. Therefore, on top of the story, one should add the kinds with wheels and eight seats.

198. The lines should be drawn clearly on the outside as well as the inside. One should make structures in the middle of the plinths.

199. By means of wheels placed in the center of the plinths and intersecting with one another, the automata all move with speed.

200. This leads to the happiness of the king, who is sitting on a swing, making his fame but not arrogance shine forth even among the gods, by these movements (of machines) among the temples, variegated like the movements of courtesans.

201. The architect should create an area and then divide it into eight parts, and then create a square cornice within that area.

202. On top of that, he should create one twice its size by counting the division of floors. There, the floor should be square as far as the height.

203. Therefore, the top floor is without the eight, six, and four parts. In proper order, those should be three, or with a half added.

204. He should make a bell, square in shape, equipped with the height of the remaining parts. The third and fourth stories are to be made in the size of six to four parts.

205. There should be a stage on the first floor or the second floor, and there should be riders standing

in the corners, and there should be pleasant swings equipped with cornices.

206. He should make very charming riders on the third story, in the cornices. He should further make a wheel and seats in the half structure and in the corners.

207. The wheel should have eight seats, with four seats for the swing and riders. There should also be a seat that may be called a seat for a young lady.

208. All those facing the wheel carry rotation. Where there are seats, that is here called *bhrama* (wheel).

209. On top of the stick and below the rotator he may attach a wheel, and he may join smaller wheels to the seats.

210. He should make strong bolts attached to the circle of the spokes of the small wheels, evenly spaced, united, and fastened to the spokes of the small wheels.[62]

211. He should attach the wheel, with riders on the front and top, and with a rotator that has spokes. The square of sticks horizontal in it may have two wheels.

212. He should make a device attached to the rotator with sticks for the riders on top of the second story or inside the third one.

213. He should make four evenly spaced rotators underneath the sticks supporting the seats, which are joined to the wheels of the riders.

214. That way, there is an evenly spaced stick in the center of the swing on the second floor. He may put down a stick inside the southern and northern wheels.

215. Thus, the four sticks that are attached to the wheel on the top of the head of the driver on the corner of the ground, which have two wheels, should be connected to two other wheels.

216. He should make the horizontal sticks, the ones that are in the center of the swing, connected to the wheels with the drivers in the corner in the middle of the outer wheels.

217. In the first cornice, he should create a door with a ladder at the bottom. On the rear side of the middle, he may introduce a swing for a deity.

218. Knowing properly the mutual attraction and separation of wheels and rotators, he should use either a fast device or a slow one.

219. We have briefly described the correct science of rotators. Even in other cases it should be done properly when it comes to the rotator.

220. Created by the establishment of pillars, sturdy, smooth, with long main supports, and with well-made joints . . .

221. . . . he should create in a proper way a *tripura* surrounded by ornaments on all sides, equipped with lion ears, made lovely by his own paintings.

222. He who understands properly the chapter on *yantras*, wherein *yantras* are designed with intelligence, he obtains his desires connected with fame, and is honored daily by kings.

223. This entire circle of twelve kings, made up of the crest-jewels of the protectors of the earth, whose circle is the joining of arms and pillars, rotates voluntarily. He, the sole joy of the earth, the divine king, quickly composed this chapter on *yantras*, by means of the mechanical devices created by his intellect.[63]

This was the thirty-first chapter, called "The Chapter on *Yantras*," of the architectural treatise called *Samarāṅgaṇasūtradhāra* composed by the great king Bhoja.

Notes

Introduction

1. Gaby Wood, *Edison's Eve: A Magical History of the Quest for Mechanical Life* (New York: Anchor, 2002), xiv.

2. V. Raghavan, *Yantras or Mechanical Contrivances in Ancient India* (Bangalore: Indian Institute of Culture, 1956).

3. Signe Cohen, "Romancing the Robot and Other Tales of Mechanical Beings in Indian Literature," *Acta Orientalia* 64 (2003): 65–75.

4. Daud Ali, "Bhoja's Mechanical Garden: Translating Wonder across the Indian Ocean, circa 800–1100 CE," *History of Religions* 55, no. 4 (2016): 460–493.

5. Davenport defines science fiction as fiction "based upon some imagined development of science, or upon the extrapolation of a tendency in society." See Basil Davenport, *Inquiry into Science Fiction* (New York: Longmans, Green, 1955), 15.

6. Although the term is based on ancient Greek, it is not itself found in ancient Greek texts. The *Oxford English Dictionary* refers to its use by Chambers in 1727, in reference to a mechanical being created by Albert Magnus. Higley points out, however, that the term is attested in Gabriel Naudé's writings as early as 1669, also in reference to Albert Magnus. See Sarah L. Higley, "The Legend of the Learned Man's Android," in *Retelling Tales* (Cambridge: D. S. Brewer, 1997), 130. This appears to be the earliest occurrence of the term *android*; see Jessica Riskin, *The Restless Clock: A History of the Centuries-Long Argument over What Makes Living Things Tick* (Chicago: University of Chicago Press, 2016), 115. The abbreviated form *droid* was first used in George Lucas's *Star Wars* films but has since become ubiquitous in science fiction literature and film.

7. Harold B. Segel, *Pinocchio's Progeny: Puppets, Marionettes, Automatons, and Robots in Modernist and Avant-Garde Drama* (Baltimore: Johns

Hopkins University Press, 1995), 297. The Czech term is cognate with the German *Arbeit*, "work."

8. Long before Clynes and Kline invented this term, the German Romantic author Jean Paul (1763–1825) wrote about *Maschinen-Männer*, whose biological organs had been replaced by mechanical devices, so although the term *cyborg* is only attested since the last half of the twentieth century, the concept is considerably older. See Manfred E. Clynes and Nathan S. Kline, "Cyborgs and Space," *Astronotics* 1960); and Horst Glaser and Sabine Rossbach, *The Artificial Human: A Tragical History* (Frankfurt: Peter Lang, 2011), 40.

9. The *Ṛgveda* (1.112; 1.116–118; 10.39) does mention a woman (or possibly a female horse?) called Viśpálā who loses a leg in battle and is given a replacement leg made of metal by the Aśvins. There is no evidence that this leg was conceptualized as a mechanical device rather than a plain metal rod, however. For the text of the *Ṛgveda*, see Barend A. van Nooten and Gary B. Holland, *The Rigveda* (Cambridge: Harvard University Press, 1994).

10. See for example *Rājataraṅginī* 6.160. See V. Bandhu, *Rājataraṅgiṇī of Kalhaṇa* (Hoshiarpur: Vishveshvaranand Vedic Research Institute, 1963).

11. *Kathāsaritsāgara* 29.1 and 18. See P. Durgâprasâd and K. P. Parab, *The Kathâsaritsâgara of Somabhatta* (Bombay: Nirnaya Sagara Press, 1903).

12. *Kathāsaritsāgara* 12.4. See Durgâprasâd and Parab, *Kathâsaritsâgara*.

13. *Kādambarī*. See R. Śāstrī, *Kādambarī* (Varanasi: Caukhamba, 1985).

14. T. Gaṇapati Śāstrī, *Samarāṅgaṇasūtradhāra by King Bhojadeva* (Baroda: Baroda Central Library, 1924).

15. *Kathāsaritsāgara* 43.33. See Durgâprasâd and Parab, *Kathâsaritsâgara*.

16. Translation from Stephanie Jamison and Joel Brereton, *The Rigveda* (Oxford: Oxford University Press, 2014), 1634.

17. *Mahābhārata* 1.176.10, but not included in the critical edition. In the text of the critical edition, this contraption containing the target is just described as a *yantra* in general, and there is no mention of a fish shape; see Vishnu S. Sukthankar et al., eds., *The Mahābhārata, for the First Time Critically Edited* (Poona: Bhandarkar Oriental Research Institute, 1933), vol. 1, part 2, 716. The *matsyayantra* episode is well known in popular Hinduism, however, and is depicted in the narrative friezes of the twelfth-century Amṛteśvara temple in Amrutapura, Karnataka; see Kirsti Evans, *Epic Narratives in the Hoysaḷa Temples: The Rāmāyaṇa, Mahābhārata and Bhāgavata Purāṇa in Haḷebīd, Belūr and Amṛtapura* (Brill: Leiden, 1997), 25 and 135. Evans suggests that the introduction of a fish motif in the depiction of the *yantra* may have originated in the Hoysala art of Karnataka (169), as does Alf Hiltebeitel in *The Cult of Draupadī*, vol. 1: *Mythologies: From Gingee*

to Kurukṣetra (Chicago: University of Chicago Press, 1988), 21. Hiltebeitel notes an intriguing parallel with the Telugu oral epic of Palnāḍu, which features a hero who must cut down a fish device suspended by a hair in order to win a bride (201).

18. *Harivaṃśa* 31.78 and 81.34, Visnu S. Sukthankar et al., eds., *The Harivaṃśa: The Khila or Supplement to the Mahābhārata* (Poona: Bhandarkar Oriental Research Institute, 1976). For a discussion of the problems of dating this text, see André Couture, *Kṛṣṇa in the Harivaṃśa*, vol. 2: *The Greatest of All Sovereigns and Masters* (Delhi: DK Printworld, 2017), 4 and 76–77. Couture concludes that the text in its current form took shape over a millennium, from around 200 CE to 1300 CE.

19. *Bhagavadgītā* 18.61 = *Mahābhārata* 6.18.61, Sukthankar, *Mahābhārata.*

20. *Yuddhakāṇḍa* 3.12, Jyotindra Markand Mehta, ed., *The Vālmīki Rāmāyaṇa, Critically Edited for the First Time* (Baroda: Oriental Institute, 1960–1975).

21. *Bālakāṇḍa* 5.10, Mehta, *The Vālmīki Rāmāyaṇa.*

22. *Sundarakāṇḍa* 3.18, Mehta, *The Vālmīki Rāmāyaṇa.*

23. Patrick Olivelle, *King, Governance, and Law in Ancient India: Kauṭilya's Arthaśāstra* (Oxford: Oxford University Press, 2013), 29. For the Sanskrit text, see R. P. Kangle, *The Kauṭilīya Arthaśāstra*, vol. 1: *A Critical Edition with a Glossary*, 2nd ed. (Bombay: University of Bombay, 1969).

24. See Olivelle, *King, Governance, and Law*, 402.

25. Olivelle, *King, Governance, and Law*, 107.

26. Olivelle, *King, Governance, and Law*, 105.

27. Olivelle, *King, Governance, and Law*, 142.

28. 10.6.50, see Olivelle, *King, Governance, and Law*, 387.

29. 2.24.18, see Olivelle, *King, Governance, and Law*, 153.

30. The dating of this text is disputed. A date of seventh to ninth centuries CE is suggested in Arthur B. Keith, "The Date of the Bṛhatkathā and the Mudrārākṣasa," *Journal of the Royal Asiatic Society of Great Britain and Ireland* (1909): 145–149. Coulson, however, proposes a potential date of composition between the fourth and the sixth centuries CE. A significant question for the dating of the text is whether the reference to king Candragupta in the final benedictory stanza of the text is to be taken as a genuine reference to Candragupta II, who reigned from about 376 to 415 CE. Coulson concludes that "the question cannot be taken as settled"; see Michael Coulson, *Rākṣasa's Ring by Viśākhadatta* (New York: New York University Press 2005), 15. For the Sanskrit text, see Ganga Sar Rai, ed., *Mudrārākṣasam* (Vārāṇasī: Caukhambhā Saṃskṛta Saṃsthāna, 1992).

31. *Kāmasūtra* chapter 3. For an edition of the Sanskrit text and Yaśodhara's commentary, see Durgāprasāda Dvivedī, ed., *Śrī-Vātsyāyana-*

praṇītaṃ Kāmasūtram: Yaśodhara-viracitayā Jayamaṅgalākhyayā ṭīkayā sametam (Bombay: Nirnaya Sagar Press, 1900). See also Raghavan, *Yantras*, 9.

32. Cited from *Bṛhatkathāślokasaṅgraha* 5.200–258 in Ram Prakash Poddar and Neelima Sinha, *Budhasvāmin's bṛhatkathā ślokasaṅgraha* (Varanasi: Tara Print, 1986). Also see the discussion in Raghavan, *Yantras*, 15–17.

33. David Gordon White, *The Alchemical Body: Siddhi Traditions in Medieval India* (Chicago: University of Chicago Press, 1996), 181; *Rasārṇava* 3.13–16. Sanskrit text in P. C. Ray and Hariscandra Kaviratna, *Rasārṇava* (Calcutta: Baptist Mission Press, 1910).

34. White, *Alchemical Body*, 160; *Rasaprakāśa Sudhākara* chapter 10. Sanskrit text in Yadavji Trikamji Acharya, *Rasaprakāśa Sudhākara* (Bombay: Venkatesvara Steam Press, 1910–1911).

35. *Rasaratnasamuccaya* 9.56, text from Ambikādatta Śāstri Vāgbhaṭṭa, ed., *Rasaratnasamuccaya* (Varanasi: Chaukhamba, 1939). See also White, *Alchemical Body*, 481. This apparatus is made from a clay pot, with compartments for heating various substances; see Oliver Hellwig, *Wörterbuch der Mittelalterlichen indischen Alchemie* (Eelde: Barkhuis, 2009), 21.

36. White, *Alchemical Body*, 248ff.

37. White, *Alchemical Body*, 250.

38. *Harṣacarita* 6.4, see Kāśīnāth Pāṇḍuraṅg Parāb, ed., *The Harṣacarita of Bāṇabhaṭṭa*, 7th ed. (Bombay: Nirnaya Sagar Press, 1946).

39. 12.4. Durgâprasâd and Parab, *Kathâsaritsâgara*.

40. From the introductory section of the *Avantisundarī*, Suranad Kunjan Pillai, ed., *Ācārya-Dandi-viracitā Avantisundarī* (Trivandrum: Trivandrum University, 1954). See discussion in Raghavan, *Yantras*, 12–13.

41. From the introductory section of the *Avantisundarī*, Pillai, *Ācārya-Dandi-viracitā Avantisundarī*.

42. Raghavan, *Yantras*, 13.

43. V. Raghavan, ed., *Nṛttaratnāvalī of Jāya Senāpati* (Madras: Government Oriental Manuscripts Library, 1965).

44. Gudrun Bühnemann, "Maṇḍalas and Yantras," *Brill's Encyclopedia of Hinduism*, vol. 2 (Leiden: Brill, 2010), 569.

45. Giuseppe Tucci, *The Theory and Practice of the Mandala* (London: Rider, 1969), 46.

46. Heinrich Zimmer, *Artistic Form and Yoga in the Sacred Images of India* (Princeton: Princeton University Press, 1984), 122.

47. Mircea Eliade, *Yoga: Immortality and Freedom*, 2nd ed. (Princeton: Princeton University Press, 1969), 219.

48. Hélène Brunner, "Maṇḍala and Yantra in the Siddhānta School of Śaivism: Definitions, Descriptions, and Ritual Use," in *Maṇḍalas and Yantras in the Hindu Traditions*, ed. Gudrun Bühnemann (Leiden: Brill, 2003), 162–163.

49. Brunner, "Maṇḍala and Yantra," 162.

50. Marion Rastelli, "Maṇḍalas and Yantras in the Pañcarātra Tradition," in *Maṇḍalas and Yantras in the Hindu Traditions*, ed. Gudrun Bühnemann (Leiden: Brill, 2003), 119.

51. Bühnemann, "Maṇḍalas and Yantras," 560.

52. Bühnemann, "Maṇḍalas and Yantras," 566.

53. Fredrick W. Bunce, *The Yantras of Deities and Their Numerological Foundations—An Iconographic Consideration* (New Delhi: D. K. Printworld, 2001), xiv; Gudrun Bühnemann, "Maṇḍala, Yantra and Cakra: Some Observations," in *Maṇḍalas and Yantras in the Hindu Traditions*, ed. Gudrun Bühnemann (Leiden: Brill, 2003), 47.

54. Bunce, *Yantras*, 27; Bühnemann, "Maṇḍala, Yantra and Cakra," 41.

55. Bühnemann, "Maṇḍala, Yantra and Cakra," 41.

56. Bühnemann, "Maṇḍala, Yantra and Cakra," 47.

57. Bunce, *Yantras*, xv.

58. Bühnemann, "Maṇḍala, Yantra and Cakra," 41.

59. Ulrich Schneider, "Tantra—Endpunkt eines strukturierten Ablaufs?" *Saeculum* 39 (1988): 100.

60. Zimmer, *Artistic Form*, 69; Arion Rosu, "*Mantra* et *yantra* dans la medicine et l'alchimie indiennes," in *Mantras et diagrammes* (Paris: Centre national de la recherché scientifique, 1986); Bunce, *Yantras*, 31.

61. Zimmer, *Artistic Form*, 69; Bunce, *Yantras*, 31.

62. Bunce, *Yantras*, 31.

63. Bunce, *Yantras*, 31.

64. Gudrun Bühnemann, Introduction to *Maṇḍalas and Yantras in the Hindu Traditions*, ed. Gudrun Bühnemann (Leiden: Brill, 2003), 1.

65. Madhu Khanna, "Yantra," in *Encyclopedia of Religion*, vol. 15 (New York: Macmillan, 1987), 500.

66. Bühnemann, Introduction, 1.

67. Bühnemann, "Maṇḍalas and Yantras," 560.

68. Khanna, "Yantra," 501.

69. See for example Stella Kramrisch, *The Hindu Temple* (Delhi: Motilal Banarsidass, 1976). Sonit Bafna, "On the Idea of the Mandala as a Governing Device in Indian Architectural Tradition," *Journal of the Society of Architectural Historians* 59 (2000): 26–49, argues, however, that there is not much evidence in favor of *maṇḍalas* being used as building diagrams.

70. Peter Gaeffke, "Hindu Maṇḍalas," in *The Encyclopedia of Religion*, ed. Mircea Eliade (New York: Macmillan, 1987), 154. See also Sanjukta Gupta, "The Maṇḍala as an Image of Man," in *Indian Ritual*, ed. Richard Gombrich (Delhi: Oxford University Press, 1988), 32–41.

71. Tucci, *Theory*, vii.

72. Tucci, *Theory*, vii.

73. Bühnemann, Introduction, 1.

74. Bühnemann, "Maṇḍala, Yantra and Cakra," 21.

75. *Chāndogya Upaniṣad* 8.1.1–2, *Kaivalya Upaniṣad* 6, *Maitrī Upaniṣad* 6.2, *Dhyānabindu Upaniṣad, passim*. For the text of the *Chāndogya Upaniṣad*, see Patrick Olivelle, *The Early Upaniṣads: Annotated Text and Translation* (Oxford: Oxford University Press, 1998). For the text of the *Kaivalya Upaniṣad*, see Bernadette Tubini, ed., *Kaivalyopaniṣad* (Paris: Adrien-Maisonneuve, 1952). For the text of the *Maitrī Upaniṣad*, see J. A. B. van Buitenen, *The Maitrāyaṇīya Upaniṣad* ('s-Gravenhage: Mouton, 1962). For the text of the *Dhyānabindu Upaniṣad*, see Hari Narayan Apte, *Śrīnārāyaṇaśaṃkarānandaviracitadīpikāsametānāmatharvaśikhādyānāṃ haṃsopaniṣadantānāṃ dvātriṃśanmitānām upaniṣadāṃ samuccayaḥ* (Puṇyākhyapattane: Ānandaśramamudraṇālaye, 1895). The heart is also compared to a lotus flower in the *Suśruta-saṃhitā* (5th–2nd c. BCE): "With the dawn of day a man wakes from sleep, and his heart unfolds like a lotus flower" (Kaviraj Kunja Lal Bhishagratna, *The Sushruta Samhita*, vol. 1 (Calcutta: J. N. Bose, 1907), 570. Cf. Bühnemann, "Maṇḍala, Yantra and Cakra," 22.

76. Gaeffke, "Hindu Maṇḍalas," 153.

77. Tucci, *Theory*, 23.

78. Raghavan, *Yantras*, 2.

Chapter 1: The History of Automata in the West

1. John Cohen, *Human Robots in Myth and Science* (London: George Allen & Unwin, 1966); Wood, *Edison's Eve*; Minsoo Kang, *Sublime Dreams of Living Machines: The Automaton in the European Imagination* (Cambridge: Harvard University Press, 2011); Adrienne Mayor, *Gods and Robots: Myths, Machines, and Ancient Dreams of Technology* (Princeton: Princeton University Press, 2018).

2. See Mayor, *Gods and Robots*, 1.

3. Cohen, *Human Robots*, 96.

4. L. Sprague De Camp, *The Ancient Engineers* (New York: Ballantine Books, 1960), 256ff.

5. Jean-Claude Beaune, "The Classical Age of Automata: An Impressionistic Survey from the Sixteenth to the Nineteenth Century," in *Fragments* (Cambridge: MIT Press, 1989), 431.

6. Cohen, *Human Robots*, 19.

7. Cohen, *Human Robots*, 20.

8. Derek J. de Solla Price, "Automata and the Origins of Mechanism and Mechanistic Philosophy," *Technology and Culture* 5 (1964): 9–23, here 10.

9. Cohen, *Human Robots*, 19.

10. The soul (*ka*) is the life force, closely associated with a person's name. The *ba*, or "shadow," is linked to the body but can reunite with it after death. The *ankh* is a third kind of soul in ancient Egyptian thought, a fusion of the *ba* and *ka*. See Rosalind David, *Religion and Magic in Ancient Egypt* (London: Penguin, 2002), 117; Jan Assmann, *Death and Salvation in Ancient Egypt* (Ithaca: Cornell University Press, 2005), 89; and Helen Strudwick, *The Encyclopedia of Ancient Egypt* (London: Amber Books, 2006), 178.

11. Cohen, *Human Robots*, 20.

12. Emma Brunner-Traut, "Ein Golem in der ägyptischen Literatur," *Studien zur Altägyptischen Kultur* 16 (1989): 21–26.

13. Brunner-Traut, "Golem," 22.

14. Brunner-Traut, "Golem," 23.

15. Denis Vidal, "Anthropomorphism or Sub-anthropomorphism? An Anthropological Approach to Gods and Robots," *Journal of the Royal Anthropological Institute* 13 (2007): 917.

16. Mayor, *Gods and Robots*, 1.

17. *Iliad* 18.414ff. For the text of the *Iliad*, see Martin L. West, *Homeri Ilias*, vol. 2 (Stuttgart: B. G. Teubner, 2000). See Cohen, *Human Robots*, 15; and Mayor, *Gods and Robots*, 149–150.

18. *Iliad* 18.369ff. See Cohen, *Human Robots*, 15; and John Humphrey et al., *Greek and Roman Technology: A Sourcebook—Annotated Translations of Greek and Latin Texts and Documents* (London: Routledge, 1998), 61.

19. Sylvia Berryman, "Ancient Automata and Mechanical Explanation," *Phronesis* 48 (2003): 351.

20. Berryman, "Ancient Automata," 351.

21. Ovid's *Metamorphoses* 10.243–297. For the Latin text, see R. J. Tarrant, ed., *Metamorphoses* (Oxford: Clarendon Press, 2004).

22. Dorothea Wender, *Hesiod: Theogony, Work and Days* (Harmondsworth: Penguin, 1973), 63. For the Greek text, see Richard Hamilton et al., *Hesiod's Work and Days* (Bryn Mawr: Bryn Mawr College, 1988).

23. For a more extensive discussion of Talos, see Mayor, *Gods and Robots*, 7–32.

24. Berryman, "Ancient Automata," 352. See also Glaser and Rossbach, *Artificial Human*, 9.

25. Cohen, *Human Robots*, 15.

26. M. R. Duffey, "The Vocal Memnon and Solar Thermal Automata," *Leonardo Music Journal* 17 (2007): 51–54; Cohen, *Human Robots*, 16.

27. Duffey, "Vocal Memnon," 51.

28. Aristotle, *On the Soul*, 1.3.406. For the Greek text, see W. D. Ross, *Aristotelis De Anima* (Oxford: Clarendon Press, 1956). See Cohen, *Human Robots*, 17; Humphrey et al., *Greek and Roman Technology*, 62; Wood, *Edison's Eve*, xv–xvi; and Mayor, *Gods and Robots*, 93.

29. Price, "Automata," 11.

30. Mayor, *Gods and Robots*, 197–199.

31. 12.13.11. For the Greek text, see W. R. Paton, ed., *Polybius: The Histories* (Chicago: University of Chicago Press, 2012). See Humphrey et al., *Greek and Roman Technology*, 63.

32. Henry Hodges, *Technology in the Ancient World* (Harmondsworth: Penguin, 1970), 180–184; E. R. Truitt, *Medieval Robots: Mechanism, Magic, Nature, and Art* (Philadelphia: University of Pennsylvania Press, 2015), 4; Mayor, *Gods and Robots*, 200.

33. Donald R. Hill, *A History of Engineering in Classical and Medieval Times* (La Salle: Open Court, 1984), 201.

34. Polybius's *Histories* 13.16. See discussion in Evan T. Sage, "An Ancient Robotette," *Classical Journal* 30, no. 5 (1935): 299–300; De Camp, *Ancient Engineers*, 153; and Mayor, *Gods and Robots*, 193–195.

35. Cohen, *Human Robots*, 17.

36. *Pneumatics* 1.15–16. For the Greek text, see W. Schmidt, *Heronis Alexandrini Opera quae supersunt omnia. 1. Pneumatica et Automata*, 2nd ed. (Stuttgart: B. G. Teubner, 1976). For the English translation, see Bennet Woodcroft, *The Pneumatics of Hero of Alexandria* (London: Taylor Walton and Maberly, 1851), 29. See also J. G. Landels, *Engineering in the Ancient World* (Berkeley: University of California Press, 2000), 203; Humphrey et al., *Greek and Roman Technology*, 63; Gerard Brett, "The Automata in the Byzantine 'Throne of Solomon,'" *Speculum* 29 (1954): 478ff.

37. Woodcroft, *Pneumatics*, 46.

38. Woodcroft, *Pneumatics*, 62; Harry M. Geduld, "Genesis II: The Evolution of Synthetic Man," in *Robots, Robots, Robots* (Boston: New York Graphic Society, 1978), 18.

39. Woodcroft, *Pneumatics*, 71.

40. De Camp, *Ancient Engineers*, 256ff.

41. In the *Civil Wars* (2.20.147) of his *Historia romana*. For the Latin text, see Paul Viereck and A. G. Roos, *Historia romana* (Leipzig: B. G. Teubner, 1962). See Humphrey et al., *Greek and Roman Technology*, 2011; and Gérard Walter, *Caesar: A Biography* (New York: Charles Scribner's Sons, 1952), 544.

42. Cohen, *Human Robots*, 18.

43. *Attic Nights* 10.12.9–10, Latin text in Peter K. Marshall, *Noctes Atticae* (Oxford: Clarendon Press, 1968). See Price, "Automata," 11; Berryman, "Ancient Automata," 354; and Humphrey et al., *Greek and Roman Technology*, 62.

44. *The Recognitions of Clement*, book 2, chapter 9. Latin text in Bernhard Rehm and Georg Strecker, eds., *Die Pseudoklementinen*, 2nd ed. (Berlin: Akademie-Verlag, 1994). See Moshe Idel, *Golem: Jewish Magical and*

Mystical Traditions of the Artificial Anthropoid (Albany: State University of New York Press, 1990).

45. Frances Yates, *Giordano Bruno and the Hermetic Tradition* (Chicago: University of Chicago Press, 1964), 37. See also Cohen, *Human Robots*, 21.

46. Hill, *History of Engineering*, 201; Truitt, *Medieval Robots*, 20.

47. Truitt, *Medieval Robots*, 20.

48. Donald R. Hill, *The Book of Ingenious Devices (Kitāb al-Ḥiyal) by the Banū (Sons of) Mūsà bin Shākir* (Dordrecht: D. Reidel, 1979), 3; Hill, *History of Engineering*, 202; Truitt, *Medieval Robots*, 20.

49. Hill, *Ingenious Devices*, 19; Ahmad Y. Hassan and Donald R. Hill, *Islamic Technology* (Cambridge: Cambridge University Press, 1986), 60; Siegfried Zielinski, "Allah's Automata: Where Ancient Oriental Learning Intersects with Early Modern Europe—A Media-Archaeological Miniature by Way of Introduction," in *Allah's Automata* (Karlsruhe: ZKM, 2016), 2021.

50. Zielinski, "Allah's Automata," 12.

51. Zielinski, "Allah's Automata," 17.

52. Donald R. Hill, *Studies in Medieval Islamic Technology: From Philo to al-Jazari, from Alexandria to Diyar Bakr* (Aldershot: Ashgate, 1998), xvii, 34.

53. Hill, *History of Engineering*, 203–204.

54. Ananda K. Coomaraswamy, *The Treatise of Al-Jazarī on Automata* (Boston: Museum of Fine Arts, 1924), 12.

55. Coomaraswamy, *Treatise*, 14.

56. Coomaraswamy, *Treatise*, 18–19.

57. Truitt, *Medieval Robots*, 31.

58. Rugaya Hashim et al., "Religious Perceptions on Use of Humanoid for Spiritual Augmentation of Children with Autism," *Procedia Computer Science* 105 (2017): 353–358.

59. Truitt, *Medieval Robots*, 5.

60. Alfred Chapuis and Edmond Droz, *Automata: A Historical and Technological Study* (Neuchâtel: Éditions du Griffon, 1958), 36; Truitt, *Medieval Robots*, 5.

61. For the French text, see Paul Aebischer, *Le voyage de Charlemagne à Jérusalem et à Constantinople* (Geneva: Libraire Droz, 1965). For discussion, see Truitt, *Medieval Robots*, 12.

62. Brett, *Automata*, 477. For the Greek text, see Albert Vogt, ed., *Le livre des cérémonies*, 2 vols. (Paris: Société d'édition "Les Belles Lettres," 1935–1940). This text is ascribed to Emperor Constantine VII Porphyrop-genetos, see Truitt, *Medieval Robots*, 23.

63. Brett, *Automata*, 477–478.

64. Marcus Rautman, *Daily Life in the Byzantine Empire* (Westport: Greenwood Press, 2006), 4.

65. A speaking head of Orpheus at Lesbos, mentioned in Ovid's *Metamorphoses*, XI.55, see Tarrant's edition.

66. Odin takes advice from Mimir's severed head in *Voluspá* 47. For the Old Norse text, see Gustav Neckel and Hans Kuhn, eds., *Edda: Die Lieder des Codex Regius nebst verwandten Denkmälern, Vol. 1, Text*, 5th ed. (Heidelberg: Carl Winter, 1983).

67. Kevin LaGrandeur, *Androids and Intelligent Networks in Early Modern Literature and Culture: Artificial Slaves* (New York: Routledge, 2013), 82.

68. J. A. Giles, *William of Malmesbury's Chronicle of the Kings of England: From the Earliest Period to the Reign of King Stephen* (Eugene: Wipf & Stock, 2004), 181; Cohen, *Human Robots*, 27; Higley "Legend," 137; Kang, *Sublime Dreams*, 68ff.

69. Todd Andrew Borlik, " 'More than Art': Clockwork Automata, the Extemporizing Actor, and the Brazen Head in *Friar Bacon and Friar Bungay*," in *The Automaton in English Renaissance Literature* (Burlington: Ashgate, 2011), 129–144.

70. Roger Bacon's creation of a speaking brazen head is described in Robert Greene's 1590 play *Friar Bacon and Friar Bungay*. See David Selzer, ed., *Friar Bacon and Friar Bungay* (Lincoln: University of Nebraska Press, 1963). See Cohen, *Human Robots*, 31; Geduld, "Genesis II"; Higley, "Legend," 137.

71. Daniel Defoe, *A Journal of the Plague Year* (London: E. Nutt, J. Roberts, A. Dodd, and J. Graves, 1722).

72. Canto 1, George Gordon Byron, *Don Juan* (London: Thomas Davison, 1819).

73. Nathaniel Hawthorne, "The Birth-Mark," *The Pioneer*, March 1843.

74. Borlik, "More than Art," 130.

75. Kang, *Sublime Dreams*, 78.

76. LaGrandeur, *Android and Intelligent Networks*, 85.

77. Higley, "Legend," 137; Borlik, " 'More than Art,' " 130; Domenico Comparetti, *Vergil in the Middle Ages* (Piscataway: Gorgias Press, 2002), 258–259.

78. Truitt, *Medieval Robots*, 65.

79. Truitt, *Medieval Robots*, 65.

80. E. R. Truitt, "Fictions of Life and Death: Tomb Automata in Medieval Romance," *Postmedieval: A Journal of Medieval Cultural Studies* 1 (2010): 195; Truitt, *Medieval Robots*, 54.

81. Higley, "Legend," 137; Comparetti, *Vergil*, 306.

82. Truitt "Fictions"; Truitt, *Medieval Robots*, 99.

83. Linda M. Strauss, "Reflections in a Mechanical Mirror: Automata as Doubles and Tools," *Knowledge and Society: Studies in the Sociology of Culture Past and Present* 10 (1996): 194. E. R. Truitt, " 'Trei poëte, sages dotors, qui mout sovent di nigromance': Knowledge and Automata in

Twelfth-Century French Literature," *Configurations* 12 (2004): 172, makes a similar observation.

84. Truitt, *Medieval Robots,* 56.

85. Truitt, *Medieval Robots,* 59.

86. Alexander Marr, "Understanding Automata in the Late Renaissance," *Journal de la Renaissance* 2 (2004): 205.

87. Geduld, "Genesis II," 18; Marr, "Understanding Automata," 205.

88. William Godwin, *Lives of the Necromancers: Or, An Account of the Most Eminent Persons in Successive Ages, Who Have Claimed for Themselves, or to Whom Has Been Imputed by Others, the Exercise of Magical Powers* (London: F. J. Mason, 1834).

89. Geduld, "Genesis II," 18.

90. Higley, "Legend," 141; Kang, *Sublime Dreams,* 70.

91. Higley, "Legend," 141. See also Arthur Dickson, *Valentine and Orson: A Study in Late Medieval Romance* (New York: Columbia University Press, 1929), 214, note 147.

92. Joachim Sighart, *Albert the Great of the Order of Friar-Preachers: His Life and Scholastic Labours,* trans. Rev. Fr. T. A. Dixon (London: R. Washborne, 1876), 147.

93. Higley, "Legend," 142.

94. Roger Sherman Loomis, *The Grail from Celtic Myth to Christian Symbol* (Cardiff: University of Wales Press, 1963), 135–136.

95. Truitt, *Medieval Robots,* 119.

96. Truitt, *Medieval Robots,* 123–124.

97. Silvio Bedini, "The Role of Automata in the History of Technology," *Technology and Culture* 5 (1964): 31.

98. Bedini, "Role of Automata," 31.

99. Bedini, "Role of Automata," 32.

100. Anthony Grafton, "The Devil as Automaton: Giovanni Fontana and the Meanings of a Fifteenth-Century Machine," in *Genesis Redux* (Chicago: University of Chicago Press, 2007), 46.

101. Grafton, "Devil as Automaton," 55.

102. Bedini, "Role of Automata," 32; Price, "Automata," 18.

103. Glaser and Rossbach, *Artificial Human,* 8.

104. Chapuis and Droz, *Automata,* 53.

105. Cohen, *Human Robots,* 38; Geduld, "Genesis II," 7; Idel, *Golem,* 27.

106. Idel, *Golem,* 185–186.

107. Idel, *Golem,* 30.

108. Idel, *Golem,* 31.

109. Esther J. Hamori, *Women's Divination in Biblical Literature: Prophecy, Necromancy, and Other Arts of Knowledge* (New Haven: Yale University Press, 2015), 190.

110. Cohen, *Human Robots,* 189.

111. Hamori, *Women's Divination*, 191.
112. Hamori, *Women's Divination*, 191.
113. *Pirke Avot* 5.7, Leonard Kravitz and Kerry M. Olitzky, eds., *Pirke Avot* (New York: UAHC Press, 1993), 80.
114. Idel, *Golem*, 232.
115. Idel, *Golem*, 34.
116. Idel, *Golem*, 34–35.
117. Idel, *Golem*, 32.
118. Cohen, *Human Robots*, 38–39; Geduld, "Genesis II," 7; Idel, *Golem*, 233.
119. Idel, *Golem*, 233.
120. Idel, *Golem*, 234.
121. Cohen, *Human Robots*, 39; Idel, *Golem*, 55.
122. Idel, *Golem*, 56.
123. Idel, *Golem*, 57.
124. Idel, *Golem*, 55.
125. Idel, *Golem*, 57.
126. Idel, *Golem*, 58.
127. Idel, *Golem*, 64.
128. Geduld, "Genesis II," 8.
129. Cohen, *Human Robots*, 40.
130. Idel, *Golem*, 208.
131. Rabbi Loew was also known as the Maharal, an acronym standing for the Hebrew phrase "Our teacher, Rabbi Leyb."
132. Cohen, *Human Robots*, 41; Geduld, "Genesis II," 8.
133. Translated in Joachim Neugroschel, *The Golem* (New York: W. W. Norton, 2006).
134. Idel, *Golem*, 219.
135. Lynsey McCullough, "Antique Myth, Early Modern Mechanism: The Secret History of Spenser's Iron Man," in *The Automaton* (Burlington: Ashgate, 2011), 76.
136. For a discussion, see Riskin, *Restless Clock*, 44ff.
137. Cohen, *Human Robots*, 69; Glaser and Rossbach, *Artificial Human*, 151; Kang, *Sublime Dreams*, 123.
138. Wood, *Edison's Eve*, 3–4.
139. Kang, *Sublime Dreams*, 123.
140. Scott Maisano, "Descartes avec Milton: The Automata in the Garden," in *The Automaton* (Burlington: Ashgate, 2011), 24.
141. Glaser and Rossbach, *Artificial Human*, 99.
142. Glaser and Rossbach, *Artificial Human*, 99.
143. Cohen, *Human Robots*, 83.
144. Bedini, "Role of Automata," 38.

145. Paula Findlen, "Scientific Spectacle in Baroque Rome: Athanasius Kircher and the Roman College Museum," in *Jesuit Science* (Cambridge: MIT Press, 2003), 253.

146. Findlen, "Scientific Spectacle," 223.

147. Findlen, "Scientific Spectacle," 241–242.

148. Brooke Conti, "The Mechanical Saint: Early Modern Devotion and the Language of Automation," in *The Automaton* (Burlington: Ashgate, 2011), 95.

149. Conti, "Mechanical Saint," 96.

150. Conti, "Mechanical Saint," 97.

151. Chapuis and Droz, *Automata,* 233; Cohen, *Human Robots,* 86.

152. Cohen, *Human Robots,* 87.

153. Bedini, "Role of Automata," 36.

154. Geduld, "Genesis II," 22.

155. Bedini, "Role of Automata," 39; Cohen, *Human Robots,* 87.

156. Chapuis and Droz, *Automata,* 280–282; Bedini, "Role of Automata," 39; Cohen, *Human Robots,* 87.

157. Chapuis and Droz, *Automata,* 292–295.

158. Chapuis and Droz, *Automata,* 297–301; Bedini, "Role of Automata," 39; Wood, *Edison's Eve,* xii–xiv.

159. Wood, *Edison's Eve,* 8.

160. Wood, *Edison's Eve,* xv.

161. Julien Offray de La Mettrie, *L'Homme machine* (Leiden: Elie Luzac, 1747).

162. Glaser and Rossbach, *Artificial Human,* 96.

163. Wood, *Edison's Eve,* 12.

164. Cohen, *Human Robots,* 72.

165. Glaser and Rossbach, *Artificial Human,* 103.

166. From *Innocents Abroad,* cited in Glaser and Rossbach, *Artificial Human,* 102.

167. Wood, *Edison's Eve,* 60–61.

168. Wood, *Edison's Eve,* 62.

169. Chapuis and Droz, *Automata,* 363–365; Cohen, *Human Robots,* 90.

170. Wood, *Edison's Eve,* 81.

171. Auguste Villiers de l'Isle-Adam, *Tomorrow's Eve* (Urbana: University of Illinois Press, 1982).

172. The author informs us that "Hadaly" is the Persian word for "Ideal," but to the best of my knowledge, this is sheer fantasy on the part of Villiers de l'Isle-Adam.

173. See for example Ira Levin's novel *The Stepford Wives* (New York: Random House, 1972) and its 1975 and 2004 film adaptations, Paolo Baci-

galupi's novel *The Windup Girl* (San Francisco: Nightshade Books, 2009), and the films *Her* (2013) and *Ex Machina* (2015).

174. Sigmund Freud, *The Uncanny* (London: Penguin, 2003), 124.

175. Freud, *The Uncanny*, 135.

176. Cf. Nicholas Royle, *The Uncanny* (New York: Routledge, 2003), 1.

177. Higley, "Legend," 128.

178. Wood, *Edison's Eve*, xv.

179. Cohen, *Human Robots*, 61.

180. J. P. Telotte, *Replications: A Robotic History of the Science Fiction Film* (Urbana: University of Illinois Press, 1995), 20.

181. For an examination of memory and humanity in *Blade Runner*, see Silke Arnold de-Simine, "Ich erinnere, also bin ich?—Menschen und Gedäctnismedien in Ridley Scott's *Blade Runner* (1982/1992)," in *Textmaschinenkörper* (Amsterdam: Rodopi, 2006), 225–242.

182. Donna Haraway, "A Cyborg Manifesto: Science, Technology, and Socialist-Feminism in the Late Twentieth Century," *Socialist Review* 15, no. 2 (1985): 65–107.

183. Cohen, *Human Robots*, 105.

184. Wendy Beth Hyman, Introduction to *The Automaton* (Burlington: Ashgate, 2011), 3.

185. Ernst Jentsch, "Zur Psychologie des Unheimlichen," *Psychiatrisch-Neurologische Wochenschrift* 8, no. 22 (1906): 195–198 and 8, no. 23 (1906): 203–205. See discussion in Lydia Liu, *The Freudian Robot: Digital Media and the Future of the Unconscious* (Chicago: University of Chicago Press, 2010), 207.

186. Freud, *The Uncanny*.

187. Kang, *Sublime Dreams*, 44.

188. Masahiro Mori, "Bukimi no tani [The Uncanny Valley]," *Energy* 4 (1970): 33–35.

189. Takeshi Kimura, "Masahiro Mori's Buddhist Philosophy of Robot," *Paladyn, Journal of Behavioral Robotics* 9 (2018): 72.

190. See Pravas Jivan Chaudhury, "The Theory of Rasa [1952]," *Journal of Aesthetics and Art Criticism* 11, no. 2 (1952): 147–150; and Pravas Jivan Chaudhury, "The Theory of Rasa [1965]," *Journal of Aesthetics and Art Criticism* 24, no. 1 (1965): 145–149.

191. *Nāṭyaśāstra* 6: 42–45, text in Manavalli Ramakrishna Kavi, ed., *Nāṭyaśāstra*, 4 vols. (Baroda: Central Library, 1926–1964). See Susan Schwartz, *Rasa: Performing the Divine in India* (New York: Columbia University Press, 2004), 15.

192. Sheldon Pollock, *A Rasa Reader: Classical Indian Aesthetics* (New York: Columbia University Press, 2016), 8–9.

193. Pollock, *Rasa Reader*, 18.

194. Ali, "Bhoja's Mechanical Garden," 474.
195. Ali, "Bhoja's Mechanical Garden," 478.
196. See Chaudhury, "Theory of Rasa [1952]," 147.
197. *Nāṭyaśāstra* 6.35, see Chaudhury, "Theory of Rasa [1952]," 147.

Chapter 2: Interlude: Yavanas and the Creation of Automata

1. Himanshu P. Ray, "The Yavana Presence in Ancient India," *Journal of the Economic and Social History of the Orient* 31, no. 3 (1988): 312.

2. Ray, "Yavana Presence," 312; Romila Thapar, "Indian Views of Europe: Representations of the Yavanas in Early Indian History," in *Cultural Pasts: Essays in Early Indian History*, ed. Romila Thapar (Delhi: Oxford University Press 2000), 539; and Matthew Adam Cobb, *Rome and the Indian Ocean Trade from Augustus to the Early Third Century CE* (Leiden: Brill 2018), 163.

3. Thapar, "Indian Views of Europe," 539.

4. *Manu* 10, 43–44 (Ganganatha Jha, *Manusmṛti with the Commentary "Manubhāṣya" of Acārya Medhātithi*, 2 vols. [Delhi: Parimal, 1998]) and *Mahābhārata* 13.33.19–21 (Sukthankar et al., *Mahābhārata*). See Thapar, "Indian Views of Europe," 542.

5. Thapar, "Indian Views of Europe," 546–448; and Cobb, *Rome and the Indian Ocean Trade*, 164–165.

6. Kamil Zvelebil, "The Yavanas in Old Tamil Literature," in *Charisteria Orientalia praecipua ad Persiam pertinenia*, edited by Felix Tauel et al., 401–409 (Prague: Nakladatelstvi Československe Akademi, 1956), 409.

7. U. V. Sāminātaiyar, *Puṟanāṉūṟu Mūlamum Ureiyum* (Madras: n.p., 1950). For the dating of this text, see Zvelebil, "Yavanas in Old Tamil Literature," 401.

8. The Tamil term *kalam* could be translated as either "bowl" or "boat," so alternatively, the Yavanas might bring wine in beautiful bowls or jars. See Zvelebil, "Yavanas," 402.

9. *Akanāṉūṟu*, 2nd ed. (Tirunelvēli, Ceṉṉai: Caivacittānta nūṟpatippuk kaḻakam, 1949). For the dating of this text, see Kamil Zvelebil, *The Smile of Murugan: On Tamil Literature of South India* (Leiden: Brill, 1973), 41–43.

10. U. V. Sāminātaiyar, *Pattuppāṭṭu mūlamum*, 3rd ed. (Ceṉṉai: Kēcari Accukkūṭam, 1931). For dating of this text, see Zvelebil, "Yavanas," 401.

11. Zvelebil, "Yavanas," 405.

12. Naṭukkāvēri Mu. Vēṅkaṭacāmi Nāṭṭār, ed., *Cīttalaic Cāttanār iyaṟṟiya Maṇimēkalai* (Ceṉṉai: Tirunelvēlit Teṉṉintiya Caivacittānta Nūṟpatippuk Kaḻakam, 1951). See also Zvelebil, "Yavanas," 406.

13. Zvelebil notes that a fragment of a Roman earthen lamp dating from the first century CE has been found in Arikamedu and implies that the poet may have seen such lamps firsthand. See Zvelebil, "Yavanas," 407.

14. *Yugapurāṇa* 47–48 and 56–57. The *Yugapurāṇa* is part of the *Gargīyajyotiṣa*. For the Sanskrit text, English translation, and discussion, see John E. Mitchiner, *The Yuga Purāṇa* (Calcutta: Asiatic Society, 1986). Mitchiner dates the brief text to around 25 BCE (16).

15. *Harivaṃśa* 25.8–27 and 80.1–8 (Sukthankar ed.).

16. See for example the fifth rock edict, E. Hultzsch, *Inscriptions of Asoka* [*Corpus Inscriptionum Indicarum I*] (Varanasi: Indological Book House, 1969), 8.

17. Romila Thapar, *Aśoka and the Decline of the Mauryas* (Oxford: Oxford University Press, 1961), 41. For the texts of Aśoka's edicts, see D. C. Sirkar, *Inscriptions of Aśoka* (Delhi: Government of India Press, 1967).

18. Text in Vilhelm Treckner, *The Milindapañho: Being Dialogues between King Milinda and the Buddhist Sage Nāgasena: The Pali Text* (London: Luzac, 1962).

19. See discussion in Jagdishchandra Jain, *Studies in Early Jainism* (New Delhi: Navrang, 1992), 20–24.

20. Jain, *Studies in Early Jainism*, 92–93.

21. *Harṣacarita* 6.4, Sanskrit text from Parāb, *The Harṣacarita of Bāṇabhaṭṭa*.

22. See Raghavan, *Yantras*, 15.

23. Pillai, *Ācārya-Dandi-viracitā Avantisundarī*.

24. Jain, *Studies in Early Jainism*, 93.

25. Cohen, *Human Robots*, 23.

26. Charles P. Eells, trans., *Life and Times of Apollonius of Tyana* (Stanford: Stanford University Press, 1923), 78.

27. Simon Swain, "Apollonius in Wonderland," in *Ethics and Rhetoric: Classical Essays for Donald Russell on His Seventy-Fifth Birthday*, ed. Doreen Innes, Harry Hine, and Christopher Pelling (Oxford: Clarendon Press, 1995), 252.

28. Swain, "Apollonius in Wonderland," 253.

Chapter 3: Robots in the Royal Garden

1. Traditionally, India is home to many kinds of puppets, including string puppets, rod puppets, glove puppets, and shadow puppets, but string puppets have always been the most popular ones. See Sampa Ghosh and Utpal K. Banerjee, *Indian Puppets* (New Delhi: Abhinav, 2006), 75 and 99.

2. Richard Pischel, *The Home of the Puppet Play* (London: Luzac, 1902), 25; M. K. Varadpande, *Ancient Indian and Indo-Greek Theatre* (New Delhi: Abhinav, 1981), 113.

3. Pischel, *Home of the Puppet Play*, 6.

4. *Mahābhārata* 5.39.1 (Sukthankar, *Mahābhārata*).

5. Pischel, *Home of the Puppet Play*, 5.

6. *Mahābhārata* 4.37.29 (Sukthankar, *Mahābhārata*). See also Pischel, *Home of the Puppet Play*, 6.

7. This episode from Ananta's pre-fifteenth-century *Vīracarita* is summarized in Hermann Jacobi, "Über das Vīracaritram," *Indische Studien* 14 (1876): 116. Jacobi consulted the original manuscript kept at the East India Company in London, but unfortunately, the Sanskrit text was never published, and the present whereabouts of the manuscript are not known. There are no other extant manuscripts of the texts.

8. Michael Schuster, "Visible Puppets and Hidden Puppeteers: Indian Gombeyata Puppetry," *Asian Theatre Journal* 18 (2001): 59–68, here 66–67.

9. The text was first edited by T. Gaṇapati Śāstrī and published in 1924 (Śāstrī, *Samarāṅgaṇasūtradhāra*). Śāstrī based his edition on three manuscripts, but none of the manuscripts were complete, so the current published text is also incomplete. Felix Otter, *Residential Architecture in Bhoja's Samarāṅgaṇasūtradhāra* (Delhi: Motilal Banarsidass, 2010), 5. A revised edition was published by V. S. Agrawala in the Gaekwad Oriental Series: Vasudeva Saran Agrawala, *Samarāṅgaṇa-Sūtradhāra of Mahārājadhirāja Bhoja, the Paramāra Ruler of Dhārā* (Baroda: Oriental Institute, 1966).

10. Otter argues based on inconsistencies of style, vocabulary, and contents that the *Samarāṅgaṇasūtradhāra* is likely a compilation of multiple authors' work. Otter, *Residential Architecture*, 31.

11. Mahesh Singh, *Bhoja Paramāra and His Times* (Delhi: Bharatiya Vidya Prakashan, 1984), 1ff.

12. Singh, *Bhoja*, 22 and 34.

13. H. C. Ray, *The Dynastic History of Northern India (Early Medieval Period)*, vol. 2. (Calcutta: University of Calcutta, 1931), 869.

14. Singh, *Bhoja*, 314.

15. Cited from Singh, *Bhoja*, 24–25.

16. Oracular heads are mentioned in William of Malmesbury's *Gesta Regum Anglorum* from around 1125 and in Gautier de Metz's *L'image du monde* from approximately 1245. The possible influence of *L'image du monde* on the Buddhist text *Lokapaññatti* is discussed later in this book.

17. V. A. K. Ayer, *Untold Stories of King Bhoja* (Bombay: Bharatiya Vidya Bhavan, 1975).

18. Louis H. Gray, *The Narrative of Bhoja (Bhojaprabandha) by Ballāla of Benares* (New Haven: American Oriental Society, 1950).

19. Gray, *Narrative of Bhoja,* 20.

20. Singh, *Bhoja,* 132ff.

21. Singh, *Bhoja,* 141.

22. Singh, *Bhoja,* 160.

23. This translation is based on the text in the edition by Gaṇapati Śāstrī, revised by Agrawala in 1966. The entire text of the *Samarāṅgaṇasūtradhāra* was translated into English by Sudarshan Kumar Sharma as *Samarāṅgaṇa Sūtradhāra of Bhojadeva (Paramāra Ruler of Dhāra): An Ancient Treatise on Architecture,* 2 vols. (Delhi: Parimal, 2007). While this translation is helpful to some extent, it is not always very literal. I have therefore included my own translation of the Sanskrit text in the appendix. Although the original text is in verse, I have not attempted to recreate the Sanskrit meter in English.

24. Roy suggests that the author of the *Samarāṅgaṇasūtradhāra* may have been influenced by Greek philosophy and points to Hero of Alexandria's discussion of air, earth, fire, and water in the creation of various mechanical devices. Mira Roy, "The Concept of Yantra in the *Samarāṅgaṇa-Sūtradhāra* of Bhoja," *Indian Journal of History of Science* 19, no. 2 (1984): 119.

25. Hellwig, *Wörterbuch,* 21.

26. Berryman, "Ancient Automata," 362.

27. *De natura deorum,* books 2, 34, and 38. For the Latin text, see Francis Brooks, *Marci Tullii Ciceronis De natura deorum* (London: Methuen, 1896).

28. Edward Dolnick, *The Clockwork Universe: Isaac Newton, the Royal Society, and the Birth of the Modern World* (New York: Harper Perennial, 2012), 182.

29. H. G. Alexander, *The Leibniz-Clarke Correspondence* (Manchester: Manchester University Press, 1956), 11–12. Cited from Steven Shapin, "Of Gods and Kings: Natural Philosophy and Politics in the Leibniz-Clarke Disputes," *Isis* 72 (1981): 187–215, here 193.

30. Cited from Dolnick, *Clockwork Universe,* vii.

31. *Taittirīya Upaniṣad* 2.1–2.5, *Praśna Upaniṣad* 4.8, *Śvetāśvatara Upaniṣad* 2.12. Olivelle, *Early Upaniṣads.*

32. See for example https://wiki2.org/en/Vaimānika_Shāstra.

33. An article by Shruti and Jairam, essentially a summary the thirty-first chapter of the *Samarāṅgaṇasūtradhāra,* argues that the technology described must have existed even prior to Bhoja's time. K. R. Shruti and Rajani Jairam, "Mechanical Contrivances and Dharu Vimanas Described in 'Samarangana Sutradhara' of Bhojadeva," *Journal of Humanities and Social Science* 20, no. 12 (2015): 16–20.

34. See for example M. Shivanandam, "Mercury Propulsion System in Vedic Vimanas and Modern Spacecraft," *International Journal of Research and Analytical Reviews* 2, no. 2 (2015): 136–144.

35. White, *Alchemical Body*, 11.

36. Peter James and Nick Thorpe, *Ancient Inventions* (New York: Ballantine Books, 1994), 131; Mayor, *Gods and Robots*, 94.

37. Mayor, *Gods and Robots*, 94.

38. *Rasaratnasamuccaya* 8. 32, text from Śāstri, *Rasaratnasamuccaya*.

39. Ali in "Bhoja's Mechanical Garden" (461) argues that the text is likely composed by a court poet rather than by King Bhoja himself.

40. Sanskrit text in Kalpalatā Munshi, *Śṛṅgāramañjarīkathā* (Bombay: Bhāratīya Vidyā Bhavana, 1959), sections 5–3.

41. In Indian literature, *cakora* birds, which are a kind of partridge, are said to subsist on moonlight.

42. See Franklin Edgerton, "A Hindu Book of Tales: The Vikramacarita," *American Journal of Philology* 33, no. 3 (1912): 249–284; and Edgerton, *Vikrama's Adventures: Or Thirty-Two Tales of the Throne* (Cambridge: Harvard University Press, 1926).

43. Ali, "Bhoja's Mechanical Garden," 465. See also Daud Ali, "Gardens in Early Indian Court Life," *Studies in History* 19, no. 2 (2003): 221–252.

44. P. Śivadatta and Kāśināth Panduraṅg Parab, *Yaśastilakacampū* (Bombay: Tūkarām

Jāvajī, 1901), 1.355–358. See also V. Raghavan, "Somadeva and King Bhoja," *Journal of the University of Gauhati* 3 (1952): 35–38; and Ali, "Bhoja's Mechanical Garden," 463.

45. Ali, "Bhoja's Mechanical Garden," 465.

46. Ali, "Bhoja's Mechanical Garden," 465.

47. Ali, "Bhoja's Mechanical Garden," 468.

48. A supernatural spirit.

Chapter 4: Body of Flesh, Body of Wood, Body of Stone: Humans, Androids, and Gods in Hinduism

1. *Ṛgveda* 10.58. See John Robert Gardner, "The Developing Terminology for the Self in Vedic India," PhD dissertation, University of Iowa, 1998.

2. Dominik Wujastyk, "Interpreting the Image of the Human Body in Premodern India," *International Journal of Hindu Studies* 13 (2009): 189–228, here 194–195.

3. Jamison and Brereton, *Rigveda*, 1540.

4. Etymologically, *ātman* is derived from a verbal root *an* that means "to breathe" and cognate with the German *Atem*, "breath."

5. See for example *Bṛhadāraṇyaka Upaniṣad* 1.1.1, 1.2.1, 1.2.3, 1.2.4, 1.2.5, 1.2.7, 1.4.4., 1.5.21, 1.6.3, 2.4.4; *Chāndogya Upaniṣad* 1.2.14, 1.6.3, 3.18.1, 4.3.3, 8.8.1, 8. 8.4; *Aitareya Upaniṣad* 2.2; and *Kauṣītaki Upaniṣad* 2.12, 4.2, and 4.10 in Olivelle, *Early Upaniṣads*. See discussion in Signe Cohen, *Text and Authority in the Older Upaniṣads* (Leiden: Brill, 2008), 40; and Jacqueline Suthren Hirst, "*Ātman* and *Brahman* in the Principal Upaniṣads," in *The Upaniṣads*, ed. Signe Cohen (London: Routledge, 2018), 107.

6. *Taittirīya Upaniṣad* 2.2–2.5 in Olivelle, *Early Upaniṣads*.

7. *Kaṭha Upaniṣad* 3.3–4 in Olivelle, *Early Upaniṣads*. This striking image has parallels in both Buddhist and ancient Greek literature. See Signe Cohen, "Conclusion," in *The Upaniṣads* (London: Routledge, 2018), 414–415.

8. See for example *Kaṭha Upaniṣad* 1.6. For a full discussion, see Dermot Killingley, "Karma and Rebirth in the Upaniṣads," in *The Upaniṣads* (London: Routledge, 2018), 121–132.

9. Gerald James Larson, "The Concept of Body in *Ayurveda* and the Hindu Philosophical Systems," in *Self as Body*, ed. Thomas P. Kasulis et al. (Albany: State University of New York Press, 1993), 107; S. Cromwell Crawford, *Hindu Bioethics for the Twenty-First Century* (Albany: State University of New York Press, 2003), 44.

10. Larson, "Concept of Body," 112.

11. White, *Alchemical Body*, 21.

12. Crawford, *Hindu Bioethics*, 56.

13. Crawford *Hindu Bioethics*, 56–57.

14. *Carakasaṃhitā* 5.3, cited in Wujastyk, "Interpreting the Image," 195. Sanskrit text in Yadavji Trikamji Acharya, *Caraka Saṃhitā* (Bombay: Chaukhambha, 1941).

15. Wendy Doniger, "Medical and Mythical Constructions of the Body in Hindu Texts," in *Religion and the Body*, ed. Sarah Coakley (Cambridge: Cambridge University Press, 1997), 171–172.

16. Doniger, "Medical and Mythical Constructions," 172.

17. *Bhagavadgītā* 2.22 (Sukthankar, *Mahābhārata*).

18. John M. Koller, "Human Embodiment: Indian Perspectives," in *Self as Body* (Albany: State University of New York Press, 1993), 46–47.

19. Wujastyk, "Interpreting the Image," 190.

20. Mark Singleton, *Yoga Body: The Origins of Modern Posture Practice* (Oxford: Oxford University Press, 2010), 26.

21. André Padoux, "Hindu Tantrism," in *The Encyclopedia of Religion*, vol. 14, ed. Mircea Eliade (New York: Macmillan, 1986), 273.

22. White, *Alchemical Body*, 4–5.

23. Wujastyk, "Interpreting the Image," 199.

24. George Weston Briggs, *Gorakhnāth and the Kānphaṭa Yogīs* (Delhi: Motilal Banarsidass, 1938), cited in Wujastyk, "Interpreting the Image," 199. See also Eliade, *Yoga*, 236–241.

25. Georg Feuerstein, *Tantra: The Path of Ecstasy* (Boston: Shambhala, 1998), 57.

26. David Gordon White, *Tantra in Practice* (Princeton: Princeton University Press, 2000), 9.

27. Madhu Khanna, "Yantra and Cakra in Tantric Meditation," in *Asian Traditions of Meditation*, ed. Halvor Eifring (Honolulu: University of Hawai'i Press, 2016), 71–72.

28. Khanna, "Yantra and Cakra," 78.

29. Bühnemann, *Maṇḍalas and Yantras in the Hindu Tradition*, 1.

30. André Padoux, "Maṇḍalas in Abhinavagupta's *Tantrāloka*," in *Maṇḍalas and Yantras in the Hindu Tradition*, ed. Gudrun Bühnemann (Leiden: Brill 2003), 232–235. See also Sthaneshwar Timalsina, *Language of Images: Visualization and Meaning in Tantras* (New York: Peter Lang, 2015), 64.

31. White, *Alchemical Body*, 6, 52.

32. Satischandra Chatterjee and Dhirendramohan Datta, *An Introduction to Indian Philosophy*, 7th ed. (Calcutta: University of Calcutta Press, 1968), 62–63.

33. Chatterjee and Datta, *Introduction to Indian Philosophy*, 61.

34. See the discussion in Eliot Deutsch, "The Concept of the Body," in *Self as Body* (Albany: State University of New York Press, 1993), 5–19.

35. Deutsch, "Concept of the Body," 7.

36. Author's translation from the Sanskrit text in Raghavan (*Yantras*, 12), who cites the verse from a manuscript at the Travancore University Oriental MSS. Library. The text is also published in Pillai, *Ācārya-Dandi-viracitā Avantisundarī*.

37. 7.9.1f. Sanskrit text in Durgâprasâd and Parab, *Kathâsaritsâgara*.

38. The name means "giver of life-breath," a suitable name for a maker of *yantras*.

39. "The inner *ātman* is a person the size of a thumb," *Taittirīya Upaniṣad* 10.38.1, *Kena Upaniṣad* 2.3.17, *Śvetāśvatara Upaniṣad* 3.13 in Olivelle, *Early Upaniṣads*.

40. Cf. *Aitareya Upaniṣad* 1.1: "The *ātman* was all this, the One, in the beginning. No one else winked. He thought: 'Let me create the worlds!' "; *Bṛhadāraṇyaka Upaniṣad* 2.1.20: "As a spider moves along the thread, as small sparks come forth from the fire, even so from this *ātman* come forth all breaths, all worlds, all divinities, all beings" in Olivelle, *Early Upaniṣads*.

41. See Diana Eck, *Darśan: Seeing the Divine Image in India*, 3rd ed. (New York: Columbia University Press, 1996).

42. Richard H. Davis, *Lives of Indian Images* (Princeton: Princeton University Press, 1997), 6; George L. Hersey, *Falling in Love with Statues: Artificial Humans from Pygmalion to the Present* (Chicago: University of Chicago Press, 2009), 10. Cf. the ritual "Opening of the Mouth and Eyes" of ancient Egyptian statues in Hersey, *Falling in Love with Statues*, 13.

43. Hersey, *Falling in Love with Statues*, 10.

44. Vidal, "Anthropomorphism," 925.

45. Vidal, "Anthropomorphism," 925.

46. Davis, *Lives of Indian Images*, 132.

47. http://www.bbc.com/news/av/magazine-38301718/the-milk-miracle-that-brought-india-to-a-standstill

48. White, *Alchemical Body*, 5–6.

49. Vidal, "Anthropomorphism," 926–929.

50. 12.4. Durgâprasâd and Parab, *Kathâsaritsâgara*.

51. *Harṣacarita* 6.4. See Parāb, *Harṣacarita*.

52. Eugene Watson Burlingame, *Buddhist Legends, Translated from the Original Pali Text of the Dhammapada Commentary*, vol. 1 (Cambridge: Harvard University Press, 1921), 270–271.

53. For dating of this text, see Patrick Olivelle, *Pañcatantra: The Book of India's Folk Wisdom* (Oxford: Oxford University Press, 1999), xii.

54. From *Pañcatantra*, chapter 5. Sanskrit text in Kāśīnāth Pāṇḍuraṅg Parāb, ed., *Pañcatantraka of Viṣṇuśarman* (Bombay: Nirnaya Sagar Press 1896).

55. https://in.news.yahoo.com/blogs/opinions/weaver-princess-goldman-sachs-20100501-015946-426.html

56. See discussion in William R. Newman, *Promethean Ambitions: Alchemy and the Quest to Perfect Nature* (Chicago: University of Chicago Press, 2004), 11.

57. See Bernhard Jülg, *Siddhi-Kür: Mongolische Märchensammlung* (Innsbruck, 1866; rpt. Hildesheim: Olms, 1973), 57.

58. Hoc Dy Khing, "Note sur le motif du cygne mécanique dans la literature populaire khmere," *Mon-Khmer Studies* 8 (1980): 91–102.

59. Khing, "Cygne mécanique," 91.

60. Khing, "Cygne mécanique," 94.

61. See for example *Śvetāśvatara Upaniṣad* 1.6 and the *Haṃsa Upaniṣad*. For the text of the *Śvetāśvatara Upaniṣad*, see Olivelle, *Early Upaniṣads*, and for the text of the *Haṃsa Upaniṣad*, see Apte, *Śrīnārāyaṇaśaṃkarānandaviracitadīpikāsametānāmatharvaśikhādyānāṃ haṃsopaniṣadantānāṃ*.

62. *Mahābhārata* 3.50.1ff. (Sukthankar et al., *Mahābhārata*).

Chapter 5: Mechanical Gardens and a Craving for Flying Machines: Androids in Jainism

1. Paul Dundas, "Pārśva and Mahāvīra in History," in *Brill's Encyclopedia of Jainism*, ed. John E. Court et al. (Boston: Brill, 2020), 118.

2. *Tattvārtha Sūtra* 7.13, cited from Robert J. Zydenbos, "Jain Ethics," in *Brill's Encyclopedia of Jainism* (Boston: Brill, 2020), 399.

3. Lawrence A. Babb, "Animals," in *Brill's Encyclopedia of Jainism*, ed. John Cort et al. (Boston: Brill, 2020), 471.

4. Padmanabh S. Jaini, *The Jaina Path of Purification* (Delhi: Motilal Banarsidass, 1979), 90–91.

5. Sinclair Stevenson, *The Heart of Jainism* (New Delhi: Munshiram Manoharlal, 1984), 97–99; Christopher Key Chapple, "The Living Cosmos in Jainism: A Traditional Science Grounded in Environmental Ethics," *Daedalus* 130, no. 4 (2001): 209.

6. Babb, "Animals," 470.

7. Babb, "Animals," 470.

8. Stevenson, *Heart of Jainism*, 99; Chapple, "Living Cosmos," 209; Babb, "Animals," 470.

9. Stevenson, *Heart of Jainism*, 99; Chapple, "Living Cosmos," 209; Babb, "Animals," 470.

10. Stevenson, *Heart of Jainism*, 100–101; Chapple, "Living Cosmos," 209; Babb, "Animals," 470.

11. Chapple, "Living Cosmos," 210.

12. Chapple, "Living Cosmos," 209.

13. Piotr Balcerowicz, "The Body and the Cosmos in Jaina Mythology and Art," in *Art, Myths, and Visual Cultures in Indian History*, ed. Piotr Balcerowicz and Jerzy Malinowski (New Delhi: Manohar, 2011), 143. Also see Kristi L. Wiley and Ruth Satinsky, "Cosmology and Cycles of Time," in *Brill's Encyclopedia of Jainism* (Boston: Brill, 2020), 9–11.

14. *Praśamaratiprakaraṇa* 210. Translation from Balcerowicz, "Body and the Cosmos," 105. Sanskrit text in Yajñeśvara Sadāśiva Śāstrī, ed., *Praśamaratiprakaraṇam* (Ahmedabad: Lālabhāī Dalapatabhāī Bhāratīya Saṃskṛti Vidyāmandira, 1989).

15. Ellen Gough, "Jain *Maṇḍalas* and *Yantras*," in *Brill's Encyclopedia of Jainism* (Boston: Brill, 2020), 585–593.

16. Gough, "Jain *Maṇḍalas* and *Yantras*," 587.

17. Jyotindra Jain and Eberhard Fischer, *Jaina Iconography, Part Two: Objects of Meditation and the Pantheon* (Leiden: E. J. Brill, 1978), 2; Gough, "Jain *Maṇḍalas* and *Yantras*," 588.

18. Jain and Fischer, *Jaina Iconography*, 2.

19. Moriz Winternitz, *A History of Indian Literature*, vol. 2 (Delhi: Motilal Banarsidass, 1993), 411.

20. *Bhagavatī-sūtra (Vyākhyāprajñapti)*, 7.9.301, in Muni Kanhaiyālāla, *Bhagavatī-sūtram* (Rājakoṭa: A. Bhā. Sv́e. Sthā Jainaśāstroddhārasamitipramukhaḥ Śreshṭhi-Śrīśāntilāla-Maṅgaladāsabhāī-Mahodayah, 1961). See Raghavan, *Yantras*, 9.

21. Raghavan, *Yantras*, 8.

22. See discussion in Jain, *Studies in Early Jainism*.

23. Author's translation, based on the text in Ludwig Alsdorf, "Zwei neue Belege zur 'indischen Herkunft' von 1001 Nacht," *Zeitschrift der deutschen morgenländische Gesellschaft*, 89 (1935): 294–297.

24. Jain, *Studies in Early Jainism*, 92–93.

25. Jain, *Studies in Early Jainism*, 93.

26. For a full discussion of this work, see K. K. Handiqui, *Yaśastilaka and Indian Culture*, 2nd ed. (Sholapur: Jaina Saṁskṛti Saṁrakshaka Sangha, 1968). See also Raghavan, *Yantras*, 14–15. For the text, see Vâsudeva Laxmaṇ Śâstrî Paṇaśikar et al., eds., *The Yaśastilaka of Somadeva Sûri*, 2 vols. (Bombay: Nirnaya Sagar Press, 1903–1916), 355–358.

27. Handiqui, *Yaśastilaka*, ix. According to Somadeva Sūri, Rachhuka has such exquisite handwriting that ladies hired him to write their love letters for them (1).

28. V. Raghavan, "Gleanings from Somadevasūri's Yaśastilaka Campū," *Journal of the Ganganatha Jha Research Institute* 1 (1944): 251; Handiqui, *Yaśastilaka*, 2.

29. See Handiqui, *Yaśastilaka*; and Ali, "Bhoja's Mechanical Garden."

30. Handiqui, *Yaśastilaka*, xii–xiii.

31. Handiqui, *Yaśastilaka*, xiii.

32. Raghavan, "Gleanings," 251.

33. Raghavan, *Yantras*, 14.

34. Raghavan, *Yantras*, 14, interprets this as a "contrivance producing an artificial waterfall."

35. See Handiqui, *Yaśastilaka*, 33.

36. Raghavan, *Yantras*, 14.

37. Handiqui, *Yaśastilaka*, 42–50.

38. See Wiley and Satinsky, "Cosmology and Cycles of Time," 3.

39. Wiley and Satinsky, "Cosmology and Cycles of Time," 11.

40. See Raghavan, *Yantras*, 3.

41. See Jerome Bauer, "Dohada (Pregnancy Cravings)," in *South Asian Folklore*, ed. Peter J. Claus, Sarah Diamond, and Margaret Mills (New York: Routledge, 2003), 163.

42. See Raghavan, *Yantras*, 15.

Chapter 6: I, *Yantra*: Androids in Buddhism

1. Translation based on Jampa Losang Panglung, *Die Erzählstoffe des Mūlasarvāstivāda-Vinaya analysiert auf Grund der tibetischen Übersetzung* (Tokyo: Reiyukai Library, 1981), 51.

2. *Madhyadeśa* or "the middle region" is one of the geographical subdivisions of ancient India, encompassing roughly the areas of north India surrounding the rivers Ganga and Yamuna.

3. Translation of text in Panglung, *Erzählstoffe*, 521–523.

4. Rendered into English from the French version in Edouard Chavannes, *Cinq cents contes et apologues extraits du Tripitaka chinois*, vol. 3 (Paris: Ernest Leroux, 1911), 12–13.

5. See Newman, *Promethean Ambitions*, 12.

6. Nalinaksha Dutt, *Gilgit Manuscripts*, vol. 3, part 1 (Delhi: Sri Satguru, 1984), 166–168.

7. Mary Douglas, *Natural Symbols: Explorations in Cosmology* (New York: Vintage Books, 1973), 93.

8. Douglas, *Natural Symbols*, 99.

9. Jambudvīpa, "the continent of the rose-apple tree," is another name for India.

10. From the Sanskrit text in Almuth Degener, *Das Kaṭhināvadāna* (Bonn: Indica et Tibetica Verlag, 1990), 27–28.

11. Based on the German translation by Hiän-lin Dschi, "Parallelversionen zur tocharischen Rezension des Puṇyavanta-Jātaka," *Zeitschrift der deutschen morgenländischen Gesellschaft* 97 (1943): 284–324.

12. Dschi, "Parallelversionen," 284.

13. Dschi, "Parallelversionen," 284.

14. Author's translation, based on the text given in G. Lane, "The Tocharian *Puṇyavantajātaka*: Text and Translation," *Journal of the American Oriental Society* 67 (1947): 33–53, who follows E. Sieg and W. Siegling, *Tocharische Sprachreste*, I: *Die Texte* (Berlin: De Gruyter, 1921). See also W. Schiefner, "Der Mechaniker und der Maler," *Mélanges Asiatiques* 7 (1859): 521–523; and E. Sieg, "Das Märchen von dem Mechaniker und dem Maler in tocharischer Fassung," *Ostasiatische Zeitschrift* 8 (1919–1920): 362–369.

15. Here, we may compare the modern novel *The Adventures of the Artificial Woman*, which opens with the sentence: "Never having found a real woman with whom he could sustain more than temporary connection, Ellery Pierce, a technician at a firm that made animatronic creatures for movie studios and theme parks, decided to fabricate one from scratch." Thomas Berger, *The Adventures of the Artificial Woman* (New York: Simon and Schuster, 2004), 1.

16. Per Schelde, *Androids, Humanoids, and Other Science Fiction Monsters: Science and Soul in Science Fiction Films* (New York: New York University Press, 1993), 208–209.

17. Robert Plank, "The Golem and the Robot," *Literature and Psychology* 15, no. 1 (1965): 13.

18. Werner Winter, "Some Aspects of Tocharian Drama: Form and Techniques," *Journal of the American Oriental Society* 75 (1955): 28.

19. Nina Beguš, "A Tale from the Silk Road: A Philological Account of The Painter and the Mechanical Maiden," accessed April 15, 2022, https://scholar.harvard.edu/nbegus/publications/tocharian-tale-silk-road-philological-account-painter-and-mechanical-maiden-and, 15.

20. Beguš, "Tale from the Silk Road," 16.

21. Beguš, "Tale from the Silk Road," 2.

22. Degener, *Kaṭhināvadāna*, 47–48; see Beguš, "Tale from the Silk Road," 4.

23. Beguš, "Tale from the Silk Road," 8.

24. Beguš, "Tale from the Silk Road," 8.

25. Śivadatta and Parab, *Yaśastilakacampū*. See also Raghavan, *Yantras*, 15.

26. This aggregate includes the four elements (earth, water, fire, air) as well as the six sense organs (eye, ear, nose, tongue, body, and mind) and their objects (visible form, sound, odor, taste, things that can be touched, and things that can be thought).

27. This includes all pleasant, unpleasant, and neutral sensations that arise through contact with sense objects.

28. There are six kinds of perceptions, corresponding to the six sense organs of eye, ear, nose, tongue, body, and mind. Note that mind is regarded as one of the sense organs, capable of producing mental perceptions in the same way that the eye produces perceptions of visible things.

29. All voluntary actions create karmic effects. Mental imprints are left behind by actions, which again create dispositions to act in certain ways in the future.

30. Consciousness is the response to the perception of an external object through one of the sense organs. Thus, when the eyes see a visible object, a visual consciousness is formed, and when the mind perceives a mental object, a mental consciousness is created.

31. See Steven Collins, "The Body in Theravāda Buddhist Monasticism," in *Religion and the Body*, edited by Sarah Coakley (Cambridge: Cambridge University Press, 1997), 185ff.

32. *Dhammapada* 148, text in P. L. Vaidya, ed., *Dhammapada* (Poona: Oriental Book Agency, 1934).

33. *Saṃuytta Nikāya* 3.86, text in Bhikkhu Jagadīsakassapo, ed., *Suttapiṭake Saṃyuttanikāyapāli* ([Nālandā]: Bihārarājakīyena Pālipakāsanamaṇḍalena, 1959).

34. Sue Hamilton, *Identity and Experience: The Constitution of the Human Being According to Early Buddhism* (Oxford: Luzac, 1996; rpt. 2001), 189.

35. See for example Sue Hamilton, "From the Buddha to Buddhaghosa," in *Religious Reflections*, edited by Jane Marie Law (Bloomington: Indiana University Press, 1995), 46–63.

36. *Dharmasaṃgīti Sūtra*, cited in Paul Williams, "Some Mahāyāna Buddhist Perspectives on the Body," in *Religion and the Body* (Cambridge: Cambridge University Press, 1997), 206.

37. See Wimal Dissanayake, "The Body in Indian Theory and Practice," in *Self as Body in Asian Theory and Practice* (Albany: State University of New York Press, 1993), 139–144; and Wujastyk, "Interpreting the Image," 198.

38. *Bodhicaryāvatāra* 10:55, translation from Stephen Batchelor, *A Guide to the Bodhisattva's Way of Life* (Dharamsala: Library of Tibetan Works and Archives, 1979).

39. Susanne Mrozik, *Virtuous Bodies: The Physical Dimensions of Morality in Buddhist Ethics* (Oxford: Oxford University Press, 2007), 65.

40. Mrozik, *Virtuous Bodies*, 67ff.

41. John Powers, *Introduction to Tibetan Buddhism* (Ithaca: Snow Lion, 2007), 392.

42. Powers, *Tibetan Buddhism*, 392.

43. A *vetāla* is created when an evil spirit possesses a corpse and brings it to life. A *vetāla* figures prominently in the eleventh- to twelfth-century Sanskrit fairy tale collection *Vetālapañcaviṃśati* (The Twenty-Five [Tales] of the *Vetāla*), which consists of a series of stories told by a *vetāla* riding on the shoulders of an unwilling king.

44. Translated from the Sanskrit text at https://www2.hf.uio.no/polyglotta/index.php?page=record&view=record&vid=441&mid=739193.

45. *Visuddhimagga* 18.31. See Henry Clarke Warren and Dharmananda Kosambi, *Visuddhimagga of Buddhaghosâcariya* (Cambridge: Harvard University Press, 1950).

46. See Lieselotte Sauer, *Marionetten, Maschinen, Automaten: Der künstliche Mensch in der deutschen und englischen Romantik* (Bonn: Bouvier, 1983).

47. Jean Baudrillard, *Simulations* (New York: Semiotext(e), 1983), 5.

48. Baudrillard, *Simulations*, 2.

Chapter 7: The Buddha, the Emperor, and the Killer Robot

1. Thapar, *Aśoka and the Decline of the Mauryas*, 41.

2. For a discussion of images of mobility and paths in early Buddhism, see Jason Neelis, *Early Buddhist Transmission and Trade Networks: Mobility and Exchange within and beyond the Northwestern Borderlands of South Asia* (Leiden: Brill, 2011), 2.

3. See Alexander Cunningham, *Corpus inscriptionum indicarum*, vol. 1: *Inscriptions of Asoka* (Varanasi: Indological Book House, 1961).

4. Patrick Olivelle, "Kings, Ascetics, and Brahmins: The Sociopolitical Context of Ancient Indian Religions," in *Dynamics in the History of Religions*, edited by Volkhard Krech and Marion Steinicke (Leiden: Brill, 2012), 131.

5. Thirteenth major rock edict, see Thapar, *Aśoka*, 255–256, and Sirkar, *Inscriptions of Aśoka*, 56–58.

6. First separate rock edict, see Thapar, *Aśoka*, 258.

7. First major rock edict, see Thapar, *Aśoka*, 250, and Sirkar, *Inscriptions*, 46; fourth major rock edict, see Thapar, *Aśoka*, 251, and Sirkar, *Inscriptions*, 46; fifth pillar edict, see Thapar, *Aśoka*, 264, and Sirkar, *Inscriptions*, 73.

8. Seventh pillar edict, see Thapar, *Aśoka*, 265, and Sirkar, *Inscriptions*, 76.

9. Seventh major rock edict, see Thapar, *Aśoka*, 253, and Sirkar, *Inscriptions*, 51; twelfth major rock edict, see Thapar, *Aśoka*, 255, and Sirkar, *Inscriptions*, 55.

10. Second major rock edict, see Thapar, *Aśoka*, 251, and Sirkar, *Inscriptions*, 47.

11. See Donald K. Swearer, *The Buddhist World of Southeast Asia* (Albany: State University of New York Press, 1995), 68.

12. Swearer, *Buddhist World*, 72–73.

13. Eugène Denis, *La Lokapaññatti et les idées cosmologiques du bouddhisme ancient*, 2 vols. (Paris: Librairie Honoré Champion, 1977), accepted by Oskar von Hinüber, *A Handbook of Pāli Literature* (Berlin: Walter de Gruyter, 1996; rpt. New Delhi: Munshiram Manoharlal, 1997), 183; and Higley, "Legend," 133. See also Denis's earlier treatment of the same text in Eugène Denis, "La *Lokapaññatti* et la légende birmane d'Asoka," *Journal Asiatique* 264 (1976): 97–116.

14. John S. Strong, *The Legend and Cult of Upagupta: Sanskrit Buddhism in North India and Southeast Asia* (Princeton: Princeton University Press, 1992), 12.

15. K. Sankarnarayan et al., *Lokaprajñapti: A Critical Exposition of Buddhist Cosmology* (Mumbai: Somaiya, 2002), 1.

16. Paul Mus, *La Lumière sur les Six Voies: Tableau de la transmigration bouddhique d'après des sources sanskrites, pāli, tibétaines et chinoises en majeures partie inédites* (Paris: Institut d'ethnologie, 1939), 93.

17. Duroiselle writes that he has only seen one manuscript of the text, but it is not clear which manuscript he refers to. Ch. Duroiselle, "Upagutta et Māra," *Bulletin d'Ecole française d'Extrême-Orient*, 4 (1904): 414.

18. Strong, *Upagupta*, 186.

19. The *Thūpavaṃsa* is ascribed to a Vācissaratthera, who can be dated to the thirteenth century. There is, for example, epigraphic evidence that a (possibly slightly earlier?) version of the *Thūpavaṃsa* was recited at the ceremonial worship of the Mahāthūpa (Great Stūpa) in 1203.

20. Thirizeyathu inscription, published in *Inscriptions of Pagan, Pinya and Ava* (Rangoon 1899), 43, cited in Duroiselle, "Upagutta et Māra," 414, note 4.

21. The following is the author's translation of the Pāli text given in Denis, *Lokapaññatti*.

22. See Jain, *Studies*, 92–93.

23. Higley, "Legend," 133.

24. City in north India, corresponds to today's Patna.

25. *Dhamma* is the cosmic law in Hindu and Buddhist thought. The term is often used in Buddhist texts for the teachings of the Buddha as well.

26. The Buddha. The relics (bones) of the Buddha are regarded as sacred and imbued with supernatural power.

27. A *kosa* is about 2.25 miles.

28. "The seven precious jewels" are not all jewels; the list usually given is gold, silver, lapis lazuli, seashell, agate, pearl, and carnelian.

29. The four assemblies are Buddhist monks, Buddhist nuns, male lay followers, and female lay followers.

30. The text's royal lineage is not historically accurate. Ajātasattu's son was Udayabhadda, the founder of Pāṭaliputta, and Udayabhadda was childless. Several kings of the Nanda dynasty ruled between Udayabhadda and Aśoka's grandfather Candragupta Maurya.

31. Jambudīpa, "the continent of the rose-apple tree," is an ancient name for India.

32. Buddhist shrines. Aśoka did indeed oversee the building of thousands of *stūpas* all over northern India.

33. This is a gesture of respect for a sacred place.

34. For a different opinion, see Ali, "Bhoja's Mechanical Garden," 484. Ali argues that "Rome" in this story likely represents the Byzantine Empire rather than Rome.

35. See Higley, "Legend," 133.

36. The text was originally written in Latin but was soon translated into French. There were also several Hebrew versions of the poem.

37. Higley, "Legend," 137. Cf. the Arthurian romance *Perlesvaus*, where Perceval visits a copper castle containing an oracular image guarded by copper warriors. Kang, *Sublime Dreams*, 65.

38. If the Pāli author was indeed familiar with the French text, this has obvious implications for the dating of the *Lokapaññatti*. The *L'image du monde* is usually dated to around 1245 CE.

39. Quoted in J. B. Trapp, "The Grave of Vergil," *Journal of the Warburg and Courtauld Institutes* 47 (1984): 5.

40. Comparetti, *Vergil*, 259.

41. Comparetti, *Vergil*, 306.

42. Comparetti, *Vergil*, 312–313.

43. "The three jewels" of Buddhism are the Buddha, the community of monks and nuns, and the dharma (law, doctrine).

44. Raimundo Panikkar, "The Destiny of Technological Civilization: An Ancient Buddhist Legend, *Romavisaya*," *Alternatives* 10 (1984): 242.

45. Panikkar, "Destiny," 252.

46. Anne Blackburn, "Buddhist Networks across the Indian Ocean: Trans-regional Strategies and Affiliations," in *Belonging across the Bay of Bengal: Religious Rites, Colonial Migrations, National Rights*, edited by Michael Laffan (London: Bloomsbury, 2017), 21.

47. Blackburn, "Buddhist Networks," 21.

48. See Blackburn, "Buddhist Networks," 19.

49. The undeciphered writing of the ancient Indus civilization in today's northwest India/Pakistan is here not taken into account. See Harry Falk, *Schrift im Alten Indien: Ein Forschungsbericht mit Anmerkungen* (Tübingen: Gunter Narr Verlag, 1993), 339.

50. See for example Distress F. Singer, "Palm Leaf Manuscripts from Burma," accessed April 15, 2022, https://www.burmese-buddhas.com/burmese-manuscripts/palm-leaf-manuscripts/.

51. Higley, "Legend," 130.

52. Blackburn, "Buddhist Networks," 15.

Chapter 8: Interpreting Indian Robot Tales

1. Tzvetan Todorov, *The Fantastic: A Structural Approach to a Literary Genre* (Ithaca: Cornell University Press, 1973).

2. Todorov, *The Fantastic*, 59.

3. Todorov, *The Fantastic*, 41.

4. Todorov, *The Fantastic*, 25.

5. J. R. R. Tolkien, "On Fairy Stories," in *Essays Presented to Charles Williams* (Oxford: Oxford University Press, 1947). Reprinted in *Tolkien On Fairy-Stories* (London: HarperCollins, 2008), 25–84, here 60.

6. Tolkien, "On Fairy Stories," 27 and 32.

7. Tolkien, "On Fairy Stories," 55.

8. Jane Mobley, "Toward a Definition of Fantasy Fiction," *Extrapolation* 15 (1974): 117–128, here 117.

9. Edward James and Farah Mendlesohn, *The Cambridge Companion to Fantasy Literature* (Cambridge: Cambridge University Press, 2012), 1.

10. Rosemary Jackson, *Fantasy: The Literature of Subversion* (London: Routledge, 1981), 4.

11. Jackson, *Fantasy*, 8.

12. Cited from Ursula K. Le Guin, *The Language of the Night: Essays on Fantasy and Science Fiction*, ed. Susan Wood (New York: Perigee, 1972), 11.

13. Davenport, *Inquiry into Science Fiction*, 15.

14. S. C. Fredericks, "Lucian's *True History* as SF," *Science Fiction Studies* 3 (1976): 49–60.

15. Srinarahari Mysore, "Indian Science Fiction: History and Contemporary Trends," accessed April 14, 2022, https://www.academia.edu/10442469/Indian_Science_Fiction_History_and_Contemporary_Trends.

16. Mysore, "Indian Science Fiction."

17. Raminder Kaur, "The Fictions of Science and Cinema in India," in *Routledge Handbook of Indian Cinemas*, ed. K. Moti Golkusing and Wimal Dissanayake (London: Routledge, 2013), 284.

18. Debjani Sengupta, "Explorers of Subversive Knowledge: The Science Fantasy of Leela Majumdar and Sukumar Ray," in *Indian Genre Fiction*, ed. Bodhisattva Chattopadhyay, Aakriti Mandhwani, and Anwesha Maity (New York: Routledge, 2019).

19. Sengupta, "Explorers of Subversive Knowledge," 84.

20. See the brief discussion in Raghavan, *Yantras*, 2.

21. https://www.youtube.com/watch?v=nb9p7QQJPeQ

22. https://www.washingtonpost.com/world/asia_pacific/indias-biggest-action-movie-star-isnt-just-an-actor-he-is-god/2016/07/22/e30fa88a-4e8f-11e6-bf27-405106836f96_story.html?noredirect=on&utm_term=.de9aaafb1c49

23. https://www.washingtonpost.com/world/asia_pacific/indias-biggest-action-movie-star-isnt-just-an-actor-he-is-god/2016/07/22/e30fa88a-4e8f-11e6-bf27-405106836f96_story.html?noredirect=on&utm_term=.de9aaafb1c49

24. https://www.washingtonpost.com/world/asia_pacific/indias-biggest-action-movie-star-isnt-just-an-actor-he-is-god/2016/07/22/e30

fa88a-4e8f-11e6-bf27-405106836f96_story.html?noredirect=on&utm_term=.de9aaafb1c49

25. Thomas C. Sutton and Marilyn Sutton, "Science Fiction as Mythology," *Western Folklore* 28 (1969): 230–237.

26. Sutton and Sutton, "Science Fiction as Mythology," 236. See also Le Guin, *Language of the Night*, 73ff.

27. Kenneth Gouwens, "Human Exceptionalism," in *The Renaissance World*, ed. John Jeffries Marin (New York: Routledge, 2007).

28. Gupta, "The Maṇḍala," 34.

29. Royle, in *The Uncanny*, touches on something similar when he refers to the uncanny as a "crisis of the proper" (1) and "a strangeness of framing and borders" (2).

30. Daniel Halpern and James E. Katz, "Unveiling Robotophobia and Cyber-dystopianism: The Role of Gender, Technology and Religion on Attitudes Towards Robots," in *Human-Robot Interaction: Proceedings of the 7th ACM/IEEE International Conference* (Boston: ACM/IEEE International, 2012), 139.

31. Kang, *Sublime Dreams*, 28.

32. Richard Hanley, *Is Data Human? The Metaphysics of Star Trek* (New York: Basic Books, 1997), 43.

33. Hanley, *Is Data Human?*, 76.

34. Similar ideas can be found in Taoist texts like the *Liezi*, where being "human" is to be self-conscious and alienated from one's true nature. See Jeffrey L. Richey, "I, Robot: Self as Machine in the *Liezi*," in *Riding the Wind with* Liezi*: New Perspectives on the Daoist Classic*, ed. Ronnie Littlejohn and Jeffrey Dippmann (Albany: State University of New York Press, 2011), 204.

35. Masahiro Mori, *The Buddha in the Robot* (Tokyo: Kosei, 1981), 13.

36. Eric G. Wilson, *The Melancholy Android: On the Psychology of Sacred Machines* (Albany: State University of New York Press, 2006), vii.

37. Wilson, *Melancholy Android*, 2.

38. Despina Kakoudaki, *Anatomy of a Robot: Literature, Cinema, and the Cultural Work of Artificial People* (New Brunswick: Rutgers University Press, 2014), 4.

39. Kimura, "Masahiro Mori's," 79.

40. Jordi Vallverdú, "The Eastern Construct of the Artificial Mind," *Enrahonar: Quaderns de Filosofia* 47 (2011): 177.

41. For a discussion of robots in Japan, see Vallverdú, "Eastern Construct."

42. Isaac Asimov, *I, Robot* (New York: Gnome Press, 1950), 228.

Appendix: Chapter 31 of Bhoja's *Samarāṅgaṇasūtradhāra*

1. "The conqueror of the God of Love" is an epithet of the god Śiva. According to Hindu myth, Kāma, the god of love, attempted to distract Śiva from his ascetic penance and meditation and shot him with an arrow of love to call his attention to the lovely maiden Pārvatī. Śiva was so annoyed at the interruption that he blasted Kāma with the fire from his third eye and reduced the god of love to a pile of ashes. Kāma had the last laugh, however; since Śiva had used up all his accumulated ascetic energy to destroy Kāma, he lost his focus and fell in love with Pārvatī. And since Kāma was now without a bodily form, he became invisible, and therefore more dangerous and difficult to avoid than ever. See *Matsya Purāṇa* 227–255.

2. These are the four goals of human existence in the Hindu tradition. *Dharma* is an individual's social and religious duty, *artha* is wealth and prosperity, *kāma* is erotic love and fulfillment, and *mokṣa* is spiritual liberation.

3. The five classical elements in Hindu philosophy are earth, water, fire, air, and ether (*ākāśa*). The term used for the elements in stanza 3 (*bhūta*) is the standard Sanskrit one, while the word used in stanza 5 (*bīja*, literally, "seed") is quite unusual. Mira Roy points out that the term *bīja* first occurs in the sense of "element" in this particular text and speculates that the use of the unusual *bīja* rather than the more common *bhūta* here is likely "analogous to the alchemist's theory of *bīja* or seed or germ, causing change of one metal into another." Roy, "Concept of Yantra," 118.

4. This likely refers to the philosophical debates about whether all living beings have separate eternal selves (*ātman*), or whether all these selves are parts of the same cosmic Self.

5. This is a reference to a wind-up machine.

6. This stanza and the previous one invoke the classic four goals of human existence (see stanza 20). The idea is that a person who lives according to *dharma* will naturally attract wealth, which will bring about love but also eventually a desire to renounce worldly possessions and seek spiritual liberation.

7. The Sanskrit text plays with the double meaning of the term *pārthiva*, which means both "related to the earth" and "royal."

8. What follows is a list of items that illustrate the importance of these constituent elements in different ways.

9. Sharma takes this as a reference to plumbing, or the measurement of the interval between the lines between the earth's center and surface. Sharma, *Samarāṅgaṇa Sūtradhāra*, 367.

10. The meaning of this Sanskrit noun is unclear, and it is not attested in any other texts. It may be derived from the root *urd* or *ūrd* with a possible meaning "measure" and mean something along the lines of "measurement" or "instrument of measurement." Sharma assumes the meaning "cap" of a wheel, likely based on context (367).

11. Sanskrit word of unclear meaning. Sharma translates "shafts," although he does not give a reason for this interpretation (367). I have translated "spindles" on the assumption that the noun, which is not elsewhere attested in Sanskrit, may be derived from the verbal root *kṛt*, "to spin."

12. Sharma translates "rotator" (368). Since the meaning "spinning top" is attested elsewhere in Sanskrit, I have chosen this translation here.

13. The term *śṛṅga* (literally, "horn") is here likely used in the sense of "water engine," a meaning that is also attested in texts like the *Rahgu-vaṃśa* and the *Śiśupālavadha*. Sharma translates "syringe" (368).

14. Presumably these items are classified as belonging to the earth element because they are made of metal, which is classified as earthly.

15. The Sanskrit word used here is *bījanādyair* of unclear meaning. It could possibly mean "by means of seed sounders" and might be a reference to a sort of prayer wheel where the *mantras* (*bījas*) are set in motion/sounded when the handles are turned. I have chosen to follow Sharma and translate "fan" simply because this translation makes the most sense in the context of the stanza (368).

16. Literally "elephant ears," likely a sort of fan or flap shaped like the ear of an elephant.

17. The Sanskrit text seems to be corrupt at this point. T. Gaṇapati Śāstrī's edition has *(chā)cāṇito*, which does not make any sense. My translation assumes that a form of the verb *cañc* (to be unsteady, to shake) underlies the corrupted term here. Sharma translates "encrackled" but does not state why he chooses to do so (368).

18. Presumably a steam-powered device of some kind, associated with both fire and water, is intended here.

19. *Alakṣatā* literally means "invisibility," but it is unlikely that this is meant literally here. Rather, the term may refer to an observer's inability to see at a glance how a machine is put together.

20. A *muhūrta* is a time interval of forty-eight minutes, or 1/30 part of a (lunar) day

21. A *kāṣṭhā* is 1/360 part of a *muhūrta*, or about eight seconds.

22. This word is not attested elsewhere, and it is unclear what sort of musical instrument it refers to.

23. The meaning is not clear here. It is possible that the text is corrupt at this point, or alternatively, that some performances of plays or dance may have involved using a device to sprinkle water on the audience.

24. The story of the gods and demons working together to churn the ocean and produce *amṛta,* the drink of immortality, is found in several Hindu texts, including the *Mahābhārata* and the *Bhāgavata Purāṇa.*

25. The story of Hiraṇyakaśipu is found in the *Bhāgavata Purāṇa* and elsewhere. The demon has received a boon that makes him impossible to kill for humans or animals, by day or night, or inside or outside a dwelling. The god Viṣṇu therefore assumes the form of the hybrid creature Nṛsiṃha (man-lion) and slays the demon on the threshold at twilight.

26. This may be a reference to a device such as a mechanical gate that can be opened to let elephants out.

27. A mechanical night watchman is presumably referred to here.

28. One *nāḍi* is half a *muhūrta,* or about twenty-four minutes.

29. This appears to be an automated serpent-bed of sorts.

30. Twenty-four minutes.

31. A *yojana* is a measure of distance, around nine miles. This seems to be a description of a clock featuring a charioteer traveling across the earth. The reference to a *yojana* here is obviously not to be taken literally, but as an estimate of how far the charioteer would have traveled had he been a real person in a real chariot rather than a figure on a clock.

32. A *sūtradhāra* literally means "one who holds the strings" and is the term for the stage manager in classical Indian theater (presumably because he would also be involved in puppet theater and hold the strings). The term *sūtradhāra* is also used to designate an architect or a woodworker in general.

33. Although *citrakṛt* literally means "one who creates pictures," it is likely that the term is used more loosely here to designate any craftsman.

34. *Pañca* literally means "five." It is unclear what is referred to here, but it may have something to do with the fivefold science of *yantras* mentioned in stanza 88. Sharma translates "a fifth one" but notes the problem of "the lines not being free from corruption" (378–379).

35. An artificially constructed bird is described here.

36. This word is not attested in classical Sanskrit but is mentioned in Puṣpadanta's *Mahāpurāṇa* 4.11.3.

37. It is a standard trope in Sanskrit literature that a male elephant in rut will release temporin through its temporal ducts. While this phenomenon is well attested in male elephants, scientists do not currently believe the phenomenon is primarily connected to mating. The reason for the release of temporin in this stanza is presumably that the roar of the automaton resembles thunder, which is linked to the mating season in Sanskrit literature.

38. Chewing areca nuts wrapped in betel leaves has been a popular pastime in India for thousands of years and is said to aid digestion. The juices produced will have to be spit out and often leave a bright red stain.

39. Sharma suggests that this may be a sort of crane (383).

40. *Nandyāvarta* (literally, "the turning of joy") is a specific design in Hindu art, based on the petals of a flower and somewhat akin to a swastika, which is sometimes used in temple construction. The design is also used as an auspicious symbol on its own in Jainism. Here, it likely refers to a specific ornate design for a water feature.

41. The Ābhīras are a tribe mentioned in several ancient Sanskrit texts.

42. Twelve is the number of the sun because the sun god (Sūrya) has twelve names in Sanskrit.

43. The term used here, *kapoṭapālī*, can also mean "dovecote," but "frieze" makes more sense in the context.

44. *Jambhaka* literally means "gaping" or "yawning" and is a term applied to demons. Sharma simply translates "gaping mouths" (386). Presumably ornaments of various kinds are meant here.

45. The *vidyādhāras* (literally, "carriers of wisdom") are supernatural beings with magical powers.

46. A *siddha* is a person who has attained enlightenment and spiritual and physical perfection.

47. A *kinnāra* is a celestial musician, half human and half horse.

48. A wishing tree (*kalpataru*) is a mythological wish-granting tree.

49. Pongamia oil is extracted from the seeds of the pongamia tree. It is toxic but has many practical uses as lamp oil and lubricant.

50. Śrī is the goddess of prosperity and good fortune. Her husband is the god Viṣṇu.

51. Rati's husband is Kāma, the god of love.

52. The *puṣpaka* is the flying chariot of Kubera, the Lord of Wealth.

53. A *karṇikā* is the pericarp, or fruit wall, in the center of the lotus plant.

54. Varuṇa is the god of water and the ocean.

55. Serpents are not associated with evil in Sanskrit literature but rather with wealth and abundance.

56. The *svastika* is an ancient auspicious symbol, attested in Indian art as far back as the Indus civilization (ca. 2500–1700 BCE). While the *svastika* was later usurped by the European Nazis, the original symbol carries no such negative connotations.

57. A cubit or *hasta* is the measure of a hand.

58. In ancient Indian architecture, a *bhadra* is a rectangular projection from a wall. But note that *bhadra* is also the term for a type of *maṇḍala* design, which underscores the idea of the garden as a *yantra* diagram. See Bühnemann, "Maṇḍalas and Yantras," 564.

59. One *dhanus* (the length of a bow) equals four *hastas*.

60. The meaning of this term is not clear, but presumably it refers to a mechanical device of some sort, shaped like an elephant and capable of picking up a jewel with its trunk. Sharma translates "sloping roof," but this does not seem likely in the context (397).

61. Presumably an elongated space.

62. There is a repetition of phrases in the original text here.

63. Sharma reads the name and title "the sole king Rāmadeva" into this verse (404). Since the two terms *rāma* (joy) and *deva* (god) are not conjoined, I find it difficult to see a reference to a personal name here. While several Indian kings have been called Rāmadeva, including the ninth-century Rāmabhadra, I see no evidence of a king by that name connected to this particular text.

Bibliography

Acharya, Yadavji Trikamji. *Caraka Saṃhitā*. Bombay: Chaukhambha, 1941.

Acharya, Yadavji Trikamji. *Rasaprakāśa Sudhākara*. Bombay: Venkatesvara Steam Press, 1910–1911.

Aebischer, Paul. *Le voyage de Charlemagne à Jérusalem et à Constantinople*. Geneva: Libraire Droz, 1965.

Agrawala, Vasudeva Saran. *Samarāṅgaṇa-Sūtradhāra of Mahārājadhirāja Bhoja, the Paramāra Ruler of Dhārā*. Baroda: Oriental Institute, 1966.

Akanāṉūṟu, 2nd ed. Tirunelvēli, Ceṉṉai: Caivacittānta nūṟpatippuk kaḻakam, 1949.

Alexander, H. G., ed. *The Leibniz-Clarke Correspondence*. Manchester: Manchester University Press, 1956.

Ali, Daud. "Bhoja's Mechanical Garden: Translating Wonder across the Indian Ocean, circa 800–1100 CE." *History of Religions* 55, no. 4 (2016): 460–493.

Ali, Daud. "Gardens in Early Indian Court Life." *Studies in History* 19, no. 2 (2003): 221–52.

Alsdorf, Ludwig. "Zwei neue Belege zur 'indischen Herkunft' von 1001 Nacht." *Zeitschrift der deutschen morgenländische Gesellschaft* 89 (1935): 275–314.

Apte, Hari Narayan. *Śrīnārāyaṇaśaṃkarānandaviracitadīpikāsametānāmatharvaśikhādyānāṃ haṃsopaniṣadantānāṃ dvātriṃśanmitānām upaniṣadāṃ samuccayaḥ*. Puṇyākhyapattane: Ānandaśramamudraṇālaye, 1895.

Arnold de-Simine, Silke. "Ich erinnere, also bin ich?—Menschen und Gedäctnismedien in Ridley Scott's *Blade Runner* (1982/1992)." In *Textmaschinenkörper: genderorientierte Lektüren der Androiden*, edited by Eva Kormann, Anke Gilleir and Angelika Schlimmer, 225–242. Amsterdam: Rodopi, 2006.

Asimov, Isaac. *I, Robot*. New York: Gnome Press, 1950.

Assmann, Jan. *Death and Salvation in Ancient Egypt*. Translated by David Lorton. Ithaca: Cornell University Press, 2005.

Ayer, V. A. K. *Untold Stories of King Bhoja*. Bombay: Bharatiya Vidya Bhavan, 1975.

Babb, Lawrence A. "Animals." In *Brill's Encyclopedia of Jainism*, edited by John E. Cort et al., 470–474. Leiden: Brill, 2020.

Bacigalupi, Paolo. *The Windup Girl*. San Francisco: Nightshade Books, 2009.

Bafna, Sonit. "On the Idea of the Mandala as a Governing Device in Indian Architectural Tradition." *Journal of the Society of Architectural Historians* 59 (2000): 26–49.

Balcerowicz, Piotr. "The Body and the Cosmos in Jaina Mythology and Art." In *Art, Myths, and Visual Cultures in Indian History*, edited by Piotr Balcerowicz and Jerzy Malinowski, 95–151. New Delhi: Manohar, 2011.

Bandhu, V. *Rājataraṅgiṇī of Kalhaṇa*, 2 vols. Hoshiarpur: Vishveshvaranand Vedic Research Institute, 1963.

Batchelor, Stephen. *A Guide to the Bodhisattva's Way of Life*. Dharamsala: Library of Tibetan Works and Archives, 1979.

Baudrillard, Jean. *Simulations*. New York: Semiotext(e), 1983.

Bauer, Jerome. "Dohada (Pregnancy Cravings)." In *South Asian Folklore: An Encyclopedia*, edited by Peter J. Claus, Sarah Diamond, and Margaret Mills, 163. New York: Routledge, 2003.

Beaune, Jean-Claude. "The Classical Age of Automata: An Impressionistic Survey from the Sixteenth to the Nineteenth Century." In *Fragments for a History of the Human Body*, edited by Michael Feher, 431–480. Cambridge: MIT Press, 1989.

Bedini, Silvio. "The Role of Automata in the History of Technology." *Technology and Culture* 5 (1964): 24–42.

Beguš, Nina. "A Tale from the Silk Road: A Philological Account of The Painter and the Mechanical Maiden." Accessed April 15, 2022. https://scholar.harvard.edu/nbegus/publications/tocharian-tale-silk-road-philological-account-painter-and-mechanical-maiden-and.

Berger, Thomas. *The Adventures of the Artificial Woman*. New York: Simon and Schuster, 2004.

Berryman, Sylvia. "Ancient Automata and Mechanical Explanation." *Phronesis* 48 (2003): 344–369.

Bhishagratna, Kaviraj Kunja Lal. *The Sushruta Samhita*, vol. 1. Calcutta: J. N. Bose, 1907.

Blackburn, Anne. "Buddhist Networks across the Indian Ocean: Transregional Strategies and Affiliations." In *Belonging across the Bay of Bengal: Religious Rites, Colonial Migrations, National Rights*, edited by Michael Laffan, 15–34. London: Bloomsbury, 2017.

Borlik, Todd Andrew. "'More than Art': Clockwork Automata, the Extemporizing Actor, and the Brazen Head in *Friar Bacon and Friar Bungay*." In *The Automaton in English Renaissance Literature*, edited by Wendy Beth Hyman, 129–144. Burlington: Ashgate, 2011.

Brett, Gerard. "The Automata in the Byzantine 'Throne of Solomon.'" *Speculum* 29 (1954): 477–487.

Briggs, George Weston. *Gorakhnāth and the Kānphaṭa Yogīs*. Delhi: Motilal Banarsidass, 1938. Reprint 1982.

Brooks, Francis. *Marci Tullii Ciceronis De natura deorum*. London: Methuen, 1896.

Brunner, Hélène. "Maṇḍala and Yantra in the Siddhānta School of Śaivism: Definitions, Descriptions, and Ritual Use." In *Maṇḍalas and Yantras in the Hindu Traditions*, edited by Gudrun Bühnemann, 153–177. Leiden: Brill, 2003.

Brunner-Traut, Emma. "Ein Golem in der ägyptischen Literatur." *Studien zur Altägyptischen Kultur* 16 (1989): 21–26.

Bühnemann, Gudrun. Introduction to *Maṇḍalas and Yantras in the Hindu Traditions*, 1–12. Leiden: Brill, 2003.

Bühnemann, Gudrun. "Maṇḍala, Yantra and Cakra: Some Observations." In *Maṇḍalas and Yantras in the Hindu Traditions*, edited by Gudrun Bühnemann, 13–56. Leiden: Brill, 2003.

Bühnemann, Gudrun. "Maṇḍalas and Yantras." In *Brill's Encyclopedia of Hinduism*, vol. 2, edited by Knut A. Jacobsen, 560–573. Leiden: Brill, 2010.

Buitenen, J. A. B. van. *The Maitrāyaṇīya Upaniṣad*. 's-Gravenhage: Mouton, 1962.

Bunce, Fredrick W. *The Yantras of Deities and Their Numerological Foundations—An Iconographic Consideration*. New Delhi: D. K. Printworld, 2001.

Burlingame, Eugene Watson. *Buddhist Legends, Translated from the Original Pali Text of the Dhammapada Commentary*, vol. 1. Cambridge: Harvard University Press, 1921.

Byron, George Gordon. *Don Juan*. London: Thomas Davison, 1819.

Chapple, Christopher Key. "The Living Cosmos in Jainism: A Traditional Science Grounded in Environmental Ethics." *Daedalus* 130, no. 4 (2001): 207–224.

Chapuis, Alfred, and Edmond Droz. *Automata: A Historical and Technological Study*. Neuchâtel: Éditions du Griffon, 1958.

Chatterjee, Satischandra, and Dhirendramohan Datta. *An Introduction to Indian Philosophy*, 7th ed. Calcutta: University of Calcutta Press, 1968.

Chaudhury, Pravas Jivan. "The Theory of Rasa." *Journal of Aesthetics and Art Criticism* 11, no. 2 (1952): 147–150.

Chaudhury, Pravas Jivan. "The Theory of Rasa." *Journal of Aesthetics and Art Criticism* 24, no. 1 (1965): 145–149.

Chavannes, Edouard. *Cinq cents contes et apologues extraits du Tripitaka chinois*, vol. 3. Paris: Ernest Leroux, 1911.

Clynes, Manfred E., and Nathan S. Kline. "Cyborgs and Space." *Astronotics*, September 1960. https://archive.nytimes.com/www.nytimes.com/library/cyber/surf/022697surf-cyborg.html.

Cobb, Matthew Adam. *Rome and the Indian Ocean Trade from Augustus to the Early Third Century CE*. Leiden: Brill, 2018.

Cohen, John. *Human Robots in Myth and Science*. London: George Allen & Unwin, 1966.

Cohen, Signe. Conclusion to *The Upaniṣads: A Complete Guide*, edited by Signe Cohen, 412–418. London: Routledge, 2018.

Cohen, Signe. "Romancing the Robot and Other Tales of Mechanical Beings in Indian Literature." *Acta Orientalia* 64 (2003): 65–75.

Cohen, Signe. *Text and Authority in the Older Upaniṣads*. Leiden: Brill, 2008.

Collins, Steven. "The Body in Theravāda Buddhist Monasticism." In *Religion and the Body*, edited by Sarah Coakley, 185–204. Cambridge: Cambridge University Press, 1997.

Comparetti, Domenico. *Vergil in the Middle Ages*. Translated by E. F. M. Benecke. Originally published 1895. Reprint Piscataway, NJ: Gorgias Press, 2002.

Conti, Brooke. "The Mechanical Saint: Early Modern Devotion and the Language of Automation." In *The Automaton in English Renaissance Literature*, edited by Wendy Beth Hyman, 95–107. Burlington: Ashgate, 2011.

Coomaraswamy, Ananda K. *The Treatise of Al-Jazarī on Automata*. Boston: Museum of Fine Arts, 1924.

Coulson, Michael. *Rākṣasa's Ring by Viśākhadatta*. New York: New York University Press, 2005.

Couture, André. *Kṛṣṇa in the Harivaṃśa*, vol. 2: *The Greatest of All Sovereigns and Masters*. Delhi: DK Printworld, 2017.

Crawford, S. Cromwell. *Hindu Bioethics for the Twenty-First Century*. Albany: State University of New York Press, 2003.

Cunningham, Alexander. *Corpus inscriptionum indicarum*, vol. 1: *Inscriptions of Asoka*. 1877. Reprint Varanasi: Indological Book House, 1961.

Davenport, Basil. *Inquiry into Science Fiction*. New York: Longmans, Green, 1955.

David, Rosalind. *Religion and Magic in Ancient Egypt*. London: Penguin, 2002.

Davis, Richard H. *Lives of Indian Images*. Princeton: Princeton University Press, 1997.

De Camp, L. Sprague. *The Ancient Engineers*. New York: Ballantine Books, 1960.

Defoe, Daniel. *A Journal of the Plague Year*. London: E. Nutt, J. Roberts, A. Dodd, and J. Graves, 1722.

Degener, Almuth. *Das Kaṭhināvadāna*. Bonn: Indica et Tibetica Verlag, 1990.

Denis, Eugène. "La *Lokapaññatti* et la légende birmane d'Asoka." *Journal Asiatique* 264 (1976): 97–116.

Denis, Eugène: *La Lokapaññatti et les idées cosmologiques du bouddhisme ancient*, 2 vols. Paris: Librairie Honoré Champion, 1977.

Deutsch, Eliot. "The Concept of the Body." In *Self as Body in Asian Theory and Practice*, edited by Thomas P. Kasulis et al., 5–19. Albany: State University of New York Press, 1993.

Dickson, Arthur. *Valentine and Orson: A Study in Late Medieval Romance*. New York: Columbia University Press, 1929.

Dissanayake, Wimal. "The Body in Indian Theory and Practice." In *Self as Body in Asian Theory and Practice*, edited by Thomas P. Kasulis et al., 39–44. Albany: State University of New York Press, 1993.

Dolnick, Edward. *The Clockwork Universe: Isaac Newton, the Royal Society, and the Birth of the Modern World*. New York: Harper Perennial, 2012.

Doniger, Wendy. "Medical and Mythical Constructions of the Body in Hindu Texts." In *Religion and the Body*, edited by Sarah Coakley, 167–184. Cambridge: Cambridge University Press, 1997.

Douglas, Mary. *Natural Symbols: Explorations in Cosmology*. New York: Vintage Books, 1973.

Dschi, Hiän-lin. "Parallelversionen zur tocharischen Rezension des Puṇyavanta-Jātaka." *Zeitschrift der deutschen morgenländischen Gesellschaft* 97 (1943): 284–324.

Duffey, M. R. "The Vocal Memnon and Solar Thermal Automata." *Leonardo Music Journal* 17 (2007): 51–54.

Dundas, Paul. "Pārśva and Mahāvīra in History." In *Brill's Encyclopedia of Jainism*, edited by John E. Cort et al., 115–135. Leiden: Brill, 2020.

Durgâprasâd, P., and K. P. Parab. *The Kathâsaritsâgara of Somabhatta*, 2nd ed. Bombay: Nirnaya Sâgara Press, 1903.

Duroiselle, Ch. "Upagutta et Māra." *Bulletin d'Ecole française d'Extrême-Orient* 4 (1904): 414–428.

Dutt, Nalinaksha. *Gilgit Manuscripts*, vol. 3, part 1. Srinagar, 1947. Reprint Delhi: Sri Satguru, 1984.

Dvivedī, Durgāprasāda, ed. *Śrī-Vātsyāyana-praṇītaṃ Kāmasūtram: Yaśodhara-viracitayā Jayamaṅgalākhyayā ṭīkayā sametam*. Bombay: Nirnaya Sagar Press, 1900.

Eck, Diana. *Darśan: Seeing the Divine Image in India*, 3rd ed. New York: Columbia University Press, 1996.

Edgerton, Franklin. "A Hindu Book of Tales: The Vikramacarita." *American Journal of Philology* 33, no. 3 (1912): 249–284.

Edgerton, Franklin. *Vikrama's Adventures: Or Thirty-Two Tales of the Throne*, 2 vols. Cambridge: Harvard University Press, 1926.

Eells, Charles P, trans. *Life and Times of Apollonius of Tyana*. Stanford: Stanford University Press, 1923.

Eliade, Mircea. *Yoga: Immortality and Freedom*, 2nd ed. Princeton: Princeton University Press, 1969.

Evans, Kirsti. *Epic Narratives in the Hoysaḷa Temples: The Rāmāyaṇa, Mahābhārata and Bhāgavata Purāṇa in Haḷebīd, Belūr and Amṛtapura*. Leiden: Brill, 1997.

Falk, Harry. *Schrift im Alten Indien: Ein Forschungsbericht mit Anmerkungen*. Tübingen: Gunter Narr Verlag, 1993.

Feuerstein, Georg. *Tantra: The Path of Ecstasy*. Boston: Shambhala, 1998.

Findlen, Paula. "Scientific Spectacle in Baroque Rome: Athanasius Kircher and the Roman College Museum." In *Jesuit Science and the Republic of Letters*, edited by Mordechai Feingold, 223–284. Cambridge: MIT Press, 2003.

Fredericks, S. C. "Lucian's *True History* as SF." *Science Fiction Studies* 3 (1976): 49–60.

Freud, Sigmund. "The Uncanny." 1919. Reprinted as Sigmund Freud, *The Uncanny*, translated by David McLintock. London: Penguin, 2003.

Gaeffke, Peter. "Hindu Maṇḍalas." In *The Encyclopedia of Religion*, edited by Mircea Eliade, 153–155. New York: Macmillan, 1987.

Gardner, John Robert. "The Developing Terminology for the Self in Vedic India." PhD dissertation, University of Iowa, 1998.

Geduld, Harry M. "Genesis II: The Evolution of Synthetic Man." In *Robots, Robots, Robots*, edited by Harry M. Geduld and Ronald Gottesman, 3–37. Boston: New York Graphic Society, 1978.

Ghosh, Sampa, and Utpal K. Banerjee. *Indian Puppets*. New Delhi: Abhinav, 2006.

Giles, J. A. *William of Malmesbury's Chronicle of the Kings of England: From the Earliest Period to the Reign of King Stephen*. 1847. Reprint Eugene: Wipf & Stock, 2004.

Glaser, Horst Albert, and Sabine Rossbach. *The Artificial Human: A Tragical History*. Frankfurt: Peter Lang, 2011.

Godwin, William. *Lives of the Necromancers: Or, An Account of the Most Eminent Persons in Successive Ages, Who Have Claimed for Themselves, or to Whom Has Been Imputed by Others, the Exercise of Magical Powers*. London: F. J. Mason, 1834.

Gough, Ellen. "Jain *Maṇḍalas* and *Yantras*." In *Brill's Encyclopedia of Jainism*, edited by John E. Cort et al., 585–593. Leiden: Brill, 2020.

Gouwens, Kenneth. "Human Exceptionalism." In *The Renaissance World*, edited by John Jeffries Marin, 415–434. New York: Routledge, 2007.

Grafton, Anthony. "The Devil as Automaton: Giovanni Fontana and the Meanings of a Fifteenth-Century Machine." In *Genesis Redux: Essays in the History and Philosophy of Artificial Life*, edited by Jessica Riskin, 46–59. Chicago: University of Chicago Press, 2007.

Gray, Louis H. *The Narrative of Bhoja (Bhojaprabandha) by Ballāla of Benares*. New Haven: American Oriental Society, 1950.

Gupta, Sanjukta. "The Maṇḍala as an Image of Man." In *Oxford University Papers on India*, vol. 2, part 1: *Indian Ritual and Its Exegesis*, edited by Richard Gombrich, 32–41. Delhi: Oxford University Press, 1988.

Halpern, Daniel, and James E. Katz. "Unveiling Robotophobia and Cyber-dystopianism: The Role of Gender, Technology and Religion on Attitudes Towards Robots." In *Human-Robot Interaction: Proceedings of the 7th ACM/IEEE International Conference*, 139–140. Boston: ACM/IEEE International, 2012.

Hamilton, Richard, et al. *Hesiod's Work and Days*. Bryn Mawr: Bryn Mawr College, 1988.

Hamilton, Sue. "From the Buddha to Buddhaghosa." In *Religious Reflections on the Human Body*, edited by Jane Marie Law, 46–63. Bloomington: Indiana University Press, 1995.

Hamilton, Sue. *Identity and Experience: The Constitution of the Human Being According to Early Buddhism*. Oxford: Luzac, 1996. Reprint 2001.

Hamori, Esther J. *Women's Divination in Biblical Literature: Prophecy, Necromancy, and Other Arts of Knowledge*. New Haven: Yale University Press, 2015.

Handiqui, K. K. *Yaśastilaka and Indian Culture*, 2nd ed. Sholapur: Jaina Saṁskṛti Saṁrakshaka Sangha, 1968.

Hanley, Richard. *Is Data Human? The Metaphysics of Star Trek*. New York: Basic Books, 1997.

Haraway, Donna. "A Cyborg Manifesto: Science, Technology, and Socialist-Feminism in the Late Twentieth Century." *Socialist Review* 15, no. 2 (1985): 65–107. Reprinted in Donna Haraway, *Simians, Cyborgs and Women: The Reinvention of Nature*, 149–181. New York: Routledge, 1991.

Hashim, Rugaya, et al. "Religious Perceptions on Use of Humanoid for Spiritual Augmentation of Children with Autism." *Procedia Computer Science* 105 (2017): 353–358.

Hassan, Ahmad Y., and Donald R. Hill. *Islamic Technology*. Cambridge: Cambridge University Press, 1986.

Hawthorne, Nathaniel. "The Birth-Mark." *The Pioneer*, March 1843. http://www.online-literature.com/hawthorne/125/.

Hellwig, Oliver. *Wörterbuch der Mittelalterlichen indischen Alchemie*. Eelde: Barkhuis, 2009.

Hersey, George L. *Falling in Love with Statues: Artificial Humans from Pygmalion to the Present*. Chicago: University of Chicago Press, 2009.

Higley, Sarah L. "The Legend of the Learned Man's Android." In *Retelling Tales: Essays in Honor of Russell Peck*, edited by T. Hahn and A. Lupack, 127–160. Cambridge: D. S. Brewer, 1997.

Hill, Donald R. *The Book of Ingenious Devices (Kitāb al-Ḥiyal) by the Banū (Sons of) Mūsà bin Shākir*. Dordrecht: D. Reidel, 1979.

Hill, Donald R. *A History of Engineering in Classical and Medieval Times*. La Salle: Open Court, 1984.

Hill, Donald R. *Studies in Medieval Islamic Technology: From Philo to al-Jazari, from Alexandria to Diyar Bakr*. Aldershot: Ashgate, 1998.

Hiltebeitel, Alf. *The Cult of Draupadī*, vol. 1: *Mythologies: From Gingee to Kurukṣetra*. Chicago: University of Chicago Press, 1988.

Hinüber, Oskar von. *A Handbook of Pāli Literature*. Berlin: Walter de Gruyter, 1996. Reprint New Delhi: Munshiram Manoharlal, 1997.

Hodges, Henry. *Technology in the Ancient World*. Harmondsworth: Penguin, 1970.

Hultzsch, E. *Inscriptions of Asoka*. [*Corpus Inscriptionum Indicarum I*]. Oxford, 1925. Reprint Varanasi: Indological Book House, 1969.

Humphrey, John W., et al. *Greek and Roman Technology: A Sourcebook—Annotated Translations of Greek and Latin Texts and Documents*. London: Routledge, 1998.

Hyman, Wendy Beth. Introduction to *The Automaton in English Renaissance Literature*, edited by Wendy Beth Hyman, 1–17. Burlington: Ashgate, 2011.

Idel, Moshe. *Golem: Jewish Magical and Mystical Traditions of the Artificial Anthropoid*. Albany: State University of New York Press, 1990.

Jackson, Rosemary. *Fantasy: The Literature of Subversion*. London: Routledge, 1981.

Jacobi, Hermann. "Über das Vīracaritram." *Indische Studien* 14 (1876): 97–160.

Jagadīsakassapo, Bhikkhu, ed. *Suttapiṭake Saṃyuttanikāyapāli*. [Nālandā]: Bihārarājakīyena Pālipakāsanamaṇḍalena, 1959.

Jain, Jagdishchandra. *Studies in Early Jainism*. New Delhi: Navrang, 1992.

Jain, Jyotindra, and Eberhard Fischer. *Jaina Iconography, Part Two: Objects of Meditation and the Pantheon*. Leiden: E. J. Brill, 1978.

Jaini, Padmanabh S. *The Jaina Path of Purification*. Delhi: Motilal Banarsidass, 1979.

James, Peter, and Nick Thorpe. *Ancient Inventions*. New York: Ballantine Books, 1994.

James, Edward, and Farah Mendlesohn. *The Cambridge Companion to Fantasy Literature*. Cambridge: Cambridge University Press, 2012.

Jamison, Stephanie, and Joel Brereton. *The Rigveda*, 3 vols. Oxford: Oxford University Press, 2014.

Jentsch, Ernst. "Zur Psychologie des Unheimlichen." *Psychiatrisch-Neurologische Wochenschrift* 8, no. 22 (1906): 195–198 and 8, no. 23 (1906): 203–205.

Jha, Ganganatha. *Manusmṛti with the Commentary "Manubhāṣya" of Acārya Medhātithi*, 2 vols. Delhi: Parimal, 1998.

Jülg, Bernhard. *Siddhi-Kür: Mongolische Märchensammlung*. Innsbruck, 1866. Reprint Hildesheim: Olms, 1973.

Kakoudaki, Despina. *Anatomy of a Robot: Literature, Cinema, and the Cultural Work of Artificial People*. New Brunswick: Rutgers University Press, 2014.

Kang, Minsoo. *Sublime Dreams of Living Machines: The Automaton in the European Imagination*. Cambridge: Harvard University Press, 2011.

Kangle, R. P. *The Kauṭilīya Arthaśāstra*, vol. 1: *A Critical Edition with a Glossary*, 2nd ed. Bombay: University of Bombay, 1969.

Kanhaiyālāla, Muni. *Bhagavatī-sūtram*. Rājakoṭa: A. Bhā. Sv'e. Sthā Jaina-śāstroddhārasamitipramukhaḥ Śreshṭhi-Śrīśāntilāla-Maṅgaladāsabhāī-Mahodayah, 1961.

Kaur, Raminder. "The Fictions of Science and Cinema in India." In *Routledge Handbook of Indian Cinemas*, edited by K. Moti Golkusing and Wimal Dissanayake, 282–296. London: Routledge, 2013.

Kavi, Manavalli Ramakrishna, ed. *Nāṭyaśāstra*, 4 vols. Baroda: Central Library, 1926–1964.

Keith, Arthur B. "The Date of the Bṛhatkathā and the Mudrārākṣasa." *Journal of the Royal Asiatic Society of Great Britain and Ireland* (1909): 145–149.

Khanna, Madhu. "Yantra." In *Encyclopedia of Religion*, vol. 15, edited by Mircea Eliade, 500–502. New York: Macmillan, 1987.

Khanna, Madhu. "Yantra and Cakra in Tantric Meditation." In *Asian Traditions of Meditation*, edited by Halvor Eifring, 71–92. Honolulu: University of Hawai'i Press, 2016.

Khing, Hoc Dy. "Note sur le motif du cygne mécanique dans la literature populaire khmere." *Mon-Khmer Studies* 8 (1980): 91–102.

Killingley, Dermot. "Karma and Rebirth in the Upaniṣads." In *The Upaniṣads: A Complete Guide*, edited by Signe Cohen, 121–132. London: Routledge, 2018.

Kimura, Takeshi. "Masahiro Mori's Buddhist Philosophy of Robot." *Paladyn, Journal of Behavioral Robotics* 9 (2018): 72–81.

Koller, John M. "Human Embodiment: Indian Perspectives." In *Self as Body in Asian Theory and Practice*, edited by Thomas P. Kasulis et al., 45–58. Albany: State University of New York Press, 1993.

Kramrisch, Stella. *The Hindu Temple*. Calcutta, 1946. Reprint Delhi: Motilal Banarsidass, 1976.

Kravitz, Leonard, and Kerry M. Olitzky, eds. *Pirke Avot*. New York: UAHC Press, 1993.

LaGrandeur, Kevin. *Androids and Intelligent Networks in Early Modern Literature and Culture: Artificial Slaves*. New York: Routledge, 2013.

La Mettrie, Julien Offray. *L'Homme machine*. Leiden: Elie Luzac, 1747.

Lane, G. "The Tocharian *Puṇyavantajātaka*: Text and Translation." *Journal of the American Oriental Society* 67 (1947): 33–53.

Landels, J. G. *Engineering in the Ancient World*. Berkeley: University of California Press, 2000.

Larson, Gerald James. "The Concept of Body in *Ayurveda* and the Hindu Philosophical Systems." In *Self as Body in Asian Theory and Practice*, edited by Thomas P. Kasulis et al., 103–121. Albany: State University of New York Press, 1993.

Le Guin, Ursula K. *The Language of the Night: Essays on Fantasy and Science Fiction*. Edited by Susan Wood. New York: Perigee, 1979.

Levin, Ira. *The Stepford Wives*. New York: Random House, 1972.

Liu, Lydia H. *The Freudian Robot: Digital Media and the Future of the Unconscious*. Chicago: University of Chicago Press, 2010.

Loomis, Roger Sherman. *The Grail from Celtic Myth to Christian Symbol*. Cardiff: University of Wales Press, 1963.

Pollock, Sheldon, ed. *A Rasa Reader: Classical Indian Aesthetics*. New York: Columbia University Press, 2016.

Maisano, Scott. "Descartes avec Milton: The Automata in the Garden." In *The Automaton in English Renaissance Literature*, edited by Wendy Beth Hyman, 21–44. Burlington: Ashgate, 2011.

Marr, Alexander. "Understanding Automata in the Late Renaissance." *Journal de la Renaissance* 2 (2004): 205–222.

Marshall, Peter K., ed. *Noctes Atticae*. Oxford: Clarendon Press, 1968.

Mayor, Adrienne. *Gods and Robots: Myths, Machines, and Ancient Dreams of Technology*. Princeton: Princeton University Press, 2018.

McCullough, Lynsey. "Antique Myth, Early Modern Mechanism: The Secret History of Spenser's Iron Man." In *The Automaton in English Renaissance Literature*, edited by Wendy Beth Hyman, 61–76. Burlington: Ashgate, 2011.

Mehta, Jyotindra Markand, ed. *The Vālmīki Rāmāyaṇa, Critically Edited for the First Time*. Baroda: Oriental Institute, 1960–1975.

Mitchiner, John E. *The Yuga Purāṇa*. Calcutta: Asiatic Society, 1986.

Mobley, Jane. "Toward a Definition of Fantasy Fiction." *Extrapolation* 15 (1974): 117–128.

Mori, Masahiro. *The Buddha in the Robot*. Tokyo: Kosei, 1981.

Mori, Masahiro. "Bukimi no tani [The Uncanny Valley]." *Energy* 4 (1970): 33–35.

Mrozik, Susanne. *Virtuous Bodies: The Physical Dimensions of Morality in Buddhist Ethics*. Oxford: Oxford University Press, 2007.

Munshi, Kalpalatā, ed. *Śṛṅgāramañjarīkathā*. Bombay: Bhāratīya Vidyā Bhavana, 1959.

Mus, Paul. *La Lumière sur les Six Voies: Tableau de la transmigration bouddhique d'après des sources sanskrites, pāli, tibétaines et chinoises en majeures partie inédites*. Paris: Institut d'ethnologie, 1939.

Mysore, Srinarahari. "Indian Science Fiction: History and Contemporary Trends." Accessed April 15, 2022. https://www.academia.edu/10442469/Indian_Science_Fiction_History_and_Contemporary_Trends.

Nāṭṭār, Naṭukkāvēri Mu Vēṅkaṭacāmi, ed. *Cīttalaic Cāttanār iyaṟṟiya Maṇimēkalai*. Ceṉṉai: Tirunelvēlit Teṉṉintiya Caivacittānta Nūṟpatippuk Kaḻakam, 1951.

Neckel, Gustav, and Hans Kuhn, eds. *Edda: Die Lieder des Codex Regius nebst verwandten Denkmälern*, vol. 1, *Text*, 5th ed. Heidelberg: Carl Winter, 1983.

Neelis, Jason. *Early Buddhist Transmission and Trade Networks: Mobility and Exchange within and beyond the Northwestern Borderlands of South Asia*. Leiden: Brill, 2011.

Neugroschel, Joachim. *The Golem*. New York: W. W. Norton, 2006.

Newman, William R. *Promethean Ambitions: Alchemy and the Quest to Perfect Nature*. Chicago: University of Chicago Press, 2004.

Nooten, Barend A. van, and Gary B. Holland, eds. *The Rigveda*. Cambridge: Harvard University Press, 1994.

Olivelle, Patrick. *The Early Upaniṣads: Annotated Text and Translation*. Oxford: University Press, 1998.

Olivelle, Patrick. "Kings, Ascetics, and Brahmins: The Socio-political Context of Ancient Indian Religions." In *Dynamics in the History of Religions between Asia and Europe*, edited by Volkhard Krech and Marion Steinicke, 117–135. Leiden: Brill, 2012.

Olivelle, Patrick. *King, Governance, and Law in Ancient India: Kauṭilya's Arthaśāstra*. Oxford: Oxford University Press, 2013.

Olivelle, Patrick. *Pañcatantra: The Book of India's Folk Wisdom*. Oxford: Oxford University Press, 1999.

Otter, Felix. *Residential Architecture in Bhoja's Samarāṅgaṇasūtradhāra*. Delhi: Motilal Banarsidass, 2010.

Padoux, André. "Hindu Tantrism." In *The Encyclopedia of Religion*, vol. 14, edited by Mircea Eliade, 273. New York: Macmillan, 1986.

Padoux, André. "Maṇḍalas in Abhinavagupta's *Tantrāloka*." In *Maṇḍalas and Yantras in the Hindu Tradition*, edited by Gudrun Bühnemann, 225–238. Leiden: Brill 2003.

Panglung, Jampa Losang. *Die Erzählstoffe des Mūlasarvāstivāda-Vinaya analysiert auf Grund der tibetischen Übersetzung*. Tokyo: Reiyukai Library, 1981.

Panikkar, Raimundo. "The Destiny of Technological Civilization: An Ancient Buddhist Legend, *Romavisaya*." *Alternatives* 10 (1984): 237–253.

Paṇaśikar, Vâsudeva Laxmaṇ Śâstrî, et al., eds. *The Yaśastilaka of Somadeva Sûri*, 2 vols. Bombay: Nirnaya Sagar Press, 1903–1916.

Parāb, Kāśīnāth Pāṇḍuraṅg, ed. *The Harṣacharita of Bāṇabhaṭṭa*, 7th ed. Bombay: Nirnaya Sagar Press, 1946.

Parāb, Kāśīnāth Pāṇḍuraṅg, ed. *Pañcatantraka of Viṣṇuśarman*. Bombay: Nirnaya Sagar Press, 1896.

Paton, W. R., ed. *Polybius: The Histories*. Chicago: University of Chicago Press, 2012.

Pillai, Suranad Kunjan, ed. *Ācārya-Dandi-viracitā Avantisundarī*. Trivandrum: Trivandrum University, 1954.

Pischel, Richard. *The Home of the Puppet Play*. London: Luzac, 1902.

Plank, Robert. "The Golem and the Robot." *Literature and Psychology* 15, no. 1 (1965): 12–27.

Poddar, Ram Prakash, and Neelima Sinha. *Budhasvāmin's bṛhatkathā ślokasaṅgraha*. Varanasi: Tara Print, 1986.

Pollock, Sheldon. *A Rasa Reader: Classical Indian Aesthetics*. New York: Columbia University Press, 2016.

Powers, John. *Introduction to Tibetan Buddhism*. Ithaca: Snow Lion, 2007.

Price, Derek J. de Solla. "Automata and the Origins of Mechanism and Mechanistic Philosophy." *Technology and Culture* 5 (1964): 9–23.

Raghavan, V. "Gleanings from Somadevasūri's Yaśastilaka Campū." *Journal of the Ganganatha Jha Research Institute* 1 (1944): 249–258, 365–380, 467–478.

Raghavan, V., ed. *Nṛttaratnāvalī of Jāya Senāpati*. Madras: Government Oriental Manuscripts Library, 1965.

Raghavan, V. "Somadeva and King Bhoja." *Journal of the University of Gauhati* 3 (1952): 35–38.

Raghavan, V. *Yantras or Mechanical Contrivances in Ancient India*, 2nd ed, revised and enlarged. Bangalore: Indian Institute of Culture, 1956.

Rai, Ganga Sar, ed. *Mudrārākṣasam*. Vārāṇasī: Caukhambhā Saṃskṛta Saṃsthāna, 1992.

Rastelli, Marion. "Maṇḍalas and Yantras in the Pañcarātra Tradition." In *Maṇḍalas and Yantras in the Hindu Traditions*, edited by Gudrun Bühnemann, 119–151. Leiden: Brill, 2003.

Rautman, Marcus. *Daily Life in the Byzantine Empire*. Westport: Greenwood Press, 2006.

Ray, H. C. *The Dynastic History of Northern India (Early Medieval Period)*, vol. 2. Calcutta: University of Calcutta, 1931.

Ray, Himanshu P. "The Yavana Presence in Ancient India." *Journal of the Economic and Social History of the Orient* 31, no. 3 (1988): 311–325.

Ray, P. C., and Hariscandra Kaviratna, eds. *Rasārṇava*. Calcutta: Baptist Mission Press, 1910.

Rehm, Bernhard, and Georg Strecker, eds. *Die Pseudoklementinen*, 2nd ed. Berlin: Akademie-Verlag, 1994.

Richey, Jeffrey L. "I, Robot: Self as Machine in the *Liezi*." In *Riding the Wind with* Liezi: *New Perspectives on the Daoist Classic*, edited by Ronnie Littlejohn and Jeffrey Dippmann, 193–208. Albany: State University of New York Press, 2011.

Riskin, Jessica. *The Restless Clock: A History of the Centuries-Long Argument over What Makes Living Things Tick*. Chicago: University of Chicago Press, 2016.

Rosu, Arion. "*Mantra* et *yantra* dans la medicine et l'alchimie indiennes." In *Mantras et diagrammes rituels dans l'hindouisme*. Paris: Centre national de la recherché scientifique, 1986.

Ross, W. D. *Aristotelis De Anima*. Oxford: Clarendon Press, 1956.

Roy, Mira. "The Concept of Yantra in the *Samarāṅgaṇa-Sūtradhāra* of Bhoja." *Indian Journal of History of Science* 19, no. 2 (1984): 118–124.

Royle, Nicholas. *The Uncanny*. New York: Routledge, 2003.

Sage, Evan T. "An Ancient Robotette." *Classical Journal* 30, no. 5 (1935): 299–300.

Sāminātaiyar, U. V., ed. *Pattuppāṭṭu mūlamum*, 3rd ed. Ce<u>nn</u>ai: Kēcari Accukkūṭam, 1931.

Sāminātaiyar, U. V., ed. *Pu<u>r</u>anānū<u>r</u>u Mūlamum Ureiyum*, 4th ed. Madras: n.p., 1950.

Sankarnarayan, K., et al. *Lokaprajñapti: A Critical Exposition of Buddhist Cosmology*. Mumbai: Somaiya, 2002.

Śāstrī, R. *Kādambarī*, 2nd ed. Varanasi: Caukhamba, 1985.

Śāstrī, T. Gaṇapati, ed. *Samarāṅgaṇasūtradhāra by King Bhojadeva*, 2 vols. Baroda: Baroda Central Library, 1924.

Śāstrī, Yajñeśvara Sadāśiva, ed. *Praśamaratiprakaraṇam*. Ahmedabad: Lālabhāī Dalapatabhāī Bhāratīya Saṃskṛti Vidyāmandira, 1989.

Sauer, Lieselotte. *Marionetten, Maschinen, Automaten: Der künstliche Mensch in der deutschen und englischen Romantik*. Bonn: Bouvier, 1983.

Schelde, Per. *Androids, Humanoids, and Other Science Fiction Monsters: Science and Soul in Science Fiction Films*. New York: New York University Press, 1993.

Schiefner, W. "Der Mechaniker und der Maler." *Mélanges Asiatiques* 7 (1859): 521–523.

Schmidt, W. *Heronis Alexandrini Opera quae supersunt omnia*, 1: *Pneumatica et Automata*, 2nd ed. Stuttgart: B. G. Teubner, 1976.

Schneider, Ulrich. "Tantra—Endpunkt eines strukturierten Ablaufs?" *Saeculum* 39 (1988): 96–104.

Schuster, Michael. "Visible Puppets and Hidden Puppeteers: Indian Gombeyata Puppetry." *Asian Theatre Journal* 18 (2001): 59–68.

Schwartz, Susan. *Rasa: Performing the Divine in India*. New York: Columbia University Press, 2004.

Segel, Harold B. *Pinocchio's Progeny: Puppets, Marionettes, Automatons, and Robots in Modernist and Avant-Garde Drama*. Baltimore: Johns Hopkins University Press, 1995.

Selzer, David, ed. *Friar Bacon and Friar Bungay*. Lincoln: University of Nebraska Press, 1963.

Sengupta, Debjani. "Explorers of Subversive Knowledge: The Science Fantasy of Leela Majumdar and Sukumar Ray." In *Indian Genre Fiction: Past and Future Histories*, edited by Bodhisattva Chattopadhyay, Aakriti Mandhwani, and Anwesha Maity, 73–85, New York: Routledge, 2019.

Shapin, Steven. "Of Gods and Kings: Natural Philosophy and Politics in the Leibniz-Clarke Disputes." *Isis* 72 (1981): 187–215.

Sharma, Sudarshan Kumar. *Samarāṅgaṇa Sūtradhāra of Bhojadeva (Paramāra ruler of Dhārā): An Ancient Treatise on Architecture*, 2 vols. Delhi: Parimal, 2007.

Shivanandam, M. "Mercury Propulsion System in Vedic Vimanas and Modern Spacecraft." *International Journal of Research and Analytical Reviews* 2, no. 2 (2015): 136–144.

Shruti, K. R., and Rajani Jairam. "Mechanical Contrivances and Dharu Vimanas Described in 'Samarangana Sutradhara' of Bhojadeva." *Journal of Humanities and Social Science* 20, no. 12 (2015): 16–20.

Sieg, E. "Das Märchen von dem Mechaniker und dem Maler in tocharischer Fassung." *Ostasiatische Zeitschrift* 8 (1919–2020): 362–369.

Sieg, E., and W. Siegling. *Tocharische Sprachreste*, 1: *Die Texte*. Berlin: De Gruyter, 1921.

Sighart, Joachim. *Albert the Great of the Order of Friar-Preachers: His Life and Scholastic Labours*. Translated by Rev. Fr. T. A. Dixon. London: R. Washborne, 1876.

Singer, Distress F. "Palm Leaf Manuscripts from Burma." Accessed April 15, 2022. https://www.burmese-buddhas.com/burmese-manuscripts/palm-leaf-manuscripts/.

Singh, Mahesh. *Bhoja Paramāra and His Times*. Delhi: Bharatiya Vidya Prakashan, 1984.

Singleton, Mark. *Yoga Body: The Origins of Modern Posture Practice*. Oxford: Oxford University Press, 2010.

Sirkar, D. C. *Inscriptions of Aśoka*. Delhi: Government of India Press, 1967.

Śivadatta, P., and Kāśināth Pandurang Parab. *Yaśastilakacampū*. Bombay: Tūkarām Jāvajī, 1901.

Stevenson, Sinclair. *The Heart of Jainism*. Oxford: Oxford University Press, 1915. Reprint New Delhi: Munshiram Manoharlal, 1984.

Strauss, Linda M. "Reflections in a Mechanical Mirror: Automata as Doubles and Tools." *Knowledge and Society: Studies in the Sociology of Culture Past and Present* 10 (1996): 179–207.

Strong, John S. *The Legend and Cult of Upagupta: Sanskrit Buddhism in North India and Southeast Asia*. Princeton: Princeton University Press, 1992.

Strudwick, Helen. *The Encyclopedia of Ancient Egypt*. London: Amber Books, 2006.

Sukthankar, Vishnu S., et al., eds. *The Harivaṃśa: The Khila or Supplement to the Mahābhārata*. Poona: Bhandarkar Oriental Research Institute, 1976.

Sukthankar, Vishnu S., et al., eds. *The Mahābhārata, for the First Time Critically Edited*. Poona: Bhandarkar Oriental Research Institute, 1933.

Suthren Hirst, Jacqueline. "*Ātman* and *Brahman* in the Principal Upaniṣads." In *The Upaniṣads: A Complete Guide*, edited by Signe Cohen, 107–120. London: Routledge, 2018.

Sutton, Thomas C., and Marilyn Sutton. "Science Fiction as Mythology." *Western Folklore* 28 (1969): 230–237.

Swain, Simon. "Apollonius in Wonderland." In *Ethics and Rhetoric: Classical Essays for Donald Russell on His Seventy-Fifth Birthday*, edited by Doreen Innes, Harry Hine, and Christopher Pelling, 251–264. Oxford: Clarendon Press, 1995.

Swearer, Donald K. *The Buddhist World of Southeast Asia*. Albany: State University of New York Press, 1995.

Tarrant, R. J., ed. *Metamorphoses*. Oxford: Clarendon Press, 2004.

Telotte, J. P. *Replications: A Robotic History of the Science Fiction Film*. Urbana: University of Illinois Press, 1995.

Thapar, Romila. *Aśoka and the Decline of the Mauryas*. Oxford: Oxford University Press, 1961.

Thapar, Romila. "Indian Views of Europe: Representations of the Yavanas in Early Indian History." In *Cultural Pasts: Essays in Early Indian*

History, edited by Romila Thapar, 536–555. Delhi: Oxford University Press 2000.

Timalsina, Staneshwar. *Language of Images: Visualization and Meaning in Tantras*. New York: Peter Lang, 2015.

Todorov, Tzvetan. *The Fantastic: A Structural Approach to a Literary Genre*. Ithaca: Cornell University Press, 1973.

Tolkien, J. R. R. "On Fairy Stories." In *Essays Presented to Charles Williams*. Oxford: Oxford University Press, 1947. Reprinted in *Tolkien on Fairy-Stories: Expanded Edition, with Commentary and Notes*, edited by Verlyn Flieger and Douglas A. Anderson, 25–84. London: HarperCollins, 2008.

Trapp, J. B. "The Grave of Vergil." *Journal of the Warburg and Courtauld Institutes* 47 (1984): 1–31.

Treckner, Vilhelm. *The Milindapañho: Being Dialogues between King Milinda and the Buddhist Sage Nāgasena—The Pali Text*. London: Luzac, 1962.

Truitt, E. R. "Fictions of Life and Death: Tomb Automata in Medieval Romance." *postmedieval: a journal of medieval cultural studies* 1 (2010): 194–198.

Truitt, E. R. *Medieval Robots: Mechanism, Magic, Nature, and Art*. Philadelphia: University of Pennsylvania Press, 2015.

Truitt, E. R. "'Trei poëte, sages dotors, qui mout sovent di nigromance': Knowledge and Automata in Twelfth-Century French Literature." *Configurations* 12 (2004): 167–193.

Tubini, Bernadette, ed. *Kaivalyopaniṣad*. Paris: Adrien-Maisonneuve, 1952.

Tucci, Giuseppe. *The Theory and Practice of the Mandala*. Originally published 1949. London: Rider, 1969.

Vāgbhaṭṭa, Ambikādatta Śāstri, ed. *Rasaratnasamuccaya*. Varanasi: Chaukhamba, 1939.

Vaidya, P. L., ed. *Dhammapada*. Poona: Oriental Book Agency, 1934.

Vallverdú, Jordi. "The Eastern Construct of the Artificial Mind." *Enrahonar: Quaderns de Filosofia* 47 (2011): 171–185.

Varadpande, M. K. *Ancient Indian and Indo-Greek Theatre*. New Delhi: Abhinav 1981.

Vidal, Denis. "Anthropomorphism or Sub-anthropomorphism? An Anthropological Approach to Gods and Robots." *Journal of the Royal Anthropological Institute* 13 (2007): 917–933.

Viereck, Paul, and A. G. Roos, eds. *Historia romana*. Leipzig: B. G. Teubner, 1962.

Villiers de l'Isle-Adam, Auguste. *Tomorrow's Eve*. Translated by Robert Martin Adams. Urbana: University of Illinois Press, 1982.

Vogt, Albert, ed. *Le livre des cérémonies*, 2 vols. Paris: Société d'édition "Les Belles Lettres," 1935–1940.

Walter, Gérard. *Caesar: A Biography*. New York: Charles Scribner's Sons, 1952.

Warren, Henry Clarke, and Dharmananda Kosambi, eds. *Visuddhimagga of Buddhaghosâcariya*. Cambridge: Harvard University Press, 1950.

Wender, Dorothea. *Hesiod: Theogony, Work and Days*. Harmondsworth: Penguin, 1973.

West, Martin L., ed. *Homeri Ilias*, vol. 2. Stuttgart: B. G. Teubner, 2000.

White, David Gordon. *The Alchemical Body: Siddhi Traditions in Medieval India*. Chicago: University of Chicago Press, 1996.

White, David Gordon. *Tantra in Practice*. Princeton: Princeton University Press, 2000.

Wiley, Kristi L., and Ruth Satinsky. "Cosmology and Cycles of Time." In *Brill's Encyclopedia of Jainism*, edited by John E. Cort et al., 3–27. Leiden: Brill, 2020.

Williams, Paul. "Some Mahāyāna Buddhist Perspectives on the Body." In *Religion and the Body*, edited by Sarah Coakley, 205–230. Cambridge: Cambridge University Press, 1997.

Wilson, Eric G. *The Melancholy Android: On the Psychology of Sacred Machines*. Albany: State University of New York Press, 2006.

Winter, Werner. "Some Aspects of Tocharian Drama: Form and Techniques." *Journal of the American Oriental Society* 75 (1955): 26–35.

Winternitz, Moriz. *A History of Indian Literature*, vol. 2: *Buddhist Literature and Jaina Literature*. Calcutta, 1933. Reprint Delhi: Motilal Banarsidass, 1993.

Wood, Gaby. *Edison's Eve: A Magical History of the Quest for Mechanical Life*. New York: Anchor, 2002.

Woodcroft, Bennet. *The Pneumatics of Hero of Alexandria*. London: Taylor Walton and Maberly, 1851.

Wujastyk, Dominik. "Interpreting the Image of the Human Body in Premodern India." *International Journal of Hindu Studies* 13 (2009): 189–228.

Yates, Frances. *Giordano Bruno and the Hermetic Tradition*. Chicago: University of Chicago Press, 1964.

Zielinski, Siegfried. "Allah's Automata: Where Ancient Oriental Learning Intersects with Early Modern Europe—A Media-Archaeological Miniature by Way of Introduction." In *Allah's Automata: Artifacts of the Arab-Islamic Renaissance (800–1200)*, edited by Siegfried Zielinski and Peter Weibel, 12–27. Karlsruhe: ZKM, 2016.

Zimmer, Heinrich. *Artistic Form and Yoga in the Sacred Images of India*. Princeton: Princeton University Press, 1984.

Zvelebil, Kamil. *The Smile of Murugan: On Tamil Literature of South India*. Leiden: Brill, 1973.

Zvelebil, Kamil. "The Yavanas in Old Tamil Literature." In *Charisteria Orientalia praecipua ad Persiam pertinenia,* edited by Felix Tauel et al., 401–409. Prague: Nakladatelstvi Československe Akademi, 1956.

Zydenbos, Robert J. "Jain Ethics." In *Brill's Encyclopedia of Jainism,* edited by John E. Cort et al., 393–406. Leiden: Brill, 2020.

Index

Abhinavabhāratī, 54
Abhinavagupta, 52, 54–55
Adbhuta, 54–55, 70, 79, 95, 176, 180, 185, 187
Advaita Vedānta, 90
ahaṃkāra, 89
ahiṃsā, 113–114, 190
A. I. (2001 film), 96
Ajātasattu (Ajātaśatru), 156, 159–160, 165, 166, 168, 169, 171
Akanāṉūṟu, 58
Albert Magnus, 24, 30, 31–32, 45, 217n6
Alchemy, 9–10, 69, 76–78, 84, 92–93, 99, 249n2, 249n3
Alexander of Epirus, 151
Ammon, 19
Ānandavardhana, 54
Ananta-Amatya, 65
Anattā, 142, 144, 188, 190
android, definition, 3
angels, 24–25, 36, 186
  mechanical, 33, 41
Antigonus Gonatas of Macedonia, 151
Antiochus II Theos of Syria, 151
Aphrodite, 21, 22, 109
Appian of Alexandria, 23
Arachne, 109
archer, mechanical, 31, 163
artha, 69–70, 193, 195
Arthaśāstra, 8
Artist, The (Jaquet-Droz automaton), 41
Asimov, Isaac, 1, 47, 48, 191–192
Aśoka (Asoka), 16, 59, 151–156, 160, 161, 164, 165–172, 245n30, 245n32
Aśokāvadāna, 154
Assaghosa, 155
Atharvaveda, 85
Athena, 109
ātman, 87, 89, 90, 93, 94, 95–97, 99, 112, 139, 140, 143, 144, 145, 185, 186, 189–190, 191, 194, 236 n4, 237, n 39, 237n40, 249 n4, see also *attā*
attā, 143
Aulus Gellius, 23
automaton, definition, 3
Avantisundarī, 10–11, 60, 94
Aymeri de Narbonne, 27
Āyurveda, 13, 87–88

Bacon, Roger, 30
Ballāla of Benares, 65
Bāṇa, 60
bathhouse, mechanical, 72, 206–208
Baudrillard, Jean, 148–149

bee, mechanical, 79
Benoît de Sainte-Maure, 31
Bertrand de Bar-sur-Aube, 27
Bhagavadgītā, 7, 88–89, 179
Bhagavatī Sūtra, 115
Bhaiṣajya-Vastu, 134
Bharata, 53–54
Bhaṭṭanāyaka, 54
Bhoja, King of Malwā, 7, 11, 15, 64–66, 68, 72–81, 84, 92, 124, 179, 193–216
Bhojaprabandha, 65
Bhojarajīyam, 65
bhūta (element), 67, 68, 89, 193–194, 249n3
bhūta (spirit), 157
bīja, 12, 68–69, 74, 75, 77–78, 184, 193, 196, 197, 249n3, 250n15
bindu, 13, 92
Bindusara, 160
bird, mechanical, 1, 10, 22, 23, 25, 27, 29, 33, 71, 72, 77, 102–109, 111–112, 117, 174, 177, 182, 183–184, 200, 202, 203, 206, 210, 251n35
  (*see also* dove, eagle, goose, peacock, and rooster)
Blade Runner (1982 film), 48–49, 129, 141
Blade Runner 2049 (2017 film), 49, 129
Bodhisattva, 145
body,
  as machine, 15, 39–40, 42, 93–94, 145
  as socially constructed, 135
  in alchemy, 10
  in Buddhism, 140, 144–147, 148
  in Hinduism, 10, 13, 14, 15, 67, 85–97, 98, 115, 148
  in Jainism, 115–116
  in Judaism, 36
  in Tantra, 14, 90–92
boy, mechanical, 15, 24, 31, 41, 93
Brah Jinavaṃs, 111–112
brahman, 87, 90
brass, 1, 23, 30, 163
  brass man, 32
brazen head, 1, 29–30, 31, 40
Bṛhatkalpabhāṣya, 60
Bṛhatkathā, 59, 60, 118, 122
Bṛhatkathāślokasaṁgraha, 9, 60, 122, 126, 157
Bronze, 21, 39, 49
  bronze cup-bearers, 61
  bronze fly, 30, 162, 182
Buddha, 2, 82, 84, 113, 130–131, 137, 143–147, 152, 153, 154, 156, 159, 162, 163, 164, 168–169, 170–172, 186, 188
Buddhaghosa, 145, 147
buddhi, 89, 94
buddhīndriya, 89
Buddhism, 3, 5, 13, 14, 16, 49, 51, 55, 59, 60, 66, 80, 91, 101, 124, 129–172, 177, 178, 185, 186, 187, 188, 189, 190, 191
Budhasvāmin, 9, 60, 122, 126
Bullmann, Hans, 33
Byron, Lord George Gordon, 30
Byzantine Empire, 29, 33, 58, 81

Caesar, 23
Cagatidīpanī, 155
cakra, 11–12, 73, 74–75, 91, 193, 196
cakravartin, 152–153, 169
Cameron, James, 49
Campantar, 98
Candragupta Maurya, 151
Čapek, Josef, 4, 46
Čapek, Karel, 4, 46, 179
Carakasaṃhitā, 87–88

Cārvāka, 93
catapult, 5, 7, 8, 10
cathedral clocks, 34
Caus, Isaac and Salomon de, 40
Caxton, William, 163
Cervantes, Miguel de, 30
chariot, mechanical, 9, 18, 59–60, 73, 95, 111, 118, 126, 178, 203, 211, 212, 213, 252, n52
Charlemagne, 27, 29
chess player, mechanical, 42–43, 100
Cicero, 74
clavichord player, mechanical, 41
Clementine *Recognitiones,* 23
clockmaker, God as, 73–75
clockwork, 1, 15, 33, 73–75
clockwork universe, 73–75
cloud, artificial, 10, 124
Constantinople, 29
Conte de Flore et Blancheflor, Le, 31
Copper, 10, 29, 31, 159, 162, 196, 197, 202, 246n37
  copper knight, 31
  copper maiden, 31
Corsini, Matteo, 32
Cox, James, 42
crocodile, mechanical, 79, 124
cyborg, 21, 49–50, 218n8
  definition, 4, 218n8
Cyborg Manifesto, A, 49–50

Daedalus, 22
Dalai Lama, 191
dancer, mechanical, 31
Daṇḍin, 10–11, 60, 94
De ceremoniis, 29
De mundo, 74
De naturis rerum, 30
Defoe, Daniel, 30
demons, 8, 15, 24–25, 43, 81–84, 175, 177, 183, 184, 186, 199, 206, 251n24, 251n25
Descartes, René, 1, 39–40, 42, 45, 89–90
  android daughter, 39–40, 45, 96
devil, 31, 33, 36, 83
  mechanical, 33
Devīmāhātmya, 182
dhamma (psychophysical atom), 141, 144, 153,
dhamma (teachings of the Buddha), 59, 158, 159, 160, 165, 169, 172, 145n25
Dhammazedi, 169–170
Dhārā, 65, 78
dharma, 69–70, 153, 193, 195, 249n2, 249n6
Dhvanyāloka, 54
Dhvanyālokalocana, 55
Don Quixote, 30
doorkeeper, mechanical, 5, 6, 31, 72
Douglas, Mary, 135
dove, mechanical, 23, 119, 122
duck, mechanical, 41, 78, 99–100, 112
Durgā, 184
Dutta, Hemlal, 178
Dzogchen, 146

eagle, mechanical, 23, 33
Edison, Thomas Alva, 44
Egypt, 1, 17, 18–12, 22, 25, 35, 51, 98, 129
eightfold path, 143
Eleazar of Worms, 37
elephant, mechanical, 1, 5, 6, 10–11, 26, 70, 71, 72, 99–102, 200, 205, 207, 212, 253n60
elephant clock, 26, 27, 71, 72
elements, 6, 13, 14, 67–69, 74, 75, 76–78, 82–84, 87, 89, 90, 91, 92, 114, 115, 184, 190, 193–198, 201, 202, 242n26, 249n3

Elijah Ba'al Shem of Chelm, 38
Enosh, 36
Enthiran (2010 film), 180–183
Enthiran 2.0 (2018 film), 183–184
Eve future, L', 44

Faerie Queene, The, 39
fantasy, genre, 22, 174–177, 179
fife and drum player, mechanical, 41
fish, mechanical, 7, 125, 163, 210, 218n17
Flavius Philostratus, 61
flute player, mechanical, 25, 71, 72, 199, 201
fly, mechanical, 30, 33, 162
flying machine, 9, 10, 16, 17–18, 59–60, 73, 95, 108, 109, 111, 112, 118–122, 126, 127, 157, 174, 177, 178, 185, 203
Fontana, Giovanni, 33
Fontanelle, Bernard de, 74
Forbidden Planet (1956 film), 47–48
fountain, mechanical, 5, 25, 40, 72, 78, 79, 81, 123, 124, 125, 142, 207, 208, 209
Frankenstein, Victor, 24, 46
Frankenstein (novel), 31, 45–46
Frankenstein (1910 film), 46
Frankenstein (1931 film), 46
Frankenstein film franchise, 46
Freud, Sigmund, 15, 44–45, 52

Gadyacintāmaṇi, 125
Galatea, 45, 109
Gaṇeśa, 64, 98
gardens, 72–73, 78–81, 83–84, 96, 122–125, 142, 175, 177, 184, 189, 205
Garuḍa, 99, 103–111, 122, 174, 177, 178, 182–185, 187
Gautier de Metz, 30, 162
gender, 50–51, 88, 135, 140
Genesis Rabbah, 36
Gerbert of Aurillac (Pope Sylvester II), 30
Gesta Regum Anglorum, 30
Godwin, William, 31, 45
golem, 14, 19–20, 34–39, 45, 50, 129, 181
goose, mechanical, 1, 5, 10, 95, 109, 110, 111, 112, 206
Greece, 17, 20–23, 57–62
Greeks, 15, 17, 18, 20–23, 25, 28, 29, 31, 41, 57–62, 63, 68, 100, 109, 118
 see also *yavana*
Grosseteste, Robert, 30
guṇas, 89

Haṃs Yant, 111–112
Hanthawaddy Kingdom, 155, 164, 169–171
Haraway, Donna, 49–50
Harivaṃśa, 7, 58
Harṣacarita, 10, 60, 101
Hārūn al-Rashīd, 29
Hawthorne, Nathaniel, 30
He, She, and It, 50
head, oracular, 1, 29–30, 31, 45, 65–66, *see also* brazen head
Hephaestus, 20, 21
Hermeticism, 24
Hero of Alexandria, 18, 23, 25, 33, 59, 72, 77, 234n24
Hesiod, 21
Hinduism, 1, 6–14, 15, 51, 57–62, 63–122, 143, 148, 175, 178–185, 186, 187, 189, 190, 191
Hoffmann, E. T. A., 44–45, 52, 140, 174, 181
Hollywood (2002 film), 180
Homme machine, L', 42
Honnecourt, Villard de, 33

horse, mechanical, 40, 70, 72, 94, 121, 122, 163, 185, 200
Hṛdayadarpaṇa, 54
hyperreality, 148–149

Ibn Mu'ādh, 26
Icarus, 109
Image du monde, L', 30, 31, 162–164
immortality, 10, 76, 77, 78, 83–84, 92–93, 175, 184, 251n24
I, Robot, 47
iron, 33, 39, 71, 178, 196, 197, 203, 204, 212
iron fly, 33
Islam, 1, 18, 25–29, 33, 50, 71, 81, 98, 186
Itinerarium cuiusdam Anglici, 163

Jaquet-Droz, Pierre and Henri, 41–42, 45
Jainism, 15–16, 59–60, 66, 72, 81, 91, 113–127, 137, 142, 143, 185, 187, 189, 190, 191
Jātakas, 2, 136–139, 141, 145
Jāyasenāpati, 11
al-Jazarī, 26–27, 71–72
jina, 113, 116, 143
jīva, 114–115, 125, 191
jīvātman, 114
Jentsch, Ernst, 44, 52
John of Sacrobosco, 74
John of Salisbury, 30, 162
Judaism, 14, 18, 20, 34–39, 45, 50, 181, 186, 187
Juvenal, 22

Kabbalah, 35, 37
kāma, 69–70, 91, 193, 195, 249n2
Kāma (god), 249n1, 252n51
Kāmasūtra, 8–9, 63
karmendriya, 89
karṇikā, 72–73, 151
Kaṭha Upaniṣad, 87, 93
Kathāsaritsāgara, 10, 15, 81–84, 87, 94–96, 100, 108, 109, 118, 175
Kaṭhināvadāna, 135, 136, 142
Kauṭilya, 8
Kempelen, Wolfgang von, 42–43, 100
Kepler, Johannes, 74
khandha, 144
Khatri, Durga Prasad, 178
Khmer literature, 111–112
killer robots, 1, 3, 16, 23, 31, 49, 145, 151–172, 177, 182
Kircher, Athanasius, 40
Kitāb al-asrār fi natā'ij al-afkār, 25
Kitāb al-ḥiyal, 25, 72
Kitāb fi ma'rifat al-ḥiyal al-handasiyya, 26, 71
Kleist, Heinrich von, 188–189
Knaus, Friedrich, 42
Kṣatracūḍāmaṇi, 125
kuṇḍalinī, 91

La Mettrie, Julien Offray de, 42
Lancelot du lac, 31
Lang, Fritz, 47
Laṅkāvatārasūtra, 147
leech, mechanical, 30
Leibniz, Gottfried Wilhelm, 74
leopards, mechanical, 1, 33
Levin, Ira, 48
Leviticus Rabbah, 36
Life and Times of Apollonius of Tyana, 61–62
liminality, 31, 45
lion, mechanical, 29, 33
Lives of the Necromancers, 31, 45
Loew, Rabbi Jehudah (Maharal), 38
Lokapaññatti, 16, 31, 151, 154–172, 177, 187
Lokaprajñapti, 155

lokapuruṣa, 115
lotus flower, 6, 11, 14, 22–23, 76, 79, 116, 124, 222n75
  mechanical, 73, 78, 209, 210, 212
Lucian, 178
lute player, mechanical, 33, 71, 78, 199, 203, 204

Magas of Cyrene, 151
Mahābhārata, 7, 63, 83, 94, 112, 125
mahābhūta, 89 (*see also* elements)
Mahāvīra, 113, 143
Mahāyāna Buddhism, 145, 146, 147
Maillardet, Henri, 41
man, mechanical, 5, 10, 15, 26, 30, 31, 33, 71, 72, 79–80, 95, 147, 156, 160, 161, 167, 168, 199, 201, 203, 204
manas, 85, 89, 149
maṇḍala, 11–14, 64, 73, 75, 91–92, 193
mandolin player, mechanical, 41
Maṇimēkalai, 58
matsya-yantra, *see* fish, mechanical
Maudgalyāyana, 130–131, 136–137, 142
Memnon, 22, 45
Menander, I, 59
mercury, 10, 22, 68, 70, 72, 76–77, 92, 99, 193–194, 195, 203
Merutuṅga, 65
Metropolis (1927 film), 47, 180, 181, 182
Meyrink, Gustav, 174
Milindapañhā, 59
"milk miracle," 98–99
Mímir, 29
mokṣa, 69–70, 125, 193, 195, 249n2
monk, mechanical, 40
monkey, mechanical, 33, 70, 72, 124, 200, 206
Mori, Masahiro, 52–53, 188, 191
Mudrārākṣasa, 8, 219n30
Mūlasarvāstivāda-Vinaya, 129, 131, 142
Mullaippāṭṭu, 58
mūrti, 15, 91, 96–99, 109, 116, 148, 182, 183, 186
Mūsā brothers, 25, 26, 72
musicians, mechanical, 25, 26, 33, 40, 41, 71, 72, 78, 79, 199, 201, 203, 204
Myrrour of the World, The, 163

Nāṭyaśāstra, 53
Navasāhasāṅkacarita, 65
Neckum, Alexander, 30
Newton, Isaac, 74
Nifla'ot Maharal, 38
Nṛttaratnavalī, 11

oracular head, *see* brazen head
organ, mechanical, 18, 25, 40
Orpheus, 29, 45
Osiris, 20
Ovid, 45

Pāli canon, 101
Pañcatantra, 10, 102–111, 112
Pārvatī, 63–64, 80, 98, 249n1
Pāṭaliputta, 152, 154, 158–159, 164, 165, 169, 171, 172
Patañjali, 90
Pattuppāṭṭu, 58
Pausanias, 22, 23
peacock, mechanical, 5, 126, 127
Philo of Byzantium, 22, 25
Philostratus, 22, 61
piano player, mechanical, 41
Piercy, Marge, 50
Pirke Avot, 36
Plato, 22
Pliny, 133

Policraticus, 30, 162
Polybius, 22, 99
Prabandhacintāmaṇi, 65
prakṛti, 89–90
prāṇa, 85, 91
prāṇapratiṣṭhā, 97, 99
Praśamaratiprakaraṇa, 115
pregnancy craving, 126–127
Prometheus, 45
Pseudo-Aristotle, 74
Ptolemy II Philadelphus, 22, 151
Puṇyavantajātaka, 136–141, 145
puppet theatre, 63–64, 66–67, 71, 82–84, 189, 232n1, 251n32
Purananuru, 58
puruṣa, 86, 88–90, 115, see also *lokapuruṣa*
puruṣārthas (the four goals of life), 69–70, 193, 195
puṣpaka, 72–73, 209, 210, 211, 213
Pygmalion, 21, 45, 109

quicksilver, *see* mercury

rabbit, mechanica,l 33
rainbow body, 146
rajas, 89
Rāmāyaṇa, 8, 183, 186
rasa (mercury), 76–77, 92, 203
rasa theory, 15, 53–55, 70, 77
Rasahṛdaya Tantra, 76
Rasamañjari, 76
Rasapaddhati, 76
Rasaprakāśa Sudhākara, 10
Rasaratnasamuccaya, 10, 77–78
Rasārṇava, 10, 76
Regiomontanus (Johannes Müller von Königsberg), 33
reincarnation, 93, 115, 131, 143, 144, 147, 159
relics, 16, 145, 147, 153–154, 156, 159–165, 168–171, 184, 186
Ṛgveda, 6–7, 67, 85–86, 88, 115, 179, 218n9
robot, definition, 4
Roman d'Eneas, Le, 30
Roman de Troie, Le, 31
Romans, 1, 15, 18, 23, 30, 31, 58, 59, 60, 118, 133, 154–169, 177, see also *yavana*
Rome, 16, 17, 31, 59, 152, 154–169, 171, 187
rooster, mechanical, 9, 10, 34
Rosaio della vita, 32
Roy, Jagadananda, 178
R.U.R. (Rossum's Universal Robots), 4, 46–47, 179

Saddhammaghosa, 154
Śāktism, 91
Samarāṅgaṇasūtradhāra, 7, 11, 15, 64–78, 80, 81, 83, 84, 92, 99, 124, 179, 184, 193–216
Sāmaveda, 85
Sāṃkhya, 89–90
Sandman, The (short story), 44–45, 52, 140, 174, 181
Saṅghadāsa, 59, 60, 118
Śaṅkara, 90
Śāntideva, 145
Śāriputra, 130–131, 136–137, 142
sattva, 89
science fiction, 3, 16, 129, 173, 175, 177–184, 188, 217 n5
Scott, Michael, 48–49
Scott, Ridley, 48–49
Sefer ha-Gematrio,t 37, 38
Sefer ha-Shem, 37
Sefer Yetzirah, 35, 37
Senses, 87, 89, 90, 95, 114–115
Shelley, Mary, 31, 45, 178
siddhacakra, 116
Siddhattha Gotama (Siddhārtha Gautama), 143, 146

Siṃhāsanadvātriṃśakā, 80
Simon Magus, 23–24
Śiva, 7, 10, 64, 66, 67, 69, 73–77, 80, 82, 83, 91, 92, 98, 99, 123, 184, 249n1
skandha, 144
snail, mechanical, 22, 99
Solomon ibn Gabirol, 37
Somadeva, 94
Somadeva Sūri, 72, 81, 122–125, 142
Sone de Nansai, 33
sorcery, 24, 28, 37, 39
Spenser, Edmund, 39
Śrī yantra (*Śrīcakra*,) 12, 92
Śṛṅgāramañjarīkathā, 15, 78–81, 83, 84, 124
Star Trek, 1, 48, 181, 187–188
Star Wars, 180, 217n6
statues, coming to life, 1, 18–19, 20, 21, 22, 23–25, 32, 35, 36, 40, 51, 80, 98, 109, 160, 161, 165, 166, 189
Stepford Wives, The (novel), 48
Stepford Wives, The (1975 film), 48
Stories of Siddhi-Kur, The, 111
Strabo, 22
stūpa, 16, 145, 153, 155, 156, 160, 164, 165, 171
subtle body, 91
Suśrutasaṃhitā, 87
swan, mechanical, 42
swing, mechanical, 72, 211

Taittirīya Upaniṣad, 87
Talmud, 34–35
Talos, 21, 39
tamas, 89
tanmātras, 89
Tantra, 12–14, 90–92, 123
Tattvaprakāśa, 66
teraphim, 35–36
Terminator (1984 film), 423, 9, 180, 182
Theravāda, 101, 133, 144
Thomas Aquinas, 31–32
Thoth, 19
Three Laws of Robotics, 47
To Asclepius, 24
Tocharian, 2, 4, 137–138, 140, 141, 142
Todorov, Tzvetan, 173–174
Tolkien, J. R. R., 174, 176
tomb, 1, 30–31, 162–163
Torriano, Gianello, 33
tortoise, mechanical, 79
Tractatus de sphaera, 74
tree, mechanical, 27–28, 79
trikāya (three body) doctrine, 146
Tripiṭaka, Chinese, 133
tripods, mechanical, 20–21, 61
True History, 178
Twain, Mark, 42

Udaipur-Praśasti, 65
Umāsvāti, 115
uncanny, 15, 42, 43, 44–45, 52–55, 173, 185, 186
uncanny valley, 52–53, 54–55, 188
Upagupta (Upagutta), 156, 163
Upaniṣads, 68, 76, 87, 90, 93
ushabti, 20

Vādībhasiṃha, 125
Vāgbhaṭṭa, 10
vāstumaṇḍala, 13
Vāstuśāstras, 13
Vasubandhu, 149
Vasudevahiṇḍī, 59–60, 118, 126
Vātsyāyana, 8, 63, 103, 104
Vaucanson, Jaques de, 41, 99–100, 112
Vedānta, 90
Vergil, 30–32, 45, 154, 162–164

Verne, Jules, 178
vetāla, 47, 111
Vetālapañcaviṃśati, 111
Vikramacarita, 80
Villiers de l'Isle-Adam, Auguste, 44
Viśākhadatta, 8
Viṣṇu, 8, 66, 98, 103–109, 183, 184
Visuddhimagga, 147
Voyage de Charlemagne, Le, 29
Vyas, Ambika Dutt, 178
Vyāsa, 94, 123

water clock, 26, 28, 29, 71, 74
water dispenser, mechanical, 25
water organ, mechanical, 40
water-powered machine, 70, 205–207
weapons, mechanical, 72
Westworld (1973 film), 48
William of Malmesbury, 30
Wilcox, Fred M., 47–48
woman, mechanical, 10, 11, 16, 22, 31, 32, 33, 37, 40, 41, 44, 47, 60, 70, 71, 72, 73 79, 95, 124, 129–142, 145, 200, 204, 207, 209, 211, 213
wooden automata, 33, 37, 63, 71, 73, 82, 93, 94–95, 96, 117, 133–142, 148, 204, 209
Writer, The (Jaquet-Droz automaton), 15, 41–42

Yajurveda, 85
yantra, definition, 4, 5–6
Yaśastilakacampū, 72, 81, 122–125
Yaśodhara Bhaṭṭa, 10
yavana, 15, 57–62, 118–119, 122, 132–136, 157
  in Buddhist literature, 59
  in Tamil literature, 57–58
Yoga, 90
Yogasūtra, 90
Yugapurāṇa, 58

zither player, mechanical, 40

www.ingramcontent.com/pod-product-compliance
Lightning Source LLC
Chambersburg PA
CBHW030527230426
43665CB00010B/795
* 9 7 8 1 4 3 8 4 9 6 6 2 7 *